Love

Lyrics

from

the

Carmina Burana

Love Lyrics from the Carmina Burana

Edited

and

translated

with a

commentary

by

P.G. Walsh

The University of

North Carolina Press

Chapel Hill

and London

© 1993 The University of North Carolina Press

Library of Congress Cataloging-in-Publication Data

Carmina Burana. English. Selections
    Love lyrics from the Carmina Burana / edited and
    translated with a commentary by P. G. Walsh.
        p.   cm.
    Includes bibliographical references and indexes.
    ISBN 0-8078-2068-7 (alk. paper).
    — ISBN 0-8078-4400-4 (pbk. : alk. paper)
        1. Love poetry, Latin (Medieval and modern)—
    Translations into English.   2. Songs, Latin (Medieval
    and modern)—Translations into English.   3. Love
    poetry, Latin (Medieval and modern)   4. Goliards—
    Songs and music—Texts.   5. Students' songs—
    Texts.   6. Love songs—Texts.   I. Walsh,
    P. G. (Patrick Gerard)   II. Title.
    PA8184.C3   1993   92-30358
    874'.0308—dc20   CIP

Manufactured in the United States of America

cloth   05   04   03   02   01   5   4   3   2   1
paper   05   04   03   02   01   6   5   4   3   2

Printed by QUESTprint

For
Stephen
and
Tricia

Contents

ix   Preface

xi   Abbreviations

xiii   Introduction

1   Love Lyrics from the
     Carmina Burana

203   Bibliography

209   Index of First Lines

211   Index of Authors
       and Passages

215   General Index

Preface

The shape of this edition has changed substantially from the typescript initially submitted to the Press. It was then intended as a companion volume to my *Thirty Poems from the Carmina Burana,* an unpretentious edition published originally by the Reading University Department of Classics and reprinted a few times before being taken over by the Bristol Classical Press. This new project, entitled *Love Lyrics from the Carmina Burana,* at that stage contained no translations but a strong apologia for their absence, which claimed that they engender lazy habits in the students for whom the book was intended; moreover, it included none of the lyrics which had appeared in *Thirty Poems.* The learned readers to whom the Press submitted the typescript were agreed that the omission of, and constant cross-reference to, the lyrics in *Thirty Poems* were both a deprivation and an annoyance. I therefore agreed to incorporate the love lyrics already covered in that volume, with some revision of the annotations there. On a second major issue the readers disagreed: one pressed strongly for the inclusion of translations, whereas the other conceded that translations were undesirable but pressed me to compose my own, if any were to appear. I have as a result appended literal translations intended to help students who are struggling with the Latin. They are not to be judged as literary artifacts. Helen Waddell once remarked, on the subject of translations, "Better a live sparrow than a stuffed eagle." But there is a case for the stuffed eagle when its purpose is to aid the student to apprehend the shape and colors of the soaring original.

This book now contains about half of the love lyrics in the original collection. Many of the remainder have little literary merit, and though the absence of individual pieces will doubtless be regretted, the selection is certainly representative of the more talented content of the anthology. In *Thirty Poems* I did not present the lyrics in the order in which they appear in the Codex Buranus, as I wished to ease the way for those approaching medieval poetry for the first time. In this longer selection I have adhered to the sequence in the Codex Buranus. Teachers of less advanced students may find it helpful to begin with the simpler and shorter lyrics in the second half of the selection.

Several new editions and translations of these poems have appeared over the past two decades. Their popularity has been stimulated in part by Carl Orff's attractive musical settings, but more fundamentally by the increasing interest in the literature of Medieval Latin. The pioneering edition of Hilka and Schumann, its text rounded off by Bischoff in 1970 (though the commentary awaits completion) has been the essential forerunner. Dronke's studies have provided a welcome literary frame, broadening scholarly interests from the more severely philological approach of the German researches. Pride of place in the recent German editions must go to Vollmann's (1987) in the Bibliothek des Mittelalters, containing texts, translations, brief annotations, and a descriptive appendix on the Benediktbeuern manuscript; a limiting factor is that the editor has sought to retain the readings of the codex even when superior versions of individual poems are found in other manuscripts. The earlier edition of Fischer, Kuhn, and Bernt (1974) is also notable. In Italian, Massa's partial edition (1979) has been followed by Rossi's anthology (texts, translations, and brief annotations) of about a hundred of the poems (1989). Earlier renderings into English verse (Symonds, Whicher, Lindsay, Zeydel) are now complemented by Parlett's attractive translations of selections in the Penguin edition, and the love lyrics have been separately translated by Blodgett and Swanson (1987); this last contains a useful introduction, but the translations leave something to be desired. At a more elementary level, Sebesta has published Orff's restricted selection of songs, again with translations and annotations.

Some poems in this selection were discussed at an informal seminar at Georgetown University, where I spent an enjoyable semester in 1989; my thanks therefore to the participants, and in general to the Classics Department there for many kindnesses. I am most grateful to John Betts of the Bristol Classical Press for generously encouraging me to incorporate the lyrics of particular relevance from *Thirty Poems* and for granting permission to reproduce them here. The readers commissioned by the University of North Carolina Press were most positive in their recommendations, and I have profited greatly by their advice. Finally I thank Lewis Bateman and the staff of the Press for their courteous cooperation, and especially my copyeditor, Laura Oaks, for the knowledge and enthusiasm she brought to this work.

University of Glasgow
August 1991

Abbreviations

Abbreviations of works by classical and medieval authors generally conform with those listed in the second edition of the *Oxford Classical Dictionary*. Biblical references are to English titles: e.g., Song of Sol. = [Vulgate] Cant.

As the abbreviations below suggest, references to modern authors by last name only usually indicate editions of the *Carmina Burana* or extensive commentaries. Many earlier editors and commentators cited occasionally by last name only (Du Méril, Ehrenthal, Fickermann, Grimm, Haupt, Heinrich, Heraeus, Herkenrath, Lundius, Manitius, Martin, Meyer, Patzig, Peiper, Pillet, Schreiber, Sedgwick, Spanke, and Strecker) may be traced through Hilka and Schumann's discussion of the poems in *CB* vol. 1.2 or Bischoff's *Nachträge, CB* vol. 1.3.

Sigla for the manuscripts mentioned are shown in the Bibliography.

Bernt	Bernt in Fischer, Kuhn, and Bernt's edition of the *Carmina Burana*
Bischoff	Bischoff in *CB*
CB	*Carmina Burana*, edd. Hilka, Schumann, and Bischoff
CL	Classical Latin
Curtius	Curtius, *European Literature and the Latin Middle Ages*
Dronke	Dronke in *Medieval Latin and the Rise of European Love-Lyric*
Du Cange	*Glossarium Mediae et Infimae Latinitatis*
Fischer	Fischer in Fischer, Kuhn, and Bernt's edition of the *Carmina Burana*
Hilka	Hilka in *CB*
Laistner	Laistner in Laistner, Brost, and Bulst's edition of *Carmina Burana*

LL	Late Latin
Manitius	Manitius, *Geschichte der lateinischen Literatur des Mittelalters*
McDonough	McDonough in *The Oxford Poems of Hugh Primas and the Arundel Lyrics*
Meyer	Meyer, *Gesammelte Abhandlungen zur mittel- lateinischen Rythmik*
Migne, *PG*	*Patrologia Graeca,* ed. Migne
Migne, *PL*	*Patrologia Latina,* ed. Migne
ML	Medieval Latin
OBMLV	*The Oxford Book of Medieval Latin Verse,* ed. Raby
OLD	*The Oxford Latin Dictionary*
Raby, *CLP*	Raby, *Christian Latin Poetry,* 2d ed.
Raby, *SLP*	Raby, *Secular Latin Poetry*
Robertson	Robertson, *Essays in Medieval Culture*
Rossi	Rossi in his edition of the *Carmina Burana*
Schmeller	Schmeller in his edition of the *Carmina Burana*
Schumann	Schumann in *CB*
Thirty Poems	*Thirty Poems from the Carmina Burana,* ed. Walsh
TLL	*Thesaurus Linguae Latinae*
Vollmann	Vollmann in his edition of *Carmina Burana*
Walther	Walther, *Lateinische Sprichwörter und Sentenzen des Mittelalters*

Introduction

I

The content of the Codex Buranus, a manuscript discovered in the Bavarian monastery of Benediktbeuern by Baron von Aretin in 1803 and later transferred to Munich, is now widely known. The original collection of 228 poems, inscribed by three different hands ca. 1230, was later augmented by a miscellany, including Latin songs of the Marner, the German poet whose floruit was the mid-thirteenth century, as well as hymns and short verse-dramas on biblical themes. As rendered in the edition of Hilka, Schumann, and Bischoff, poems 1–55, consisting of moralizing and satirical pieces, form volume 1; volume 3 takes in poems 187–228, a random assemblage of drinking songs and other compositions, supplemented by the material added at a later date. Between these blocks, poems 56–186 comprise volume 2, conventionally labeled the "love lyrics"; in fact, poems 122–34 do not belong to the genre and were probably inserted in the codex at this point in haste, from a manuscript only temporarily available to the scribe. When these are removed from the reckoning, there remains a collection of about 120 love lyrics, the most impressive single anthology of this genre of Medieval Latin poetry to have survived.[1]

Though many of the lyrics were composed to be sung, it would be an oversimplification to label the codex a scholars' songbook, as a number of the poems do not lend themselves to the medium of song; these include not only compositions in Classical hexameters but also poems too technical in content or too complex in their metrical schemes. Nine of the poems have neumes (musical notations in plainchant) placed above them by the same scribe who had copied out the words, and other melodies have been gathered from poems that also appear in other codices. Thus far tunes for forty-six of the pieces in the collection have been recovered.[2]

It is impossible to establish from where or how the scribes gathered the poems. Many of them appear in superior versions in other manuscripts; inferior readings in the Codex Buranus prompt the guess that some have been written down from personal recollection or hurried dictation, rather than carefully copied. Bischoff has drawn attention to a few pairs of consist of Latin poems followed by a stanza in German; several of the authors of these German supplements have been identified.[4] The precise relation between the Latin and the German compositions cannot be established. It seems probable that the German stanzas were added to allow participants in a German locale, who were ignorant of Latin, to join in the singing.[5] It does not follow, however, that the composers of the German stanzas also wrote the Latin poems, or indeed that they were written at the same date. It may be that in the odd instance the German was composed first (*CB* 149 is a possible example) and that an occasional Latin composition was written in the same ambience as the German.[6] But the inference must not be made that all these poems originate from a German-speaking area or that the Latin stanzas can be dated from the German supplements. A combination of evidence—above all, our knowledge of individual contributors, but also courtly motifs characteristic of French vernacular literature, and even descriptions of nature more appropriate to the countryside of southern France—supports the case for the French provenance of the great majority of these lyrics. *Hebet sidus* (no. 57 [*CB* 169]), for example, has a supplementary stanza in German attributed to Walther von der Vogelweide, and *Annualis mea* (*CB* 168), to which Neidhart von Reuental appended a German stanza, should not be imagined to have been written in Germany or to be dated as late as 1217–20. In short, the Latin stanzas can be legitimately detached from the German supplements and evaluated as autonomous creations.

2

Romantic myths about the authors of these poems have long been dispelled. The vision of jolly students composing them as they wandered from one center of learning to another—in the medieval formula, to Paris for the liberal arts, to Orléans for law, to Salerno for medicine, and to nowhere for manners and morals—gave way before the insistence of Wilhelm Meyer and Karl Strecker that the bulk of the poems is to be ascribed to learned craftsmen-poets, whose formative background lay in the great schools of the French cities. In this sense the *vagantes* or "wandering scholars" are to be envisioned not as *die verlumpten Vaganten,* down-at-heel vagrants, but as the learned teachers and students from many countries who attended those schools.[7]

lyrics. Golias originates as the Philistine giant slain by David (1 Kings 17). As David in patristic exegesis became a type of Christ, Golias duly became a type of Satan and of the heretics who assaulted Christ's Church. As early as the Carolingian age the term *familia Goliae* was used to describe groups of socially aberrant clerics. But in the middle of the twelfth century Golias suddenly became a literary figure; in his morals he remained a glutton and a lecher, but as a poet he was now witty and well-read. To him are confusingly attributed compositions known to be by the Archpoet, by Hugh Primas of Orléans, and by Walter of Châtillon. It seems clear that this literary persona, which transformed him into a composite of the leading satirists of the age, arose out of the bitter controversy which erupted between Peter Abelard and Bernard of Clairvaux. Bernard expressly compared Abelard with Goliath; and the anonymous "Golias episcopus" to whom are attributed two long poems, *Metamorphosis Goliae* and *Apocalypse,* attained the status of a reforming leader in the Church by vigorously defending Abelard and by bitterly denouncing Bernard and the Cistercian Order which he founded. From this base "Golias" was credited with a widening range of satirical and comic poetic creations and simultaneously attained his legendary status as head of a sect whose "Rule" was a scathing parody of the strict observances of the Gray Monks. The name Goliards was gladly adopted by the army of *vagantes* perpetually on the move through northern Europe, bands reminiscent of the hippies of the 1960s at their internationally recognized gathering places. It is worth stressing that the terms "Goliard" and "goliardic" were never used in the High Middle Ages to describe the authors of love lyrics or their learned productions. The tendency among modern critics to use the words indiscriminately of all rhythmical, rhyming Latin poetry of that era, and its creators, should be discouraged.[8]

In the French schools, particularly at Paris in the 1130s and 1140s, grammar and rhetoric (as John of Salisbury informs us) were taught as earnestly as theology; training in philosophy and theology was by way of the seven liberal arts. This grounding equipped its students with a formidable literary competence. As a result Greek philosophy (read in Latin translation) and to a lesser degree Latin poetry were accorded a veneration scarcely less respectful than that shown to the sacred Scriptures. Abelard, for example, claimed that secular learning was an instrument of divine revelation comparable to the two biblical testaments; Thierry of Chartres in his account of the Creation sought to harmonize Genesis with Plato's

Timaeus. Such attempts to canonize pagan authors as providing an alternative route for the divine dispensation soon withered in the schools of philosophy and theology under the attacks of orthodox theologians, only to emerge under the aegis of creative literature—hence the emergence of the philosophical epic in the shape of Bernard Silvestris' *Cosmographia* and Alan of Lille's *Anticlaudianus*, ideas from which spill over into the lyrics of the era. Others exploited their literary and linguistic training by excursions into historical epic, mini-comedies, verse satire, and personal lyric.[9] One early example of love lyrics emanating from such centers of learning is provided by Peter Abelard. Heloïse remarked in a letter to him: *Frequenti carmine tuam in ore omnium Heloissam ponebas.* The influence of Hilarius, a pupil of Abelard, can be reasonably inferred from the topic and treatment of *Cur suspectum me tenet domina?* (no. 31 [CB95]).[10]

Teachers and students trained in the schools frequently gained positions at royal or ecclesiastical courts which themselves became centers of literary activity. A well-known example in France was the literary circle at the court of Champagne in the days of Henry the Liberal. Countess Marie, daughter of Louis VII and Eleanor of Aquitaine, surrounded herself with literary figures, some of them engaged with scriptural and theological studies but others preoccupied with secular themes. Prominent among these connections of Marie were Chrétien de Troyes (who not only wrote vernacular romances but also translated Ovid's *Ars Amatoria*) and Gautier of Arras, another writer of romances. The presence at court of Andreas Capellanus, author of the courtly love treatise *De Amore*, can be inferred from internal and external evidence. It would not have been surprising if courtly love lyrics had been composed at this and other courts in central and northern France.[11] Other centers where similar preoccupations with love theory are manifest can be inferred from the love judgments in Andreas' *De Amore*, in which he cites as adjudicators of disputes not only Queen Eleanor but also Viscountess Ermengarde of Narbonne (who was closely associated with the troubadours Peire Rogier, Bernard de Ventadour, and Peire d'Auvergne), and Isobel of Flanders, likewise known to have connections with troubadours.[12]

Such centers of literary activity were not confined to France; the most brilliant of them in the 1150s and 1160s was the court of Henry II of England. The historian Gerald of Wales, the court functionary Walter Map (rightly or wrongly credited with numerous satirical verse compositions), and four of the leading Latin poets of the day—Walter of Châtillon, Peter of Blois, Joseph of Exeter, and Nigel of Longchamps—all had connections there at various times.[13] In Germany, Reinald Dassel, archchancellor of Frederick I Barbarossa and archbishop of Cologne, was the patron of the

Archpoet, the greatest German-born poet writing in Latin at that time. When Reinald died near Rome in 1167, John of Salisbury states, "the news cast its shadow even in Paris; Maecenas is dead." Barbarossa's successor, Frederick II, attracted a literary circle around him in the early thirteenth century which included the court poet Henry of Avranches.[14]

Attempts to identify individual authors of these love lyrics, however, have met with little success. Some scholars have claimed to detect the pen of Peter Abelard in *Hebet sidus* (no. 57 [CB 169]) and a few other lyrics, but this is no more than attractive speculation.[15] Several authors of satirical and moralizing poems in the collection have been identified, but most of them have no likely connection with the love lyrics. Philip the Chancellor (author of *CB* 21, 27, 34, 131, 189, and perhaps 26) is accounted too sober a Christian to have indulged in such diversions. Hugh Primas, credited with the epigrams assembled as *CB* 194, and the Archpoet, author of the celebrated *Confession* (CB 191), might be considered as possible authors of the more risqué lyrics in view of their alleged activities of drinking and whoring, but Hugh's distinctive metrical techniques are nowhere mirrored in the collection, and the works of the Archpoet assembled from other manuscripts have no counterparts in the *Carmina Burana*.[16]

Walter of Châtillon, author of four satirical and moralizing poems in the codex (*CB* 3, 8, 41, 123), did achieve fame as a composer of love lyrics as well as for his satirical poetry and his epic, the *Alexandreis*. Some of this love poetry has survived; of particular interest to us is his exploitation of the pastourelle, because of the similarity in structure and texture between his creations and those in the *Carmina Burana*. Walter's eminence as a lyric poet attracted imitators dignified with the label of his "school." It would be no surprise if he or these followers were at some date identified as authors of some love lyrics as yet unattributed.[17]

The single candidate who can confidently be proposed as author of some of the love lyrics is Peter of Blois, whose correspondence contains six moralizing poems with distinctive techniques of metrical composition. Schumann demonstrated that *CB* 29–31 are strikingly similar and indicated that one of the love lyrics, *Olim sudor Herculis* (no. 6 [CB 63]), is closely comparable. Scrutiny of the Arundel lyrics has established further connections. In pursuing Bischoff's suggestion that several lyrics in that collection were from the same pen, Spanke observed that the initial letters of the stanzas of Arundel 7 (*Plaudit humus, Boree*) form the acrostic PETRI. Four of these Arundel lyrics appear in the *Carmina Burana*: *A globo veteri* (no. 7 [CB 67]), *Grates ago Veneri* (no. 12 [72]), *Sevit aure spiritus* (no. 23 [83]), and *Vacillantis trutine* (no. 33 [108]). Closely similar to the theme and style of *A globo veteri* is *Estas in exsilium* (no. 9

[69]); *Dum prius inculta* (no. 24 [84]) is likewise close to *Grates ago Veneri*. A strong if not wholly watertight case can thus be made for assigning seven of the love lyrics to Peter of Blois.[18]

It is a curious fact that the seven lyrics form a cycle not totally dissimilar to the Lesbia cycle in the poems of Catullus. This can hardly be deliberate, given the order in which the pieces appear and the random way in which the anthology of love poetry was collected. The solution must be that Peter, visualizing himself in the role of the Ovid of the *Amores,* sought to depict different facets of the face of love but within the frame of courtly love convention. In *Vacillantis trutine* the spokesman ponders the alternatives of commitment to study or to the enticements of love and opts to devote himself to Venus. In this pursuit of love *A globo veteri* and *Estas in exsilium* are a linked pair of poems describing the preliminary stage. In the first, the spokesman contents himself with detailing the charms of Coronis; in the second, he similarly glorifies the beauty of the unnamed girl. Propriety is the keynote in these two poems. In *Sevit aure spiritus* the spokesman has advanced to the contemplation and fondling of Flora's naked form; he is here at the limits of *amor purus* (see below, sections 3 and 5). *Grates ago Veneri* is the celebration of total conquest in which the girl, resuming the name Coronis from *A globo veteri,* is induced to yield to sexual intercourse. Finally *Dum prius inculta* is a cynical and clinical description of the abhorrent rape of the innocent Phyllis. Having thus methodically covered all stages of the love encounter, Peter in *Olim sudor Herculis* allows the spokesman to proclaim an end to lovemaking in order to avoid the fate of Hercules.

Peter's career well exemplifies the characteristic background of the composers of these lyrics. Born about 1135, he was a student at Tours, Chartres, Bologna, and Paris before serving for a time in Sicily as tutor to the young king William II. He subsequently became secretary of Henry II of England and later of his widow, Eleanor. After being ordained priest about 1190, he was successively archdeacon of Bath and London and finally chancellor of Canterbury under the archbishops Richard and Baldwin. This combination of diplomatic and ecclesiastical posts lends his surviving correspondence some historical importance, and in addition to these letters his studies in the liberal arts, philosophy, and theology enabled him to write on a wide range of subjects, both religious and secular. Opinions on his stature as a man of letters have varied from a dismissive judgment of his shallow conventionality to the claim that he was one of the most original litterateurs of the age. The former seems to me the juster; the range of his literary interests is impressive, and his skill as Latinist is manifest in both the prose of his letters and the virtuosity of his verses. His writings do, however, leave the impression of literary opportunism rather than of deep or constructive reflection on the issues which engaged him.[19]

3

Though precise identification of individual authors has proved difficult except in the single case of Peter of Blois, one may speak of a generic approach to the theme of love animating the whole collection. These poems were written predominantly by and for clerics. Repeatedly this social milieu is emphasized, and its sophistication flaunted: "This band of ours, steeped in learned letters, must campaign and follow Venus' banners, but the laity must be accounted oafish, for they are deaf and dumb in the art of love" (no. 52 [CB 162], stanza 5). In the love contest between Phyllis and Flora (no. 29 [92]), Flora, who loves a cleric, wins a crushing victory over Phyllis, the knight's lady.

Those who were clerics could marry and preserve that status, but if they did so they were debarred from ordination and thus from advancement to a career in the Church. Hence there is a tendency in these lyrics to advocate *amor purus*, the relationship which falls short of consummation, and to condemn *amor mixtus*, which embraces intercourse. So, for example, in no. 26 (CB 88) the spokesman proclaims himself a virgin among virgins, loathing prostitutes and married women alike because both indulge in *turpis voluptas*. Andreas Capellanus devotes a chapter to "the love of clerics"; he emphasizes that they must distance themselves from all acts of love in their service of the Lord, but then hastily pleads on their behalf for indulgence, as a life of leisure and good eating puts greater temptation in their way.[20] The celibacy prescribed for the more literate and ambitious clerics leads to a vision of love that is idealized and theoretical; the pleasure gained from the writing and the reading of these poems is the pleasure of intellectual play in relaxation. The critic must accordingly respond to them by envisioning them as rhetorical creations in which the authors devise variations of situation and presentation while frequently adhering to a basic formula.

4

This basic scheme, as is well known, consists of a sustained comparison between the coming of spring, with its transformation achieved in nature by the warming sun, and the burgeoning of love in the hearts of the young. The stereotype allots an exact balance of lines to the two sub-themes: so, for example, *Ecce gratum* (no. 46 [CB 143) devotes a stanza and a half each to the manifestations of the new season and to the consequent stirrings of human love. In some poems closer attention is devoted to the changes in nature (e.g., nos. 14 [74], 21 [81], 42 [135]); in others (e.g., 18 [78], 35 [113]) the human aspects are lent greater prominence, with detailed description of the lady's beauty often dominant. In some lyrics a triple structure is devised: the poet begins with the theme of nature's transformation, passes to general observation of the corresponding quickening in human emotions, and finally makes the spokesman particularize about his own affair of the heart (nos. 22 [82], 43 [136], 45 [139], 49 [151]). In other poems the two motifs are not presented in sequence but intermingled within the stanzas (e.g., no. 36 [114]). Many of the simpler lyrics derive from folk tradition, identifiable by their content as dance lyrics (nos. 20 [80], 21 [81]; CB 179).

In other compositions more fundamental variations are sought. Peter of Blois provides striking examples in nos. 9 (69) and 23 (83), where he stands the conventional comparison on its head to describe not the onset of spring but its opposite, the grip of winter, in which, however, the heat of human love rises unabated. Perhaps the commonest of these thematic variations lies in the "sorrows of love" motif, in which the spokesman, so far from identifying his own feelings with the joyous rebirth of nature, feels himself to be at odds with the re-created world. The anthologizer(s) seem to have grouped some of these "sorrows of love" compositions closely together (nos. 34–36 [111, 113, 114]). Elegant variations on this motif are worked into no. 45 (139), where the spokesman warns that love may be transient and that tears may follow joy in nature's way, and more strikingly in no. 11 (71), where agony in an unreciprocated love is compounded by aversion from a second relationship. The model for this second theme, Ovid's *Amores* 2.19, warns of the hazard of interpreting such sorrows as the expression of personal emotion.

5

Many lyrics incorporate leading motifs of courtly love theory.[21] What Dronke has happily called "the courtly experience" permeates the poetic sensibilities of the age, whether expressed in the learning of Latin or in the vernacular. Central to the courtly theory is the idealized depiction of the lady as on a higher pedestal, a motif pervasive in troubadour poetry, where it is reinforced by the disparate social status of wooer and wooed; so *O comes amoris, dolor* (no. 34 [*CB* 111]) laments that the lady is so venerable that the spokesman must not presume even to name her. But even without the obvious presence of such social distinctions, the theory enjoins that the suitor adopt a posture of humiliating obsequy, in which he defers wholly to the lady's wishes and promises devoted service in her name. No. 55 (166) offers a particularly significant account of such a relationship, as the spokesman on the one hand emphasizes the disparity in social status between the lady and himself but, on the other, introduces the controversy of natural versus inherited nobility, a dispute resurrected from antiquity in Andreas Capellanus' discussions of the conventions of courtship.[22]

The *De Amore* of Andreas provides many points of reference relevant to these lyrics. No. 10 (70) is cast in the form of a lovers' dialogue, the setting, introduction, and tone of which are strongly reminiscent of Andreas' technique of dialogue presentation. A leading theme in Andreas' treatment of love is the controversy between the rival merits of *amor purus* and *amor mixtus*; in the republic of clerics *amor purus* finds readier favor. A signal indication of this is provided in no. 4 (59), where the poet depicts a *controversia* between maidens about the merits of the two forms. When taken to a court of love, the dispute is settled by the presiding goddesses in favor of chaste love (*amor purus*) against the alternative which goes all the way.[23]

One of the facets of courtly love theory which emerges most obsessively in these lyrics is the motif of *spes* (hope). The lover's fear that his love may not be reciprocated is perennial, but in this era it is rooted particularly in the courtly discretion accorded to the lady, by which she can offer or deny the suitor such hope at will. Even if she offers him hope, this is only on a probationary basis, and the resultant tension between the joy of possible acceptance and the fear of dismissal offers versifiers a fruitful theme. *Longa spes et dubia* (no. 53 [163]) is an outstanding exploration of this neurosis, in which the "sorrows of love" motif is born of the depression induced by a long period of anxious waiting. *De pollicito* (no. 59 [171]) initially appears to describe the obverse side of the coin, for the spokesman here has been granted hope, and this elates him; but the possibility that the lady may later withdraw her favor again introduces the familiar tension between *spes* and *timor*.

What may be termed the *amor de lonh* motif, a situation explored in (and perhaps borrowed from) the vernacular poetry of the age, offers the prospect of a sunnier theme. The spokesman transcends his physical separation from his beloved by asserting his spiritual intimacy with her. In the words of *Omnia sol temperat* (no. 43 [136]), *sum presentialiter / absens in remota*. This is the theme of the first poem in no. 56 (167a): *corporis distantia / merens, tamen gaudeo / absentis presentia*.

The condemnation of malicious gossip which broadcasts to the world a secret love liaison is another frequent theme in these poems, as in the courtly love theory and the vernacular lyrics. In his treatise, Andreas Capellanus in his twelve precepts for lovers sternly enjoins *Amantium noli existere propalator,* and later, in the thirty-one Rules for Love appended to the Arthurian romance, he proclaims: *Amor raro consuevit durare vulgatus.* The theme is exploited for both its serious and its comic potentialities. *Rumor letalis* (no. 39 [120]) is an outstanding example of the former. This is not a mere plea for confidentiality such as we meet in *Si linguis angelicis* (no. 17 [77], stanza 2) but an expression of pain at the promiscuous behavior of a former lover, a pain exacerbated by the gossip which now blackens her reputation. An outstandingly witty example of the comic treatment of the theme is observable in *Lingua mendax et dolosa* (no. 37 [117]), in which it is all too clear that the gossip is not idly based.

Another theme prominent in courtly love theory as reflected in the treatise of Andreas is the role of the cleric in courtship. Close parallels exist between the dialogue in *De Amore* 1.6H (a conversation between a man of higher nobility, who assumes the persona of a cleric, and a lady of the same rank) and the *disputatio* in no. 29 (92) on the respective merits of cleric and knight as lovers. In Andreas the cleric makes a ruffled response to the lady's wounding comments about his unsightly demeanor and dress (1.6.478–99), and these opposing arguments surface also in the poetic contest between Phyllis and Flora (no. 29 [92], stanzas 12–41). A similar controversy is enacted in no. 22 (82), in which Thyme and Sorrel likewise explore the rival merits of knight and cleric, with emphasis duly placed, as in Andreas and no. 29 (92), on the athleticism and bravery of the knight and the availability and superior learning of the cleric, who is both available at home while the knight campaigns abroad and more skilled in the conduct of a love affair (*clerus scit diligere / virginem plus milite*).

It should be clear from these latter examples that the conventions of courtly love are not always treated seriously by the poets in the collection. Just as Ovid's didactic role in the *Ars Amatoria* and *Remedia Amoris,* with his injunctions on how to win and keep and get rid of a lady (and more off-handedly how to win and keep a man), is ironically sustained, so several of these poems are humorous and sardonic observations on what strikes their authors as an academic doctrine remote from reality. One clearly comic treatment of male subservience is *Volo virum vivere viriliter* (no. 60 [178]), in which the spokesman exploits the conventions to have his way with the lady. In *Dum curata vegetarem* (no. 32 [105]) the disregard for the decencies (!) of Ovidian manners is tearfully deplored.[24]

6

In the *De Amore* Andreas distinguishes sharply between the need for a deferential approach to courtly ladies and the possibility of casual encounters with country girls. "Should you find a suitable spot," he recommends with regard to the second category, "you should not delay in taking what you seek, gaining it by rough embraces. You will find it hard so to soften their outwardly brusque attitude as to make them quietly to consent to grant you embraces, . . . unless the remedy of at least some compulsion is first applied, to take advantage of their modesty" (1.11.3). The pastourelle or shepherdess song qualifies for inclusion in the twelfth-century love lyric by virtue of its inclusion in the canon of courtly love theory. There are four clear examples of the pastourelle in the *Carmina Burana*: *Estivali sub fervore* (no. 19 [79]), *Exiit diluculo* (no. 28 [90]), *Lucis orto sidere* (no. 50 [157]), and *Vere dulci mediante* (no. 51 [158]).[25]

This genre, developing out of folk tradition,[26] has many examples in the contemporary vernacular poetry as well as in Latin. The poems regularly begin with the description of a *locus amoenus* in which either the shepherdess or the gallant who is to court her sits resting in the shade from the summer's heat. The gallant initiates a dialogue, in which he attempts to persuade the girl to indulge in dalliance with him. She is usually reluctant and seeks to fend him off, invoking the specter of punitive members of her family. In some vernacular poems a wolf appears on the scene and carries off a sheep; she appeals to the gallant or to her rustic fiancé to rescue it. In bawdier vernacular versions, after Robin the rustic fiancé has gone in pursuit of the wolf, the girl and the gallant disport themselves.[27]

Two pastourelles by Walter of Châtillon, representing early examples of the Latin version of the genre, can be set alongside the four poems in the *Carmina Burana* to indicate the evolution of this type of lyric. In one of Walter's poems, *Sole regente lora,* the girl sits under an elm; the boy approaches her and propositions her crudely. The shepherdess rejects him, pleading her extreme youth and the fear of a beating from her mother if she gets home late. The boy counters that there is plenty of time and offers her gifts; when she further refuses, he lays hands on her, and she does not resist. In Walter's second pastourelle, *Declinante frigore,* the gallant is sitting under the tree as the girl Glycerium comes into view. Again the boy makes the approach direct; in this instance the girl readily accedes (*dum vix moram patitur*). The name Glycerium, adopted from the pregnant heroine in Terence's *Andria*, has a licentious ring in the poetry of the era.[28]

Of the four clear pastourelles in the *Carmina Burana*, *Vere dulci mediante* is recognizably in this mold. It opens with the girl standing under a tree playing her pipe; she flees at the approach of the gallant, but he overtakes her and offers her a gift. She refuses both this and his further attentions, but he wrestles her to the ground and takes her against her will. She rebukes him, but not resentfully, and is more concerned that her mother and family do not hear of it. Of the other three examples *Exiit diluculo* is too small a fragment to categorize it, but the other two reflect both a more refined sensitivity and a greater literary sophistication. In *Estivali sub fervore* the boy sits under a tree as in Walter's *Declinante frigore,* but the *locus amoenus* has clear Classical echoes. The gallant attempts to court the shepherdess, but she rebuts him by pleading her innocence and her strict parents, and there the poem ends, contrasting with the crude close of Walter's compositions. In *Lucis orto sidere* the evolution of the genre has advanced further. Not only does the gallant refrain from molesting the girl, but there is evidence here of a species of religious allegory.

7

In this twelfth-century clerical ambience homosexual love occasionally rears its head. In a society dominated by Christian morality it is hardly surprising that it was repeatedly condemned not only in theological treatises and sermons but also in the creative writing of the day. Alan of Lille adverts to it not only in his *Liber Poenitentialis* but also in his allegorical epic *De Planctu Naturae*.[29] The prevalence of courtly love theory later in the twelfth century intensifies this censorious attitude; homosexuality is roundly condemned in Andreas Capellanus' treatise.[30]

It is true that traces of a more indulgent attitude inherited from earlier times are still to be observed. Christian versifiers like Baudri and Marbod, who both attained episcopal status earlier in the twelfth century, had written admiringly of the beauty of boys, and Hilarius, student of Abelard, devoted a number of poems to this theme.[31] Walter of Châtillon in one of his satirical poems suggests that God smiles mockingly at, rather than harshly condemns, such deviation: *Ex his esse novimus plures Sodomeos / deas non recipere, sed amare deos; / sed quotquot invenerit huius rei reos / qui in celis habitat irridebit eos.* (It is, however, an error to call in evidence the conclusion of Walter's pastourelle *Declinante frigore*.)[32]

In the *Carmina Burana* the subject is rarely raised except in a humorously oblique way.[33] The one poem devoted to the topic in this present selection, *Cur suspectum me tenet domina?* (no. 31 [95]), indignantly repudiates the charge of such male association; it is significant that the complaint is said to emanate from the spokesman's lady. The poem reflects clear stylistic parallels with *Lingua mendax et dolosa* (no. 37 [117]), a composition whose jocular tone reveals the light-hearted approach of the detached scholar. If *Cur suspectum* is not the work of the same author, it is at any rate composed in the same jocular spirit.

8

We have noted that the prevalence of courtly theory attracted more satirical and even more coarsely risqué treatment from less reverent souls. *Tange, sodes, citharam* (no. 40 [CB 121]) flies directly in the face of the courtly conventions. The initial theme is the desertion of the spokesman by an earlier mistress, and the acquisition of another. The core of the poem lies in the spokesman's contrast between the two, with the virtues of the new lady shown as victorious on every count. But so far from treating her deferentially, the suitor depicts her with the image of a farm animal whose only drawback is her unwillingness to come to heel. In the splendidly ironic final stanza, the friend whose counsel is being sought is able to offer advice from his own experience: the allegedly *verecunda* and *pudibunda* maiden turns out to be not so reluctant after all.

It is to be noted that this poem begins each stanza with four lines in the "goliardic" meter, which is regularly (though not invariably) employed in narrative poems of a satirical or humorous nature.[34] Into this category of "goliardic" satire falls no. 16 (76), describing a protracted visit to a high-class bordello. *Si linguis angelicis* (no. 17 [77]) presents more difficulties of interpretation; but the "goliardic" meter, and the juxtaposition of the poem with *Dum caupona verterem*, support the arguments which I advance in the commentary for regarding this as a playful rather than a serious composition.

9

Perhaps the most arresting facet of the intellectual life of the twelfth century lies in the scholastic attempt to reconcile the Christian theology with the philosophical insights of the pre-Christian world. "To theologize," claimed Clarembald of Arras, "is to philosophize." At Chartres, under the

Breton brothers Bernard and Thierry, the veneration accorded to the Christian revelation of the Bible was extended to embrace the philosophers of antiquity, in particular Plato and Aristotle in their Latin dress; philosophy was thought to offer an alternative path to ultimate truth.[35] In this synthesis of theology and philosophy man and the natural world around him were visualized as the supreme mark of God's creative presence; the nature of God and the eternal *patria* of heaven were to be glimpsed by closer understanding of the physical world. A most influential document for an understanding of this central significance of man and nature is the *Cosmographia* of Bernard Silvestris, composed probably in the 1140s.[36]

Given that many of the authors of these lyrics were scholars writing in relaxation, it is hardly surprising that many of the lyrics reflect this philosophical outlook. An outstanding example of this is *A globo veteri* (no. 7 [67]), attributed to Peter of Blois. In this poem Nature, visualized as God's agent in the creation of the world, has lent order and cohesion to matter and, in particular, has endowed the spokesman's lady, Coronis, with features which transcend the beauty of the rest of creation. What is notable here is not merely that created woman is depicted as God's crowning achievement; there is also the initial postulate, inherited from Greek philosophy and from Ovid's *Metamorphoses,* that matter is eternal, and that creation lay in the act of lending order to the existing shapeless mass—a striking contrast with the Hebraic-Christian doctrine of divine creation *ex nihilo.*

10

Discussion of these several subgenres of love lyric must accord space to the occasional poem which breaks free of the conventions and achieves a distinctive originality. Such a composition is *Dum Diane vitrea* (no. 5 [CB 62]), in which the poet substitutes the onset of night for the "coming of spring" motif: the gentle Zephyr soothes the lover's care-laden heart, and sleep brings in its train restful images of waving corn, tinkling rills, and the motion of millstones. Tribute to its originality is bestowed not only by the parody *Dum domus lapidea* (197) but also by the incorporation of its imagery into no. 8 (CB 68). Another original creation is *Hebet sidus* (no. 57 [169]), in which the poet contrasts the suitor's clouded countenance and joyless utterance with the bright radiance of his lady. Though the attribution to Abelard cannot be confirmed, the theme is apposite to his personal situation of separation from Heloïse, and the subtlety of the imagery is in no way inferior to that achieved in his splendid hymns.[37]

One of the main purposes of this Introduction has been to demonstrate the wide range of approaches and situations in a genre sometimes considered to be cloying through its stylized pattern. Such variety is matched by subtle variation in presentation: one poem is a minstrel's song (no. 2 [57]), others are poetic dialogues (10 [70], 17 [77], 29 [92]). The songs which contain a refrain sometimes vary their words (1 [56], 24 [84]) and sometimes have recourse to the French vernacular. The pleasure of reading the poems is greatly enhanced by conscious attention to this striving for *variatio* in content and presentation.

II

The unique flavor of medieval Latin lyrics is achieved by the confluence of the Christian vision of the world (absorbed from continual study of the Latin Vulgate and the Fathers) and the effect of concentrated study of the authors of Roman antiquity in the schools. Perhaps the outstanding example of this synthesis is the Archpoet's *Confession,* in which the spokesman wears the mantle of Job while affecting sorrow for his sins detailed with evocations of the Classical authors, especially Ovid.[38] This tension between profoundly contrasting world views is frequently notable in the love lyrics, where the secular attractions of courtly loving compete with ideals of Christian chastity. The authors' familiarity with biblical and patristic texts proclaiming that Christian ideal can be taken for granted. What Classical poets were chiefly influential in the projection of the religion of secular love?

One name stands out above all others, that of Ovid. Courtly love in the twelfth century is a fashion in literature rather than in real life, and Ovid presides over it as *magister amoris curialis,* introducing into the feudal, highly Christianized twelfth-century world the more permissive standards of Augustan Rome. The *Ars Amatoria* and the *Remedia Amoris* are the bible, so to say, of courtly love, and the *Amores,* offering the practice to complement the theory, is equally prominent. Influential too is Ovid's *Metamorphoses,* a veritable encyclopedia of mythological lore; the *Heroides* was less popular but "was in general circulation north of the Alps," as were the *Epistulae ex Ponto* and the *Fasti.*[39] After Ovid, Virgil is the poet most frequently cited; his *Eclogues, Georgics,* and especially the *Aeneid* (notably for the Dido-Aeneas affair) were all well known at this time. Lucan and Statius are other epic poets popular in the twelfth century. Horace's *Odes* had likewise become familiar to literate scholars in addition to his *Satires,* which together with Juvenal and Martial were popular reading before and during the twelfth century. Of the dramatists Plautus was known to only a limited readership, but Terence was widely read and imitated.[40]

Other Classical poets present tantalizing problems. Lucretius, for example, was little known in the twelfth century, yet *Dum Diane vitrea* (no. 5 [*CB 62*]) seems to offer a clear evocation, and there were copies of *De Rerum Natura* at Corbie and Lobbes.[41] The love-elegists Propertius and Tibullus were similarly little known, yet evocations of Propertius in John of Salisbury and in the *Pamphilus,* and traces of Tibullus at Orléans, permit speculation that some creative spirits read them.[42] Catullus remains the most enigmatic figure of all; in spite of suggested evidences of knowledge of him,[43] it would be imprudent to assume that he is cited directly. It is salutary to remember that parallels with Classical authors do not necessarily presuppose a direct acquaintance. Study of Walther's *Lateinische Sprichwörter und Sentenzen des Mittelalters* shows how widely their *sententiae* were mediated through later writers and *florilegia* to become the common property of literati in the High Middle Ages.

12

In Latin versification the transition from quantitative to rhythmic verse was a gradual process which began in the early centuries of the Christian era. As the stress accent in Latin became increasingly strong, the distinction between long and short syllables began to be obscured, especially among the less educated. Even in the case of the highly literate Ambrose (d. 397), whose hymns conform strictly to the quantitative norms of the iambic dimeter, it is possible to observe rhythmical patterns which emerge from the strength of the stress accent: *Spléndor patérnae glóriáe, / de lúce lúcem proferens, / lux lúcis et fóns lúminis, / díes diérum inlúminans.*[44]

By the twelfth century, rhythmic verse had attained its full flowering. The quantity of syllables had ceased to exercise its effect, and elision had been almost wholly discarded; the result is a regular number of syllables per line. Its other conspicuous feature is the frequency of rhyme. This had been no more than occasional ornament in the quantitative meters of Latin poetry until the fifth and sixth centuries, when Sedulius and Venantius Fortunatus began to devote more attention to it, though even then it was not systematic. During the Carolingian age the internally rhyming ("leonine") hexameter and (less frequently) pentameter, are in evidence; some versifiers also attempted rhyme between successive hexameters. The long period of experiment with rhyme reached its apogee in the rhythmic "se-

quences" of the twelfth century, when Adam of St. Victor perfected tro-
chaic measures. The sequence was an extended meditation sung especially
on feast days between the readings of the epistle and of the gospel in the
Mass, and there is little doubt that this tradition of liturgical singing im-
pressed its patterns on the secular lyrics.[45]

Though most commentators conventionally append to each poem the
rhythmic scheme which has been followed, and though an agreed method
of recording such patterns has been evolved, such detail is hardly necessary for an appreciation of the sound of the lines. On the one hand, the
rhythmical basis of the simpler poems is obvious to any reader of modern
poetry; on the other, the more complex schemes do not yield easily to
such formal analysis, and different editors order the lines in slightly different ways. For this reason, readers desirous of such information must have
recourse to other modern editions.[46]

13

Readers who approach these poems without experience of the norms of
language in Medieval Latin, but with some knowledge of the workings of
Classical Latin, will have little difficulty in making the adjustment. When
Traube averred that there was no such beast as Medieval Latin, he was
uttering a profound truth; there is only Latin. But it is true that in its
development the language underwent modifications. The reader of Classical texts is well aware that beneath such literary productions lies the
underside of common speech. The evidence of inscriptions and of works
such as the *Satyricon* of Petronius and the *Appendix Probi* recalls us to
the realization that this Vulgar Latin, existing side by side with the literary
productions, was (like every living language) in a continual process of development, in which regional peculiarities played their part. A crucial as-
pect of this development was the emergence of ecclesiastical Latin. The
Old and New Testaments were first translated from the Greek into the
Latin of the common people, and even when the scholarly Jerome later
rendered the Old Testament from the Hebrew and retranslated the New
Testament from the Greek, he was still constrained by the sacredness of
the texts (*et ordo verborum mysterium est*) and by the conservatism of his
readers. The Latin of the Christianized West thus emerged as the combination of three strands: the "pure" Latin of the Classical authors, the con-
tinually developing language of common speech, and Ecclesiastical Latin
with its strong infusion of Hebraic and Greek modes of expression.

By the Carolingian age the isolation of regional Latin-speaking communities was heralding the emergence of the vernaculars. Charlemagne's inauguration of reform of Latin in the liturgy and in the education in monastic schools gradually led to a "refrigerated" Latin as the polite international language of western Europe. The twelfth-century clerics who wrote these love lyrics had been subjected to rigorous study of the Classical authors, so that the Latin which they compose does not differ in any considerable degree from that of the Classical period. Their studies had, however, in many cases included writers of Late Latin from Apuleius to Boethius, with their wider range of vocabulary and more relaxed standards of syntax, and their religious life embraced regular acquaintance with the Latin Bible and the Latin Fathers. For these reasons, and also because of more limited development of literary Latin after the Carolingian age, the reader may find the following basic observations of some use.

Orthography. The most troublesome feature is the simplification of *ae* and *oe* into *e*. As early as the sixth century Cassiodorus was urging his monks when copying: *"A" casui genetivo non subtrahas* (*Inst.* 1.15.9). Thus at 23.2 *leto letor premio* would be *laeto laetor praemio* in Classical Latin. Confusion can arise from such forms as *cepi* = *coepi* (17.13), *equis* = *aequis* (29.2), and genitives which look like adverbs (*caste, pudice,* 4.5, 4.7). *Mihi* and *nihil* become *michi, nichil* for greater ease of pronunciation, especially in singing. Various letters and combinations of letters are interchangeable: *o/u* as in *infronita* for *infrunita* (8.4), *e/i* as in *delinio* for *delenio* (8.2). Most others—*i/y, di/z* (*zabulus* for *diabolus*), *r/l* (*fraglant* for *fragrant,* 29.66), *ci/ti, c/ch,* and the curious *philomena* for *philomela* (3.1, 19.3, etc.)—do not cause difficulty. The occasional tendency to simplify a double consonant with a single one may cause confusion, as in the case *imo* for *immo.*

Morphology. Some nouns change their gender: for example, *aquila* is masculine at 3.4, and *thymum* in Classical Latin becomes *thymus* at 47.5. There is a sublime indifference to the correctness of ablatives in *-e* or *-i,* so that *vesperi* becomes *vespere*; the ablative of the comparative adjective is regularly written in *-i* (*uberiori, alacriori,* 8.3, 8.4; *molliori,* 26.2). Proper names are declined with the greatest freedom: Dione and Semele are genitives at 2.3 and 11.1b, and Cronos is a genitive at 13.1; Daphnes is nominative at 1.5, and Dione is dative at 29.47. So far as verbs are concerned, there is a tendency to form hitherto nonexistent deponents from active verbs: for example, *propinatur* at 44.1. The adverb *inpalam* appears at 41.4 as a result of a biblical expression; see the note there.

Syntax. The instrumental ablative is occasionally replaced by *a* + ablative (*a sagitta,* 16.6; cf. 22.3). Hebraisms and Graecisms affect pronominal use: *quidam* and *unus* are used indifferently for Greek *tis,* "a certain." *Quivis* and *quilibet* are used for *quisque*, "each and every" (19.2, 58.1, etc.). *In tempore,* a Vulgate usage, replaces ablative of "time when" at 25.1 and 49.2. The infinitive frequently becomes a substantive: *eius letum vivere* = "her happy life" (1.4; cf. 13.6, 17.20, etc.). *Suus* and *se* are much more loosely used: at 2.4 *suo iugo* would be *iugo eius* in Classical Latin, and *se* is similarly used loosely at 16.3 and 16.21.

The commonest changes of construction are

1. the use of *dum* where Classical Latin would have *cum* (with pluperfect subjunctive at 1.3, 16.1, 24.1; with present subjunctive [causal] at 4.4)
2. the use of *quod, quia,* and *quoniam* with either indicative or subjunctive, replacing accusative and infinitive in Classical Latin (for example, *aestimabam quod essent,* 16.2, cf. 50.6; *cerno quod noscis,* 16.11, cf. 17.10, 21.1, etc.)
3. the replacement of *tam/ita . . . ut* + subjunctive with *tam . . . quod* + indicative in result clauses (10.11a, 29.24, etc.)
4. the ablative of gerund/gerundive used in a purely participial sense (*eundo* = *euntes,* 29.65, cf. 48.3, 51.3)
5. the infinitive of purpose (2.8), already present in colloquial contexts in Classical Latin.

Note also *dignus* + infinitive for *dignus qui* + subjunctive (again colloquial earlier) at 17.13, 37.1. The natural development of the language leads to some verbs being used transitively for the first time (*benedicere,* 10.13; *acclinare,* 8.5; *vernare,* 47.3).

Vocabulary. Naturally enough, the vocabulary in Medieval Latin has been greatly extended, partly by natural development, partly to take account of new social circumstances. Thus the Christian religion is responsible for new words for its ministers and its liturgy: *sollemnizare* (1.2), *privilegiata* (7.5b), *clericus* and *clericalis* (29.4, 29.24, etc.). Scholastic philosophy introduces such vocabulary as *causatum* (17.2). Many new words are extensions from existing roots: *domicella* (29.67, 48.3b) begins as *dominicella,* diminutive of *domina,* and *pastorella* is formed as feminine of *pastor* (19.4). Many words—for example, names of birds in no. 3— emerged from common speech.

Many words retained from Classical Latin now have changed meanings, some owing to the influence of the Christian religion: *salus* = "salvation," *pudor* = "virginity," *tonsura* = the tonsure, etc. Some scriptural expressions like *oleum* bear a metaphorical meaning (59.2). Courtly and feudal contexts affect the meaning of *miles,* "knight" (39.4, etc.), and of *curialis* (40.2). More generally, *parum* ("too little" in Classical Latin) is often found meaning *paulum* (16.3, 23.3, 29.4, etc.). It is interesting to observe how the deferential plural is found in addressing an individual of higher social status (51.4, etc.).[47]

MOST OF THE LYRICS in this selection are extant solely in the Codex Buranus. Where a poem appears in another manuscript (or more) I have indicated that at the beginning of the notes to its text and have adopted the superior readings from such versions.

Notes

1. This is a deliberately bare summary, as details of the collection are given in the various editions and translations. See especially Bischoff's introduction to his facsimile edition (1967). Vollmann (906ff.) offers a more detailed account of the ordering of the poems.

2. See Clemencie, *Carmina Burana: Gesamtausgabe,* and (earlier) Lipphardt, "Unbekannte Weisen zu den *Carmina Burana.*"

3. See now Vollmann (901ff.).

4. They include Dietmar von Aist (*CB* 113a), Heinrich von Morungen (150a), Neidhart von Reuental (168a); Reinmar der Alte (147a, 166a, [perhaps] 143a), Walther von der Vogelweide (151a, 169a, 211a). On these poets see Bäuml, *Medieval Civilization in Germany,* 126ff.

5. Spanke, "Der Codex Buranus als Liederbuch," 246.

6. On *CB* 149 see Sayce, *The Medieval German Lyric,* 239–40. For the claim of a German ambience for *CB* 147 see Ashcroft, " 'Venus' Clerk.' "

7. A full bibliography of the earlier literature is assembled in *CB* 1.1–2, brought up to date by Bischoff in *CB* 1.3 (including Meyer and Strecker). The controversy about the nature of the authors of the poems is outlined in Laistner, Brost, and Bulst. Waddell, *The Wandering Scholars,* chap. 8, is fundamental.

8. I resume here the arguments which I presented in "Golias and Goliardic Poetry." An exhaustive study of the attributions to "Golias" in medieval manuscripts may be found in Rigg, "Golias and Other Pseudonyms," together with full bibliography of earlier contributions.

9. For the prominence lent to the liberal arts, and the resultant outflow of creative literature, see Wetherbee, *Platonism and Poetry.* For Abelard's encomium of secular literature, see Migne, *PL* 178:998. On Thierry's *De Sex Dierum Operibus* see Häring, "The Creation and Creator of the World."

10. Abelard *Ep.* 2 (*PL* 178:188). For Hilarius see introductory comments to no. 31 (*CB* 95). For Heloïse's letter see Migne, *PL,* 178:188.

11. See Benton, "The Court of Champagne." Benton is skeptical of the presence of Andreas; but see my comments in *Andreas Capellanus on Love,* pp. 2–3.

12. Eleanor: Andreas 2.7, 2.17, 2.19, 2.42, 2.47. Ermengarde: 2.20ff., 2.35. Isobel: 2.30. See Bezzola, *Les origines,* 3:2, 334ff., 429.

13. See Dronke, "Peter of Blois," and Bate, "La littérature d'imagination." Earlier in the century visiting scholastics crowded the court of Queen Matilda at Westminster: *Turmatim huc adventabant scholastici, tum canticis tum verbis famosi, felicemque se putabat qui carminis novitate aures mulceret domine* (William of Malmesbury *Gesta Regum* 5.4.18).

14. For Reinald as patron of the Archpoet see Watenphul and Krefeld, *Die Gedichte des Archipoeta*, 30ff.; and Raby, *SLP*, 2:180ff. For the literary circle of Frederick II see Haskins, *Studies*, chap. 6.

15. The most ambitious claims for Abelard are made by Allen, *Medieval Latin Lyrics*, 107ff.

16. On Philip the Chancellor's religious zeal as a writer of satirical and devotional poetry see Raby, *SLP*, 2:227ff. The poetry of Hugh Primas can be conveniently examined in McDonough, *Poems of Hugh Primas and the Arundel Lyrics*; the distinctive style of nos. 18 and 23 cannot be paralleled in *CB*. For the Archpoet's surviving poems see Watenphul and Krefeld, *Die Gedichte des Archipoeta*.

17. For Walter's love lyrics see Strecker, *Die Lieder Walters von Châtillon*. Recent accounts of his career appear in Colker's edition of the *Alexandreis* and Pritchard's translation.

18. The six moral-religious poems were appended to *Ep.* 57 under the headings *Cantilena de lucta carnis et spiritus* and *Contra clericos voluptati deditos*. Giles printed the poems separately in volume 4 of his edition (Oxford, 1846), unfortunately assembling the last five under one heading. They were unscrambled by Schumann in *CB* 2.1:47. Schumann followed Unger's lead in attaching *CB* 63 to this group. Details of the ascription of the Arundel lyrics can be conveniently consulted in McDonough, *Poems of Hugh Primas and the Arundel Lyrics*; he cites additional arguments of R. W. Lenzen to support Peter's authorship. Dronke, "Peter of Blois," has resumed and developed these Petrine claims.

19. A good summary of his career appears in De Ghellinck, *L'essor de la littérature latine*, 132ff. The varying judgments of his worth—by Southern, *Medieval Humanism*, 106–7 (critical) and by Bezzola, *Les origines*, 3:1, 31ff. (admiring)— are cited in Dronke, "Peter of Blois." I have translated Peter's scholastic *Twelve Advantages of Tribulation* (from *PL* 207:989, not in Giles) in *Divine Providence and Human Suffering*, 141ff., an exercise which has influenced my opinion.

20. *De amore* 1.7.3.

21. On the theory of courtly love C. S. Lewis's *Allegory of Love*, chap. 1, offers the classic *point de départ* for English-speaking students. It should be read with Dronke's criticisms (*Medieval Latin and the Rise of European Love-Lyric*) in mind. Bezzola's monumental study (*Les origines*) and Lazar's (*Amour courtois*) are fundamental. On the *Carmina Burana* specifically see Walsh, *Courtly Love in the Carmina Burana*. Boase, *Origin and Meaning of Courtly Love*, and Newman, *Meaning of Courtly Love*, offer further guidance.

22. See comments at no. 55 (*CB* 166).

23. On the purely literary status of such courts of love, and their absence from the historical stage in the twelfth and thirteenth centuries, see Benton, "Clio and Venus."

24. See Elliott's perceptive articles "The Bedraggled Cupid" and "The Art of the Inept *Exemplum*."

25. On these see Piguet, *L'évolution de la pastourelle*; Jones, *The Pastourelle*;

Raby, *SLP*, 2:334ff.; Jackson, "The Medieval Pastourelle"; Dronke, "Poetic Meaning," 116ff.; and Bate, "Ovid, Medieval Latin and the Pastourelle." To the four examples listed here Jackson would add *Grates ago Veneri* (no. 12 [72]). Spanke, "Die älteste lateinische Pastorelle," considers *Nos duo boni* (*CB* 89) to be a pastourelle. Allen, *Medieval Latin Lyrics,* would include *Florent omnes arbores* (*CB* 141). None of these seem to me to qualify as clear examples of the genre.

26. The bibliography for and against this thesis (the great majority supporting it) has been assembled in Bate, "Ovid, Medieval Latin and the Pastourelle."

27. All this is well documented in Piguet, *L'évolution de la pastourelle.*

28. Bate, "Ovid, Medieval Latin, and the Pastourelle," 23–24, quotes Baudri 207 (ed. K. Hilbert, *Baldricus Burgulianus: Carmina,* Heidelberg, 1979), the twelfth-century comedy *Pamphilus,* and *CB* 226 for citations of Glycerium as a lady of easy virtue.

29. See Longère's edition of the *Liber Poenitentialis* and, on *De Planctu Naturae,* my introductory notes to no. 31 (95).

30. *De Amore* 1.2.1, cited further in introductory remarks to no. 31 (95).

31. Documentation and citations can be conveniently consulted in Curtius, *European Literature and the Latin Middle Ages,* 114ff.

32. For recent discussion of homosexuality in the Christian centuries see Boswell, *Christianity, Social Tolerance and Homosexuality*; and Ziolkowski, *Alain of Lille's Grammar of Sex.* Levine, "How to Read Walter Map," cites further evidence of a more tolerant attitude toward homosexuality, but he is mistaken in adducing the close of Walter of Châtillon's pastourelle *Declinante frigore* by reading *sed quis nescit cetera? / pedicatus vincitur.* Raby, *SLP,* 2:192, condemned Meyer's emendation from *predicatus* ("Description is surpassed . . .") on the grounds that it is "contrary to the whole intention of the poem." This could perhaps be disputed, but Bate's observation ("Ovid, Medieval Latin and the Pastourelle," 25) that *subici compellitur . . . predicatus vincitur* is an instance of punning erotic grammar can hardly be gainsaid.

33. See, for example, *Deus pater, adiuva* (*CB* 127 = *Thirty Poems,* no. 6) with my commentary there.

34. Exceptions worth noting are *CB* 49 (moralizing) and 50 (crusade poem).

35. See note 9 above.

36. See the excellent accounts of Wetherbee, *Platonism and Poetry,* chap. 1; and Stock, *Myth and Science.* The fundamental study is Chenu's *Théologie au douzième siècle.*

37. On the hymns see Szövérffy, *Abelard's Hymnarius Paraclitensis.*

38. See Dronke, "The Archpoet and the Classics," rightly refuting the simplistic thesis of Cairns ("The Archpoet's Confession").

39. See R. J. Tarrant's survey of Ovidian manuscripts in Reynolds, *Texts and Transmission,* 262ff.

40. See, for example, De Ghellinck, *L'essor de la littérature latine,* 297.

41. Cf. Reynolds's review of Lucretius manuscripts in *Texts and Transmission,* 220–21.

42. See R. J. Tarrant (on Propertius) and R. H. Rouse and L. D. Reynolds (on Tibullus) in Reynolds, *Texts and Transmission,* 324, 421–22; and Dronke, "The Archpoet and the Classics," 72.

43. See R. J. Tarrant in Reynolds, *Texts and Transmission*, 43, with further bibliography.

44. Walpole, *Early Latin Hymns*, no. 3. The origin of rhythmic verse is a disputed question; for a useful summary in English see Beare, *Latin Verse and European Song*, chap. 17. Some French scholars have argued that as Latin was increasingly spoken by non-natives, the pronunciation changed and the length of vowels was disregarded. German- and English-speaking students have tended to claim that the strong stress accent naturally evolved into accentual verse. A third view, proposed by Meyer, connects the change with the singing of hymns at Milan and elsewhere "after the manner of the Eastern Churches" (Augustine *Confessions* 9.7), so that he attributes its origins to Syriac hymnology, an exotic solution; but undoubtedly antiphonal singing furthered the rhythmic development.

45. The origin of rhyme is no less contentious than that of rhythmic verse. Meyer again connects it with Syriac religious poetry, and Sedgwick with Hebraic hymnology. But there is abundance of *homoioteleuton* in the rhythmic prose of the Second Sophistic, which is a more probable influence on Augustine's rhyming *Psalm against the Donatists*. For surveys of these scholarly views see Raby, *CLP*, 20ff.; Beare, *Latin Verse and European Song*, chap. 23.

46. For the system of notation see Schaller, "Bauformeln für akzentrhythmische Verse und Strophen"; and McDonough, *Poems of Hugh Primas and the Arundel Lyrics*, 12ff. Vollmann (and, earlier, Hilka, Schumann, and Bischoff) offer such metrical analyses.

47. For schematic treatments of the texture of Medieval Latin see Norberg, *Manuel pratique*; Cremaschi, *Guida allo studio del latino medievale*; Löfstedt, *Late Latin*; and Blaise, *Manuel du latin chrétien*. Strecker's *Introduction to Medieval Latin*, a useful earlier study, contains bibliography of previous works.

1 (56)

1. Ianus annum circinat,
   ver estatem nuntiat;
   calcat Phebus ungula,
   dum in Taurum flectitur,
   Arietis repagula.

   Refl. Amor cuncta superat,
       Amor dura terebrat.

2. Procul sint omnia tristia!
       dulcia gaudia
   sollemnizent Veneris gymnasia!
       decet iocundari
   quos militare contigit
       Dioneo lari.

   Refl. Amor cuncta . . .

3. Dum alumnus Palladis
       Cytheree scolam
   introissem, inter multas
       bene cultas
   vidi unam solam
   facie Tyndaridi
   ac Veneri secundam,
   plenam elegantie
   et magis pudibundam.

   Refl. Amor cuncta . . .

4. Differentem omnibus
   amo differenter;
   novus ignis in me furit
       et adurit
   indeficienter.
   nulla magis nobilis,
       habilis,
   pulchra vel amabilis;
   nulla minus mobilis,
         instabilis,
   infronita reperitur,
   vel fide mutabilis.
   eius letum vivere
   est meum delectari;
   diligi si merear,
   hoc meum est beari.

   Refl. Vincit Amor omnia,
       regit Amor omnia.

5. Parce, puer, puero!
   fave, Venus, tenero,
       ignem movens,
       ignem fovens,
   ne mori sit quod vixero,
   nec sit ⟨ut⟩ Daphnes Phebo,
   cui me ipsum dedo!
   olim tiro Palladis,
   nunc tuo iuri cedo.

   Refl. Vincit Amor . . .

1. Janus compasses the circle of the year. Spring announces summer; Phoebus, while turning into Taurus, treads underfoot with his hoof the bars of Aries.

   Refrain. Love conquers all, Love penetrates all that is hard.

2. All sadness must retire far off. The schools of Venus must celebrate sweet joys. Those granted service in the house of Dione can fittingly rejoice.

   Refrain. Love conquers all . . .

3. When as the pupil of Pallas I entered the Cytherean's school, amongst many well-cultivated ladies I saw one second in beauty only to Tyndareus' daughter and to Venus, full of refinement and more modest than them.

Refrain. Love conquers all . . .

4. She is unique among all, and I love her uniquely. A new fire rages within me and scorches me unceasingly. No girl known is nobler, more presentable, more beautiful, or more lovable; none is less fickle, unreliable, foolish, or wavering in fidelity. A happy life for her is my delight. If I deserve to win her love, that is my blessedness.

Refrain. Love prevails over all, Love governs all.

5. Boy, spare this boy! Venus, be kind to this innocent youth! Stir the love-flame, feed the love-flame, so that my future life be not death, so that she to whom I surrender myself may not play Daphne to my Apollo! Once I was the novice of Pallas, but now I pass under your rightful control.

Refrain. Love prevails over all . . .

THIS POEM CONFORMS with the commonest pattern in medieval love lyric. Beginning with a stanza in celebration of the advent of spring, it then forges a connection with the burgeoning joys of youthful love. The spokesman next devotes two stanzas to hymning the beauty and the sterling qualities of his ideal woman, and ends the poem with exhortations to Cupid and Venus to promote his love. The "ring composition," by which he reverts in the final stanza to his change of status from scholar to courtly lover proclaimed in stanza 3, and the learned Ovidian evocations (stanzas 1 and 5) emphasize his credentials as a learned suitor.

1. **circinat:** Janus is envisaged as at work with the compasses (*circinus*), constructing the cycle of the coming year. The meaning of the verb extends the senses found in CL.
Taurum . . . Arietis: The sun passes from Aries into Taurus on 17 April, so this first stanza describes the three stages of the advent of fine weather.
repagula: The description of the sun's passage out of Aries is inspired by Ovid *Met.* 2.155, where the horses of the sun *pedibusque repagula pulsant.*

Ref. **Amor cuncta superat:** Cf. Virgil *Ecl.* 10.69, *omnia vincit Amor, et nos cedamus Amori.*
terebrat: The image is that of the gimlet boring through hard wood.

2. **sollemnizent . . . gymnasia:** The verb, a ML creation, is frequent in contexts of liturgy and canon law from the twelfth century onward. *Gymnasia* bears the general sense of schools, but with a hint of the original meaning of "wrestling grounds" of love.

   militare: The notion of campaigning in love is especially popular in Augustan love elegy; see, above all, Ovid *Am.* 1.9.

   Dioneo lari: Dione, mother of Aphrodite/Venus, is often found as an alternative title for her daughter, both in CL and in ML. Horace's *Dionaeo sub antro* (*Carm.* 2.1.39) may be in our poet's mind here. It is of interest that the same phrase is used by Walter of Châtillon (*Lieder*, ed. Strecker, no. 32).

3. **alumnus . . . scolam:** Fosterling of Pallas Athene, goddess of wisdom, the clerical student now enrolls himself in the school of the Cytherean. Venus is so labeled because of her celebrated shrine on Cythera, the island off the southern coast of Greece.

   unam solam . . . secundam: Helen, familiar as Tyndareus' daughter from Virgil and Ovid, is repeatedly cited in these lyrics as the ideal of physical perfection.

   magis pudibundam: The sexual exploits of Helen, paramour of Paris at Troy, and of Venus, caught in adultery with Mars by her husband Vulcan (Ovid *Met.* 4.173ff.), are in the poet's mind.

4. **differenter:** First in LL.

   indeficienter: First in Christian Latin; cf. Augustine *Conf.* 12.11.

   infronita: CL *infrunita*, used of a woman by Seneca (*Ben.* 3.13.3) but here more probably inspired by Biblical Latin (Ecclus. 23:6, etc.).

   letum vivere: *letum = laetum*, and *vivere* is here used as a substantive, a frequent use of the infinitive in ML. *Delectari* in the following line is a similar example; so too is *beari* in this stanza, and *mori* in the next.

5. **puer:** Cupid.

   tenero: Often also in CL in this sense of "innocent."

   ne mori sit quod vixero: *quod vixero = vita futura.* The notion that life after rejection in love is a type of death is a common motif both in these lyrics and in the contemporary love theory. See, e.g., 9.2, 13.7a, etc.; Andreas Capellanus 1.6.39, 1.6.77.

   sit: Supply *ea* from *cui* in the following line as subject.

   ⟨ut⟩: This is Schumann's insertion, who has further emended *quid* in the manuscript to *cui.* Vollmann retains the readings in B, punctuating *nec sit Daphnes Phebo! quid me ipsum dedo?*—but this is clearly unsatisfactory.

Daphnes Phebo: If Daphnes, not Daphne, is the true reading, it is to be regarded as an eccentric form of the nominative, not paralleled in CL; such forms are found in ML elsewhere, e.g., *Agapes* in Hrothsvitha's drama *Dulcitius*. The famous episode of Apollo's fruitless pursuit of Daphne, who was transformed into a laurel tree, is told by Ovid at *Met.* 1.452ff.

2 (57)

1. "Bruma, veris emula,
    sua iam repagula
        dolet demoliri;
    demandat Februario
    ne se a solis radio
        sinat deliniri.

2. Omnis nexus elementorum
    legem blandam sentit amorum.
    sed Hymeneus eorum
    iugalem ordinat torum,
    votis allubescens deorum
                piorum.

3.   Sed Aquilonis
            ira predonis
        elementis officit
    ne pariant; nec tamen in hoc proficit.
        sed Hymeneus obicit
        eius se turbini;
        in hoc enim numini
        deserviunt Dione.

4. Felicibus stipendiis
    Dione freta, gaudiis
    gaudet suos extollere.
    qui se suo iugo libere
    non denegant submittere,
        quam felici vivere
        vult eos pro munere!

5.   Optat Thetis
            auram quietis,
    ut celo caput exerat
    suosque fructus proferat.
    Ceres quoque secus undam cursitat,
    et tristia sollicitat
            inferorum numina
            pro surrepta Proserpina.

6.   Elementa supera
            coeunt et infera.
            hinc illis vocabula
            sunt attributa mascula;
            illis vero feminina
    congrue sunt deputata nomina,
            quia rerum semina
            concipiunt ut femina.

7. Sol, quia regnat in Piscibus
                celestibus,
            dat copiam
            plenariam
            piscationi
    reddens formam turbide Iunoni."

8. Ista Phrison decantabat
        iuxta regis filiam,
    egram que se simulabat
        dum perrexit per viam
    desponsari. sed hec gnanus
        notans sponso retulit;
    mox truncatur ut profanus.
        tandem sponso detulit.

1. "Winter, jealous of spring, grieves that her bars are now broken. She bids February not to allow itself to be softened by the sun's rays.

2. All the elements intermingled experience the caressing law of love. But Hymenaeus arranges their nuptial couch, thus gratifying the aspirations of the devoted gods.

3. But the anger of the piratical North Wind seeks to impede the elements from giving birth, but does not succeed in this aim. Instead Hymenaeus confronts his storm, for in this the elements obey the will of Venus.

4. Venus relies on their blessed service and is pleased to elate her followers with joys. When men do not refuse freely to submit themselves to her yoke, how keen is her wish that they live in accord with that blessed service!

5. Thetis longs for a tranquil breeze so that she may raise her head to heaven and bring forth her produce. Ceres too rushes to and fro beside the waters, and importunes the grim powers of the dead on behalf of Proserpina, who was snatched away.

6. The elements above and on the earth below are wedded. By reason of this intercourse, to the first are allotted male titles; the second are aptly accorded female names, because like a woman they conceive the seeds of things.

7. Because the Sun rules in Pisces in the heavens, he grants full opportunity for fishing, and restores to disheveled Juno her beauty."

8. This was the song Phrison sang in the company of the king's daughter. She counterfeited illness as she proceeded along the road to her betrothal. But a dwarf marked these events and reported them to the bridegroom: he was promptly beheaded as one impious. [But Phrison] finally delivered the girl to the bridegroom.

THIS POEM IS wholly dissimilar in form from all the other love lyrics in the *Carmina Burana*. As the final stanza indicates, it is sung by a certain Phrison. Patzig ("Zu Guiraut de Cabreira," 549–50) identifies him with the Frizon mentioned in Guiraut de Cabreira's minstrel song *Cabra juglar*, but the identification is disputed; cf. Riquer, *Les chansons de geste*, 349; Pirot, *Recherches*, 14:399. As Raby observes (*SLP* 2:270 n. 1), the story of the minstrel and the dwarf accompanying the king's daughter on her betrothal journey was presumably familiar to the poet's contemporaries, though it is obscure to us. The obvious meaning of the final stanza is that the dwarf was beheaded for giving ear to and divulging the content of the minstrel's song, which was intended for a lover's ear alone; he thus showed himself to be *profanus*. If this is the case, the subject of *detulit* in the final line must be Phrison the minstrel.

The sacred theme of Phrison, designed to reveal to the girl her future participation in the love which animates the cosmos, begins with the motif of the advent of spring, but with a minor variation: the winter, already in February, shows resentment at being dislodged. The following two stanzas describe the stirring influence of the marriage god, Hymenaeus, throughout the universe; the poet has derived inspiration from Martianus Capella here. Stanza 4 turns from the world of nature to the human species, encouraged by Venus to play its allotted role in this love transformation. Then Phrison turns back in stanzas 5–7 to the various provinces of nature—the sea (Thetis), the land-harvest (Ceres), the intercourse between heaven and earth—and with a final flourish of ring composition closes as he began (stanza 2) with another reminiscence from Martianus Capella. Structural variation in the conventional comparison between the quickening in nature and love in the human breast is attained here by setting human love at the center (stanza 4) and flanking it with three stanzas on each side which detail the activity of cosmic Amor.

1. **repagula**: For the Ovidian reminiscence see comments at 1.1.
   deliniri: = *deleniri*, as occasionally in CL.

2. **omnis nexus . . . deorum piorum**: The whole stanza is inspired by the verse invocation to Hymenaeus, god of marriage, at the outset of Martianus Capella's *Marriage of Philology and Mercury*:

> . . . semina qui arcanis stringens pugnantia vinclis
>   complexuque sacro dissona *nexa* foves,
> namque *elementa* ligas vicibus . . .
> foedere complacito sub qua natura iugatur . . .
> O Hymenaee decens. . . .

Similar descriptions appear in Alan of Lille *De Planctu Naturae* 8.208ff., and in Bernardus Silvestris *Cosmographia* 2.9–10.
votis: This is the emendation of Schumann, who cites Arundel 1.1.4: *et amantum teneris / votis allubescit*. The reading in the manuscript is *thetis*, retained by Vollmann as a pseudo-Greek formulation meaning "ordinances."
allubescens: The word is taken over from Martianus Capella. Cf. 1.25, *conubiorum copulis allubescat* [sc. Iuppiter]; 2.181, . . . *Venere, quae nuptiis allubescebat*.

6 ✤ 2 (57) *Bruma, veris emula*

3. **in hoc . . . Dione:** Dione is genitive here and at 11.7a. For Dione as Venus see comments at 1.2.

4. **freta . . . gaudet:** Bischoff's *sueta* for *freta* seems hardly necessary.
   suo: Clearly = Venus'. ML frequently overrides the Classical canons of grammar.
   felici pro munere: The phrase picks up and underlines *felicibus stipendiis* in 4.1.

5. The poet now suggests that the sea (personified in the sea nymph Thetis) and the cornfields (personified as Ceres) impatiently await the coming of calm, bright weather. Neptune and Ceres are among the gathered deities at Martianus Capella 1.49ff.
   fructus: The fish that can be trawled in the fine weather. See stanza 7 below.
   Ceres . . . Proserpina: For Calliope's song of how Dis, god of the underworld, was inflamed by Cupid's arrow with love for Proserpina see Ovid *Met.* 5.341ff. Proserpina was finally permitted to spend summer on earth with her mother but was consigned to the shades below during the winter.

6. **vocabula mascula . . . feminina:** The sky is personified as a male god under the old masculine form Caelus (see Cicero *Nat. D.* 3.44, etc.), and Iuppiter is likewise commonly used for the heavens. The earth is personified as female under the titles Terra and Tellus; Cybele, the Magna Mater, is also regarded as the earth goddess.

7. **in Piscibus:** Pisces, the twelfth sign of the zodiac, is entered by the sun 21 February–20 March before it passes into Aries. The time is consistent with that in stanza 1 above, where winter in February laments the presence of the sun.
   piscationi: Fishing becomes possible again under the sun in Pisces!
   reddens formam turbidae Iunoni: See Martianus Capella 1.67. Juno (here as Luna, the moon) has been storm-tossed all winter, but now regains her beauty.

8. **truncatur . . . detulit:** For a suggested solution to this cryptic stanza see the introductory note above. I take Phrison as the subject of *detulit*. The manuscript has the further word *piorum* after *detulit*: I follow Schumann in excising it. Vollmann emends to *hec parari* and thus provides a rhyme for *desponsari*, which he prints unaccompanied as line 5 of the stanza.

3 (58)

1. Iam ver oritur;
   veris flore variata
      tellus redimitur.
   excitat in gaudium
   cor concentus avium
      voce relativa
   Iovem salutantium.
      in his philomena
   Tereum reiterat,
   et iam fatum   antiquatum
      querule retractat.
   sed dum Fatis obicit
      Itym perditum,
   merula   choraulica
      carmina coaptat.

2. Istis insultantibus
   casibus fatalibus,
   in choree speciem
      res reciprocatur.
   his autem conciliis
   noster adest Iupiter
      cum sua Iunone,
      Cupido cum Dione.
   post hos Argus stellifer,
   et Narcissus floriger,
   Orphëusque plectriger,
   Faunus quoque corniger.

3. Inter hec sollemnia
         communia
   alterno motu laterum
   lascive iactant corpora
         collata,
         nunc occurrens
         nunc procurrens
   contio pennata:

4. Mergus aquaticus,
   aquila munificus,
   bubo noctivagus,
   cygnus flumineus,
   phenix unica,
   perdix lethargica,
   hirundo domestica,
   columba turtisona,
   upupa galigera,
         anser sagax,
         vultur edax,
   psitacus gelboicus,
   milvus gyrovagus,
   alaudula garrula,
   ciconia rostrisona.

5.   His et consimilibus
         paria sunt gaudia;
   demulcet enim omnia
   hec concors consonantia.

6. Tempus est letitie;
   nostro tempore
      vernant flores
   in pratis virentibus,
      et suis rebus
   decus auget Phebus
   in nostris finibus.

1. Now spring is dawning; the earth is dappled and wreathed with the blossoms of spring. The chorus of birds, greeting the clear sky with their commentary in song, rouses the heart to joy. Among them the nightingale repeats Tereus' name and now plaintively tells again her fate of long ago. But as she reproaches the Fates with the loss of Itys, the blackbird joins in with fluting song.

2. As the story of these fatal mishaps strikes the air, the theme is reiterated like a chorus. These councils our Jupiter attends with his Juno, and Cupid with Venus. Behind them come starry Argus, flower-bearing Narcissus, Orpheus with his plectrum, and Faunus with his horn.

3. During these shared rituals, the feathered assembly playfully sway their gathered bodies, moving each flank in turn. Now they meet each other, and now they dart outwards:

4. Waterfowl, bounteous eagle, night-roaming owl, river swan, phoenix without parallel, effete partridge, house swallow, dove with its turtle's note, crested hoopoe, wise goose, gluttonous vulture, bright yellow parrot, circling kite, chattering wee lark, beak-rattling stork—all are there.

5. Through these and others like them equal joys are won; for this united harmony charms the whole of creation.

6. It is the time of gladness; in this our season the flowers bloom in the verdant meadows, and Phoebus in our borders enhances the beauty of the creation that is his.

IN THESE LYRICS the contribution of birdsong in the celebration of spring's coming is an integral strand (see no. 47). Here the birds are the main focus of the poem to the exclusion of explicit mention of the love theme; but the deities and heroes in stanza 2, among them Venus and Cupid, symbolize the quickening of cosmic love and thus justify the inclusion of the composition among the love lyrics. The birds are visualized as participating in human fashion in the ritual dance of spring (stanza 3). It might even be imagined that the poet describes a pageant in which the human participants enact the roles of birds, deities, and heroes.

Bird lore is a prominent feature in the encyclopedic literature of the period. Twelfth-century compilers were able to build upon the earlier learning of the Elder Pliny's *Natural History*, the Latin translations (ca. 400 A.D.) of the *Physiologus*, and Isidore's *Etymologies*. Bestiaries such as *The Book of Beasts* (ed. White), Theobald's eleventh- or twelfth-century *Physiologus* (ed. Eden), and Hugh of Fouilloy's *De Bestiis et Aliis Rebus* (in Migne, *PL* 177) attest the popularity of the subject. Such bird catalogues as in stanza 4 are frequently found not only in these lyrics but also in the philosophical epics of the day; Bernard Silvestris' *Cosmographia* 3.445ff., and Alan of Lille's *De Planctu Naturae*, prosa 1 (where birds and other creatures adorn Nature's dress) are notable examples.

1. **Iovem:** Jupiter the sky god is frequently used by metonymy for the sky itself; here with the dispelling of winter's clouds the birds greet the open heavens.

   philomena . . . Itym perditum: The celebrated myth of Philomena (CL Philomela) was best known to twelfth-century poets through the version of Ovid *Met.* 6.438ff. The plaintive cry of the nightingale (*tereu, tereu*) recalls the rape of Philomela by her brother-in-law Tereus, king of Thrace. In revenge for this outrage, Philomela in company with her sister Procne, the king's wife, served up his son Itys to Tereus in an Irish stew, and was delivered from revenge when all three were transformed into birds. The myth is evoked repeatedly in these lyrics (see 11.2b, etc.) and in other twelfth-century poems.

   choraulica: The word *choraula* can mean a precentor or soloist in ML, but in origin it is a transliteration of the Greek for a flute-accompanist, and the sense of "fluting" is more appropriate here.

2. **his conciliis:** Chaucer's *Parliament of Fowls*, 316ff., comes to mind.

   Iupiter cum Iunone, etc.: As Vollmann suggests, these deities have an allegorical purport. Jupiter may signify the warmth and light of heaven, Venus and Cupid the love that propagates the world, Narcissus and Faunus plant life and animal life, and Orpheus the musical harmony animating and uniting these participants in the cosmos, thus embracing the whole creation.

   Argus stellifer: Vollmann retains Arcus in B, and translates as the zodiac. But Argus of the hundred eyes, symbolic of the stars of heaven, fits more aptly into a list of mythological heroes. Like other characters in this list, Argus evokes a facet of the love experience; he is persecutor of Jupiter's favorite, Io (Ovid *Met.* 1.622ff.). Jupiter and Juno represent the wedlock of deities, Narcissus the love of self (Ovid *Met.* 3.402ff.), Orpheus the tragic traducer of Eurydice (*Met.* 10.3ff.), Faunus the promiscuous satyr with the appendages of a goat (hence *corniger*).

3. **alterno motu laterum:** Compare the sinuous movements of girls in other lyrics, e.g., *Omittamus studia*, 15.4: *ibi fulget mobilis / membrorum lascivia / dum puelle se movendo / gestibus lasciviunt.* . . .

10 ✠ 3 (58) *Iam ver oritur*

4. **aquila munificus**: (Note the indifference to traditional gender.) The epithet "bountiful" is hardly characteristic of the eagle in CL (though the bird plays a kindly role in the Cupid and Psyche story, Apuleius *Met.* 6.15) and more probably evokes scriptural contexts (Exod. 19:4, Deut. 32:11, etc.), reporting its tenderness to the young.

phenix unica: So Isidore *Etym.* 12.7.22, *singularis et unica*. Ovid explains this uniqueness (*Met.* 15.392): *una est, quae reparet seque ipsa reseminet, ales.*

perdix lethargica: This ill repute arises from the partridge's tendency not to rise in flight. Cf. Ovid *Met.* 8.256ff., *non tamen haec alte volucris sua corpora tollit.*

turtisona: The onomatopoeic word does not appear in CL.

galigera: Heraeus' intelligent emendation of *galligera* in the manuscript.

anser sagax: The epithet is borrowed from Ovid (*Met.* 11.599, *canibusve sagacior anser*) to describe the goose's proverbial vigilance (Livy 5.47.4, etc.).

gelboicus: The sense is uncertain. Fischer suggests that it refers to the parrot's power of speech, Vollmann to its bright color.

gyrovagus: Amusingly used of the restless monk in Benedict's *Rule* 1.

alaudula garrula: The diminutive is favored in ML for this *parva avis* (Pliny *HN* 11.121, etc.). *Garrulus* is frequently applied to birds; see *TLL* s.v. garrulus 2.

ciconia rostrisona: Cf. Ovid *Met.* 6.97, *crepitante ciconia rostro.*

6. **suis rebus**: The creation is "his" because the sun has transformed the world.

4 (59)

1. Ecce, chorus virginum
   tempore vernali,
   dum solis incendium
   radios equali
   moderatur ordine,
   nubilo semoto,
   fronde pausat tilie
   Cypridis in voto!

   Refl. Cypridis in voto
   fronde pausat tilie
   Cypridis in voto!

2. In hac valle florida
   floreus flagratus,
   inter septa lilia
   locus purpuratus.
   dum garritus merule
   dulciter alludit,
   philomena carmine
   dulcia concludit.

   Refl.

3. Acies virginea
    redimita flore;
quis enarret talia,
    quantoque decore
prenitent ad libitum
    Veneris occulta?
Dido necis meritum
    proferat inulta.

Refl.

4. Per florenta nemorum
    me fortuna vexit;
arcum Cupidineum
    vernula retexit.
quam inter Veneream
    diligo cohortem,
langueo, dum videam,
    libiti consortem.

Refl.

5. Questio per singulas
    oritur: honesta
potiorque dignitas
    casta vel incesta?
Flora, consors Phyllidis,
    est sententiata:
"caste non est similis
    turpiter amata."

Refl.

6. Iuno, Pallas, Clyope,
    Cytherea dura
affirmant interprete
    Flora verbi iura:
"flagrabit felicius
    nectare mellito
castam amans potius
    quam in infinito."

Refl.

7. Iura grata refero
    puellarum ludis;
vigeant in prospero
    pudice futuris!
actibus temeritas
    nulla salutaris,
contingat iocunditas,
    spes adulta caris!

Refl.

1. See how in the season of spring, as the sun's heat orders its rays equally between day and night, and the clouds are dispersed, a band of maidens in the lime tree's shade seeks rest in paying vows to Venus!

Refrain. In paying vows to Venus, seeks rest in the lime tree's shade, in paying vows to Venus!

2. In this blossoming valley lies a flame of flowers, a becrimsoned place amid an enclosure of lilies. As the blackbird's chattering makes pleasant play, the nightingale closes the sweet notes in her song.

Refrain.

3. The line of maidens is wreathed in flowers. Who could describe such a scene, or tell in what beauty the hidden powers of Venus shine out at will? A Dido could here recount the death which she merited unavenged.

Refrain.

4. Fortune has borne me through these blossoming groves; the home-born slave has uncovered his Cupid's bow. I faint when I behold the one I love, the partner of my choice, among the band of Venus.

Refrain.

5. The question is posed between each and all: Is the state that is chaste, or that which is not chaste, worthy and preferable? Flora, companion of Phyllis, opines: "She who is loved basely is not to be compared with her who is chaste."

Refrain.

6. Juno, Pallas, Calliope, [and] unbending Venus pronounce judgment according to Flora's interpretation: "The man who loves a chaste girl will burn more blessedly with honeyed nectar than he whose love seeks no limit."

Refrain.

7. I recount this welcome judgment to the maidens' frolics. May chaste girls wax and flourish in days to come! No rashness in intercourse brings salvation; may pleasant days and hope full-formed accrue to their dear ones!

Refrain.

SCHUMANN WAS troubled by the apparently disjointed nature of this composition and feared that stanzas had fallen out or that the order was confused. But the sequence as it stands is defensible if considered as an exploration of the controversy raised in courtly love discussion of *amor purus* versus *amor mixtus*, the love falling short of intercourse versus the love that goes all the way. This controversy is prominent in the treatise of Andreas Capellanus (1.6H.470ff., 2.6.24–25). The second of these passages, in which Andreas speaks *propria persona*, maintains that there is no essential difference between the two, but that view is controverted here and in other poems in this collection (notably no. 26). The spokesman here is a cleric whose sympathy lies with *amor purus,* often to be equated with *amor clericalis.* It is helpful to have no. 29 in mind when reading this poem, for

Flora and Phyllis, the friends cited here in stanza 5, are there the contestants arguing respectively the merits of the cleric and the knight as the ideal lover. Flora, the cleric's lady in no. 29, is the apologist for *amor purus* here (though when cited unaccompanied in other poems the name does not invariably symbolize the chaste lover).

The sequence of ideas here may be explained as follows. The scene is conventionally set in stanzas 1–3 with a band of maidens reclining in a *locus amoenus*. In stanza 4 the spokesman chances upon them and sees there the girl of his choice. The girls conduct a *controversia* in which Flora argues for *amor purus*, maintaining that one who is *turpiter amata* (*turpis amor* is the *amor mixtus* in which courtesans and matrons alike indulge; see 26.3) is unworthy to be compared with the one who confines herself to *amor purus*. The issue is referred to the court of love, at which four judges with sobriquets of goddesses pronounce in Flora's favor (perhaps against Phyllis' arguing for *amor mixtus*?). The spokesman bears this judgment back to the maidens with warnings against *amor mixtus*. It should be stressed that such a court is a literary fiction rather than a reality in the world of the twelfth century.

1. **equali . . . ordine:** A reference to the spring equinox (about 20 March), when hours of daylight and darkness are equal.
   nubilo: Sedgwick's emendation of *iubilo*; this manuscript reading is defensible (the chorus "abandons its glad song") but is clearly less appropriate.
   pausat: So Patzig for *pausa* in the manuscript.
   Cypridis: This Greek form of "the Cyprian" (Cyprus is the island of Aphrodite) is not found in CL, occurring first in Ausonius.

2. **flagratus:** Best taken as a ML noun. The contrast between white and crimson is a favorite theme in both CL and ML (cf. 7.5a, 18.2, etc.).
   purpuratus: See comments at 46.1.

3. **Dido . . . inulta:** Cf. Virgil *Aen.* 4.659–60, *dixit, et os impressa toro, "moriemur inultae, / sed moriemur" ait.* Dido is introduced as an exemplar of the hidden powers of Venus, depicted so memorably by Virgil with the imagery of arrow and flame. Perhaps too Dido's case history is relevant to the adjudication, a warning against *turpis amor* (cf. CB 99.10).

4. **vernula:** The home-born slave is Cupid, depicted as agent of Venus.
   langueo, etc.: Construe as *langueo, dum videam (eam) quam diligo, libiti consortem, inter Veneream cohortem.*

5. **caste:** = *castae* (dative).

6. In no. 29 the issue of cleric versus knight as ideal lover is taken to the court of Cupid and decided there. Here the arbiters are Juno, Pallas, Calliope, and unbending Venus. Calliope is chosen as Muse of amatory poetry (Bischoff's emendation to Dione is overbold, as Calliope and Pallas Athene are associated at Ovid *Met.* 5.336ff., as are Juno and Venus at Virgil *Aen.* 4.90ff., both pairs in love contexts). Sedgwick would read *Cytheree* (dative) to render "Calliope hostile to Venus," which would reduce the panel to three and emphasize the hostility of the Muse of studious learning toward the distracting Venus, but the change seems otiose.

7. **ludis:** The word bears the sense of innocent flirtation in these poems.
pudice: = CL *pudicae*, Bischoff's fine emendation of *iudice*.
futuris: For the sense "in future days" cf. 29.79.
actibus temeritas: So Schumann for *actibus emeritas* in the manuscript. For *actibus* = "acts of sexual intercourse" see 26.8.
contingat . . . caris: *Spes* has a technical sense in courtly love theory. A lady can either dismiss wholly the attentions of a suitor, or grant him hope. In this second instance he must justify himself by deeds of worth undertaken for and in the name of the lady, who may then consent to accept him, in which case his *spes* is *adulta*.

5 (62)

1. Dum Diane vitrea
   sero lampas oritur,
   et a fratris rosea
   luce dum succenditur,
   dulcis aura Zephiri
   spirans omnes etheri
   nubes tollit; sic emollit
   vi chordarum pectora,
   et immutat   cor, quod nutat
   ad amoris pignora.

2. Letum iubar Hesperi
   gratiorem   dat humorem
   roris soporiferi
   mortalium generi.

3. O quam felix est antidotum soporis!
   quot curarum tempestates sedat et doloris!
   dum surrepit clausis oculorum poris,
   ipsum gaudio equiperat dulcedini amoris.

4. Morpheus in mentem
   trahit impellentem
   ventum lenem segetes maturas,
   murmura rivorum per harenas puras,
   circulares ambitus molendin⟨ari⟩orum
   qui furantur somno lumen oculorum.

[5. Post blanda Veneris commercia
   lassatur cerebri substantia;
   hinc caligant mira novitate
   oculi nantes in palpebrarum rate.
   hei, quam felix transitus
   amoris ad soporem,
   sed suavior
   regressus ad amorem.

6. Ex alvo leta fumus evaporat,
   qui capitis tres cellulas irrorat.
   hic infumat oculos   ad soporem pendulos,
   et palpebras sua fumositate
   replet, ne visus exspacietur late.
   unde ligant oculos virtutes animales,
   que sunt magis vise ministeriales.

7. Fronde sub arboris amena,
   dum querens canit philomena,
   suave est quiescere;   suavius ludere
   in gramine cum virgine speciosa
   si variarum   odor herbarum
   spiraverit, si dederit thorum rosa,
   dulciter soporis alimonia
   post Veneris defessa commercia
   captatur, dum lassis instillatur.

8. O in quantis
   animus amantis
   variatur vacillantis!
   ut vaga ratis per equora,   dum caret anchora,
   fluctuat inter spem metumque dubia,
   sic Veneris milicia.]

1. When the glistening torch of Diana rises late in the day and is ignited by
   the rosy light of her brother, the sweet breath of the West Wind with its ex-
   halation removes all clouds from the sky. In the same way that wind by the
   power of his strings relieves men's breasts and transforms the heart that is
   wilting in the face of love's pledges.

2. The joyful radiance of the evening star brings to the race of mortals the
   more welcome moisture of sleep-inducing dew.

3. How blessed is the antidote of sleep! What storms of cares and griefs it assuages! As it creeps along the closed passages of the eyes, it equals with its
   joy the sweetness of love.

4. Morpheus draws into the mind a gentle wind inclining the ripe harvest, the
   murmur of rills along glistening courses of sand, the circling movement of
   the beasts of the mill, which in sleep steal the sight from our eyes.

[5. After the pleasurable interchange of love, the brain matter is fatigued. By
   reason of this the eyes, swimming in the barque of the lids, darken in a
   strange and novel way. Oh, how blessed is the passage from love to sleep,
   but sweeter the return to love!

6. Steam wells forth from the exultant belly and bedews the three cells of the
   brain. Here it wreathes the eyes as they droop in sleep and fills the lids
   with its fumes, so that the sight may not journey far. So the physical powers, which appear stronger in their service, bind the eyes.

7. It is sweet to relax under the lovely foliage of a tree to the plaintive song of
   the nightingale. But it is sweeter to sport on the grass with a beautiful
   maiden. If the scent of mingled plants breathes forth, if rose petals provide
   a couch, once the wearying intercourse of love is over it is sweet to win the
   nurture of sleep as it seeps into our languid bodies.

8. In what depths does the mind of the unstable lover shift! Love's army is like
   a ship without an anchor, wandering over the sea, wavering hesitant between hope and fear.]

IN THIRTY POEMS 90ff., I argued against Dronke's restoration (*Medieval Latin and the Rise of European Love-Lyric*, 306ff.) of stanzas 5–8 to this poem, which is deservedly recognized as the most original in its theme, and the most arresting in its presentation, of the entire collection. Because subsequent editors, including Vollmann, have followed Dronke, I have appended these stanzas with a translation to allow readers to form their own judgment of the justification for Hilka and Schumann's excluding them. Dronke suggests that the well-known parody *Dum domus lapidea* (*CB* 197) incorporates echoes of stanzas 6 and 8; but such echoes, not strikingly close, can be explained by the hypothesis that *Dum Diane vitrea* had already been complemented by other hands by the time the parody was composed. The decisive criterion must be study of the additional stanzas themselves; though 5–6 and 7–8 resume the theme of sleep and love, the treatment and tone differ notably not only from 1–4 but also from each other. Stanzas 5–6 read like a technical discourse on the physiological effects of lovemaking on the eyes; 7–8 incorporate banal borrowings from other lyrics and also from earlier stanzas (compare 7.8 and 5.1). Hence my support for Schumann's conclusion that these are inferior supplements contributed by two different hands.

Stanzas 1–4 form a miniature masterpiece on the single theme of the blessings of night for the wearied lover. Lovemaking, so conspicuous in the appended stanzas, is irrelevant to the treatment. The cooling influence of the Zephyr and the falling dew promote the sleep which affords relief and indeed a joy equal to that experienced in the act of love. In that blessed sleep the tranquility is delineated through the images of the breeze inclining the cornfields, the stream coursing smoothly over its sandy channel, and the circular movements of the beasts that turn the millstones.

1. **Diane . . . fratris:** Diana and Apollo, the moon and the sun, were the twin children of Leto, born on Delos.
   lampas . . . rosea luce: The language is strikingly reminiscent of Lucretius 5.610, *rosea sol alte lampade lucens*.
   etheri: Ablative; the -*i* form, common in ML, is required for the rhyme.
   vi chordarum: I retain *vi* from the manuscript (against Meyer's *vis*), taking the gentle breeze of the Zephyr as the subject.
   pignora: Schumann emends to *pondera*, believing that *pignora* has entered the text from the parody in *CB* 197, *et immutet . . . vestes in pignora*. Vollmann persuades me that there is a case for retaining *pignora*, but he construes *ad . . . pignora* with *immutat* as in the parody. My interpretation of the theme of the poem as sleep as consolation from the pressures of love makes it more appropriate to take it with *nutat*.

2. **iubar**: The word depicts the bright glow of the Evening Star accompanying the moon in its course. Ovid *Fasti* 2.149 uses it of the Morning Star, equally aptly.

3. **quot**: Manitius' emendation of *quod* may not be strictly necessary (Vollmann retains *quod*), but it certainly adds rhetorical force to the stanza. **surrepit**: Probably influenced by Ovid *Fasti* 3.19, *blanda quies furtim victis obrepit ocellis* (*surrepit* is an alternative reading in the manuscripts).

4. **Morpheus**: Schmeller's emendation of *Orpheus* is certainly more appropriate to the theme of 1–4. *Orpheus*, retained by Dronke (*Medieval Latin and the Rise of European Love-Lyric*, 307) and Vollmann, has no clear connection with the celebration of sleep.
   molendin⟨ari⟩orum: The *qui furantur* suggests that the mill beasts would be a more appropriate antecedent than the millstones, and the rhythm of the line is arguably improved by the change. In *Thirty Poems* I further suggest that there may be a pleasant play in the idea that the mill beasts (normally blinded or blindfolded for this task; cf. Apuleius *Met.* 9.11.3, Paulinus of Nola *Ep.* 23.12) rob us of the sight of our eyes.

6 (63)

1a. Olim sudor Herculis,
    monstra late conterens,
    pestes orbis auferens,
    claris longe titulis
                enituit;
    sed tandem defloruit
    fama prius celebris,
    cecis clausa tenebris,
    Ioles illecebris
    Alcide captivato.

1b. Hydra damno capitum
    facta locupletior,
    omni peste sevior,
    reddere sollicitum
                non potuit,
    quem puella domuit.
    iugo cessit Veneris
    vir, qui maior superis
    celum tulit humeris
    Atlante fatigato.

Refl.

    Amor fame meritum   deflorat;
amans tempus perditum   non plorat,
        sed temere   diffluere
             sub Venere
            laborat.

Refl.

2a. Caco tristis halitus
et flammarum vomitus
vel fuga Nesso duplici
     non profuit;
Geryon Hesperius
ianitorque Stygius
uterque forma triplici
     non terruit,
quem captivum tenuit
risu puella simplici.

  Refl.

2b. Iugo cessit tenero,
somno qui letifero
horti custodem divitis
     implicuit,
frontis Acheloie
cornu dedit Copie,
apro, leone domitis
     enituit,
Thraces equos imbuit
cruenti cede hospitis.

  Refl.

3a. Antei Libyci
luctam sustinuit,
casus sophistici
fraudes cohibuit,
cadere dum vetuit;
sed qui sic explicuit
lucte nodosos nexus,
vincitur et vincitur,
     dum labitur
magna Iovis soboles
ad Ioles amplexus.

  Refl.

3b. Tantis floruerat
laborum titulis,
quem blandis carcerat
puella vinculis.
et dum lambit osculis,
nectar huic labellulis
Venereum propinat;
vir solutus otiis
     Venereis
laborum memoriam
et gloriam inclinat.

  Refl.

4a. Sed Alcide fortior
     aggredior
pugnam contra Venerem.
     ut superem,
     hanc fugio;
in hoc enim prelio
fugiendo fortius
     et melius
     pugnatur,
sicque Venus vincitur:
     dum fugitur,
          fugatur.

  Refl.

4b. Dulces nodos Veneris
     et carceris
blandi seras resero,
     de cetero
     ad alia
dum traducor studia.
o Lycori, valeas
     et voveas
     quod vovi;
ab amore spiritum
     sollicitum
          removi.

  Refl.

1a. The sweat of Hercules of old, treading monsters underfoot far and wide, and removing the banes of the world, shone out with outstandingly bright glory. But finally his earlier-famed renown lost its bloom when it was engulfed in blinding darkness, since that descendant of Alceus was in thrall to the enticements of Iole.

Refrain. Love strips the bloom from the meed of glory. The lover does not lament the waste of time, but rashly toils to squander it in service to Venus.

1b. The Hydra, which was enriched by loss of its heads and was fiercer than any bane, could not trouble him, but a girl subdued him. He who was greater than the gods, and who bore the sky on his shoulders when Atlas tired, yielded to the yoke of love.

Refrain.

2a. Cacus' oppressive breath, vomiting forth fire, did not avail him, nor did flight aid the two-faced Nessus. Spanish Geryon, and the Stygian doorman, each with threefold shape, did not frighten the one whom a girl with her ingenuous smile enslaved.

Refrain.

2b. The man who enfolded the guardian of the rich garden in death-bearing sleep, who presented to the goddess Abundance the horn of Achelous' forehead, who became glorious by subduing the boar and the lion, and who steeped the Thracian horses in the slaughter of the bloodstained host, yielded to the soft yoke of love.

Refrain.

3a. He endured the wrestling of African Antaeus and checked the deceits of his crafty tumbling when he forbade him to fall. But though he thus loosed the entangling knots of that wrestling, the mighty offspring of Jupiter was conquered and enchained when he fell to Iole's embraces.

Refrain.

3b. Such were the great glories of the labors through which that man prospered, whom a maiden imprisoned with her enticing bonds. And while she gave him tongue-kisses and with her dear lips served him Venus' nectar, he was undone through his vacation in love, and let slip the recollection and fame of his labors.

Refrain.

4a. But I am stronger than Hercules, and I take up the fight against Venus. I shun her to overcome her; for in this engagement it is better and braver to fight by flight, and this is how Venus is overcome. She is routed when we flee from her.

Refrain.

4b. I undo the sweet knots of Venus and draw back the bars of her alluring prison; for the future I devote myself to other pursuits. Farewell, Lycoris! take the vow which I have taken. I have sundered my troubled soul from love.

Refrain.

THIS POEM survives in four other manuscripts besides B (see details in Hilka and Schumann's *CB*), thus providing a more satisfactory text.

In this composition, which exemplifies the mythological lyric, Peter of Blois (see Introduction, section 2) exploits the Hercules theme to announce in mannered lines the renunciation of love. In his best-known poem, *Vacillantis trutine* (no. 33), the spokesman weighs reason against love and pronounces love the heavier; in this poem he comes to the opposite resolution (stanza 4b, *ad alia / dum traducor studia*). Such variation on a similar theme suggests the imprint of the detached craftsman rather than that of the passionate lover.

The poem incorporates twelve exploits of Hercules, seven of them his labors. All twelve are included in the single narrative of Ovid *Metamorphoses* 9, with the exception of the Cacus episode, familiar to twelfth-century readers from Virgil *Aeneid* 8. Ovid *Heroides* 9 is less in evidence as a source.

1a. **Ioles illecebris:** Ovid *Met.* 9.136ff. recounts how the rumored passion of Hercules for Iole, daughter of King Eurytus of Oechalia, led his wife to send him the shirt of Nessus as an aphrodisiac, and thereby unwittingly caused his death.

1b. **Hydra:** The seven-headed dragon that sprouted two heads when one was cut off was familiar from Ovid *Met.* 9.192–93, Horace *Carm.* 4.4.61, etc. **celum tulit, etc.:** Ovid *Met.* 9.198 has *hac caelum cervice tuli.*

2a. **Caco:** The destruction of Cacus, the giant oppressing Evander's kingdom of Pallanteum on the site of Rome, is recounted at Virgil *Aen.* 8.193ff., Livy 1.7.4, Ovid *Fasti* 1.543–44, etc.

Nesso duplici: The adjective may bear a punning sense, as Nessus was a centaur, two-shaped as well as two-faced (Ovid *Met.* 9.119–20, *Nessoque paranti / fallere depositum . . .*).

Geryon Hesperius / ianitorque Stygius: They are likewise juxtaposed in Ovid *Met.* 9.184–85, *Nec me pastoris Hiberi / forma triplex, nec forma triplex tua, Cerbere, movit.*

2b. **horti custodem:** The garden of the Hesperides was guarded by a sleepless dragon (Ovid *Met.* 9.190), which in some versions was killed by Hercules (e.g., Hyginus *Fab.* 30.12).

frontis Acheloie cornu dedit Copie: For the struggle with the river god Achelous, who transformed himself into a bull and had his horn broken off and presented to Copia, see Ovid *Met.* 9.1–88.

apro, leone domitis: Hercules' slaughter of the Erymanthian boar and the Nemean lion are recounted by Ovid at *Met.* 9.192 and 9.197.

Thraces equos . . . hospitis: The reading in F, *Traces,* is much superior to *truces* in B. At *Met.* 9.194ff. Ovid recounts how Hercules slew the Thracian horses and their master Diomedes.

3a. **Antei Libyci . . . dum vetuit:** Antaeus was the son of Earth; he compelled guests to wrestle with him and slew them when they were worsted. Each time he fell, he drew fresh strength from his mother (Ovid *Met.* 9.183–84). As Vollmann suggests, there may be scholastic punning in *casus sophistici fraudes,* with its possible sense of a problem solved by a false conclusion.

vincitur et vincitur: The embrace of Antaeus in the wrestling match is amusingly contrasted with that of Iole in the love match. Whereas Hercules disengaged himself from the grasp of Antaeus to prevail, he enchained himself with Iole and was overcome.

magna Iovis soboles: Alcmena bore Hercules when impregnated by Jupiter in the absence of her husband Amphitryon, as Plautus' play of that name narrates. Cf. Ovid *Met.* 9.23ff.

3b. **inclinat:** The sense of "cause to decline" is found occasionally in CL.

4a. **fugio . . . fugiendo . . . dum fugitur, fugatur:** The motif of survival through flight is found in two compositions by Peter of Blois earlier in the *Carmina Burana*: *CB* 29.13–14, *et qui novit cedere, fugiendo fugitur*; and *CB* 31.8.

4b. **ad alia . . . studia:** Contrast 1.5, in which Minerva is deserted in favor of Venus.

Lycoris: The girl is given a name familiar from Roman elegy (cf. Ovid *Am.* 1.15.30, *Ars Am.* 3.537, etc.), just as in other poems Peter exploits the name Coronis (see nos. 7, 12).

1a. A globo veteri
cum rerum faciem
traxissent superi,
mundique seriem
prudens explicuit
et texuit
Natura,
iam preconceperat
quod fuerat
factura.

1b. Que causas machine
mundane suscitans,
de nostra virgine
iam dudum cogitans,
plus hanc excoluit,
plus prebuit
honoris,
dans privilegium
et pretium
laboris.

2a. In hac pre ceteris
totius operis
Nature lucet opera.
tot munera
nulli favoris contulit,
sed extulit
hanc ultra cetera.

2b. Et, que puellulis
avara singulis
solet partiri singula,
huic sedula
impendit copiosius
et plenius
forme munuscula.

3a. Nature studio
longe venustata,
contendit lilio
rugis non crispata
frons nivea.
simplices siderea
luce micant ocelli.

3b. Omnes amantium
trahit in se visus,
spondens remedium
verecunda risus
lascivia.
arcus supercilia
discriminant gemelli.

4a. Ab utriusque luminis
confinio,
moderati libraminis
iudicio,
naris eminentia
producitur venuste
quadam temperantia;
nec nimis erigitur
nec premitur
iniuste.

4b. Allicit verbis dulcibus
et osculis
castigate tumentibus
labellulis,
roseo nectareus
odor infusus ori.
pariter eburneus
sedet ordo dentium
par nivium
candori.

5a. Certant nivi, micant lene
    pectus, mentum, colla, gene;
    sed, ne candore nimio
       evanescant in pallorem,
       precastigat hunc candorem
    rosam maritans lilio
       prudentior Natura,
    ut ex his fiat aptior
       et gratior
          mixtura.

5b. Rapit michi me Coronis
    privilegiata donis
    et Gratiarum flosculis.
       nam Natura, dulcioris
       alimenta dans erroris,
    dum in stuporem populis
       hanc omnibus ostendit,
    in risu blando retia
       Veneria
          tetendit.

1a. When the gods above extracted the shape of the world from the ancient mass, and Nature sagaciously unfolded and interwove the chain of the universe, she had already visualized what she had intended to create.

1b. As she set in motion the causes of the world's fabric, she had long been pondering my maiden, and she adorned her the more and gave her more distinction, presenting her as the preferment and reward of her toil.

2a. In her the work of Nature shines forth more brightly than in the rest of her entire labors. On no other did Nature bestow so many gifts of favor, but raised her above all else.

2b. And those dainty gifts of beauty which she usually bestows in miserly fashion on each and every maiden, she diligently imparted more lavishly and fully on her.

3a. The girl's snowy brow, lent boundless charm by Nature's zeal, rivals the lily and is unlined with wrinkles. Her ingenuous dear eyes shine with starry brightness.

3b. The modest playfulness of her smile attracts to itself all the eyes of her suitors, promising them deliverance. Twin delicate arches mark her eyebrows.

4a. From the vicinity of each eye with studied and controlled balance the line of her nose extends charmingly with a certain restraint. It neither juts out too sharply nor is unduly bulbous.

4b. The aroma of nectar breathed into her rosy mouth lends enticement to the sweet words and kisses from her dear lips, with their controlled pouting. The line of her teeth, like ivory, sits evenly, matching the whiteness of snow.

5a. Her breast, chin, neck, and cheeks vie with snow in their gentle glow. But so that they may not fade into pallor through excessive whiteness, Nature in her greater wisdom disciplines this whiteness by marrying the rose to the lily, so that the two may form a more suitable and pleasant compound.

5b. Coronis steals my heart from me, endowed as she is with the preferment of gifts and sweet blossoms of the Graces; for Nature, nurturing my waywardness more sweet, whilst flaunting her before all folks to astound them, has stretched out her love nets in that charming smile.

THIS POEM is found in Heidelberg 357, London Arundel 384, and Florence Laur. Plut. 29.1 (F) (in part), as well as in B.

The poet (probably Peter of Blois; see Introduction, section 2) draws the inspiration for his composition from contemporary philosophical writing. Of particular significance is Bernard Silvestris' *Cosmographia* (ed. Dronke, trans. Wetherbee; useful analyses in Wetherbee, *Platonism and Poetry,* and in Stock, *Myth and Science*). In Bernard's poem "Nature pleads that something more beautiful be made of the primal chaos" (Wetherbee). Like Ovid in his *Metamorphoses,* Bernard depicts a creation not *ex nihilo* as in Genesis but *a globo veteri.* Noys, the divine Wisdom personified in the *Cosmographia,* describes Nature as *uteri mei beata fecunditas,* which "oversees the processes of generation and renewal in the universe" (Wetherbee). This comes close to her role in the first stanza of this poem. The *Cosmographia* was published probably in the 1140s (according to Stock); Peter of Blois, born ca. 1135, could have been composing his amatory poetry within twenty years of its publication. A second work reflecting close similarities with this poem is Gerald of Wales' *De Mundi Creatione* (ed. Brewer), as the comments below indicate. Thirdly, though it would be hazardous to suggest direct influence from Alan of Lille's *De Planctu Naturae* (ed. Häring, trans. Sheridan) or his *Anticlaudianus* (ed. Bossuat, trans. Sheridan), it is notable that the first of these poems projects Nature as God's deputy and the source of moral law, and the second depicts Nature's design of creating the perfect man—as, here, she creates Coronis—as the crowning glory of her work. Hence the awareness of the existence of these philosophical works clarifies the backdrop of intellectual ideas against which this poem can be read.

1a. **globo**: For the sense of "mass" see Virgil G. 1.473. Munari ("Mediaevalia I–II," 288) rightly cites Bernard Silvestris' *Cosmographia: Megacosmos* 1.1ff: *congeries informis adhuc, cum silva teneret, / sub veteri confusa globo primordia rerum / visa Deo Natura queri.* . . .
superi: The non-Christian flavor of the myth of creation is reinforced by the Classical aura of the plurality of gods.
mundique seriem: In his excellent edition of the Arundel manuscript, in which this poem appears, McDonough prints *mundi que seriem / prudens explicuit / et texuit, / Natura iam preconceperat.* . . .

1b. **causas machine mundane:** Cf. Prudentius *Hamart.* 247ff., *nec mirum, si membra orbis concussa rotantur, / si vitiis agitata suis mundana laborat / machina.* This itself is perhaps a reminiscence of Lucretius 5.96, *moles et machina mundi.*

dans privilegium: McDonough well compares Bernard Silvestris' *Cosmographia: Microcosmos* 3.1, where Noys in promising man a unique endowment speaks of *quodam quasi dignitatis privilegio et singularitate.*

2a. **extulit hanc super cetera:** The possible reminiscence of Paul (Phil. 2:9, *nomen quod est super omne nomen*) suggests a divine status for the lady.

2b. **puellulis:** "Mere maidens," in contrast to the excellence of his favorite.

3–5. The description of the girl's beauty is a conventional feature paralleled in many of these lyrics. Systematic analysis of the physiognomy of the loved one is a feature of the instruction offered by the rhetorical manuals of the period. Matthew of Vendôme's *Ars Versificatoria* 1.56ff. (ca. 1175) (ed. Munari, trans. Galyon) gives two formal examples of how to describe women's beauty. Geoffrey of Vinsauf's *Poetria Nova* (ca. 1200) (ed. Faral, trans. Nims), in retailing such details (554ff.), calls the practice *res quasi trita / et vetus.* Such close descriptions of female beauty are found as early as Maximian *Elegies* 1.93 in the sixth century, and in less concentrated form earlier in the Classical poets. See Brewer, "The Ideal of Feminine Beauty"; and Häring, "Die Gedichte und Mysterienspiele des Hilarius von Orléans."

3a. **crispata:** Cf. Persius 3.87.
siderea luce: The phrase is borrowed from Ovid *Met.* 4.169.

3b. **omnes ... visus:** Cf. 9.3, *omnes in se trahit visus.*
verecunda risus lascivia: In this oxymoron too the parallel with 9.3 is manifest, prompting the suggestion of identical authorship. See further stanza 4b below.
arcus ... gemelli: McDonough well compares Gerald of Wales' *De mundi creatione* 1.347 throughout this description: *prodit in arcum / forma supercilii ... naris naturae vultum supereminet arte, / nec trahit hanc modicam, nec nimis in vitium.*

4a. **naris eminentia ... quadam temperantia:** See the previous note. Matthew of Vendôme (1.56) likewise defines the ideal nose as neither too big nor too small. In his allegiance to this rhetorical theory our poet comes perilously close to bathos.

4b. **castigate tumentibus labellulis:** The correspondence with 9.3, *labia Veneria tumentia,* cannot be fortuitous. Maximian (see note at 3–5 above) has *modicumque tumentia labra.*

roseo ori: Cf. Ovid *Met.* 7.705, *roseo spectabilis ore;* Virgil *Aen.* 9.5, *roseo Thaumantius ore.*

nectareus odor . . . eburneus ordo: Gerald of Wales (see 3b above) has *nectaris odor . . . eburneus ordo.*

5a. **nivi:** Ablative, = CL *nive.* Cf. 17.15, *tamquam massa nivea gula candescebat.* The throat is singled out for separate treatment in Matthew of Vendôme's *exempla* (see notes for stanzas 3–5 above).

precastigat: First in ML.

rosam maritans lilio: See comments at 4.2.

5b. **rapit michi me:** Cf. 15.4 (and Horace *Carm.* 4.13.20; also *CB* 104.2.1, *michi me subripuit*).

me Coronis: This is the superior reading in the Arundel manuscript; B has *nectar diis.* The literary pseudonym, which reappears in 12.3a, is adopted from Ovid *Met.* 2.542. The girl in Ovid was loved by Apollo; when she was unfaithful to him, she was delated to him by a bird and, though pregnant, was transfixed by the god's arrow. The parallel is hardly apposite here, though Coronis in no. 12 is a girl who yields.

privilegiata: The verb is a ML creation from *privilegium.*

dulcioris . . . erroris: The "sweeter sin" is the spokesman's, not the girl's.

in risu blando . . . retia Veneria tetendit: The parallel with 9.3, *blandi risus . . . labia Veneris,* is again close. Cf. Ovid *Her.* 20.45ff., *retia . . . quae tetendit Amor.*

8 (68)

1. Saturni sidus lividum, Mercurio micante,
   fugatur ab Apolline risum Iovis nudante;
   ⟨iam⟩ redit ab exilio ver coma rutilante.

2.   Cantu nemus avium
         lascive canentium
         suave delinitur,
         fronde redimitur;
   vernant spine floribus
            micantibus,
            signantibus
   Venerem, quia spina pungit, flos blanditur.

3. Mater Venus subditis amori
        dulcia
        stipendia
        copia
    largiri delectatur uberiori.

4. Dulcis aura Zephyri
    spirans ab occidente
    Iovis favet sideri
    alacriori mente,
    Aquilonem carceri
    Eolo nolente
    deputans; sic ceteri
    glaciales spiritus diffugiunt repente.
    redit calor etheri,
    dum caligo nubium rarescit sole Taurum tenente.

5. Sic beati spes, halitus flagrans oris tenelli
        dum acclinat basium,
        scindit nubem omnium
        curarum, sed avelli
    nescit, ni congressio sit arcani medica duelli.

6. Felix hora huius duelli,
    cui contingit nectar adunare melli!
        quam felix unio,
        cuius suavitatis poculo
    sopiuntur sensus et ocelli!

1. When Mercury shines, the louring star of Saturn is put to flight by Phoebus, who uncovers heaven's smile. Spring returns from exile with its glowing tresses.

2. The grove is sweetly soothed by the song of birds singing a sportive melody, and is wreathed with foliage. The thorns sprout with gleaming blooms
   which symbolize love, for the thorn pricks as the blossom entices.

3. Mother Venus takes delight in bestowing with more fruitful abundance her
   sweet wages on those subject to love.

4. The sweet breeze of the Zephyr breathing from the west nurtures Jupiter's star with more eager spirit, consigning the North Wind to prison against the will of Aeolus; thus the other icy blasts suddenly disperse. Warmth returns to the upper air as the darkness of clouds thins away when the Sun lays hold of Taurus.

5. The blessed man's hope is like that; it cleaves the cloud of universal cares, when the burning breath of a young mouth bends to kiss. It cannot be sundered unless there be the healing union of a secret duel.

6. Happy the occasion of this duel, in which nectar is happily mingled with honey! How happy that union, for by the draught of its sweetness, feelings and poor eyes are drugged in sleep!

IN THIS LYRIC the initial description of the advent of spring exploits the astronomical motif prominent also in no. 27. This lore, defining the position of the planets at the coming of spring, contrasts the glacial and hostile Saturn with the temperate warmth of Jupiter. The standard themes of nature's renewal and the onset of human love are strikingly interlinked. Venus and her rewards are introduced by the rose-thorn topos (stanzas 2–3); the poet then resumes the theme of the transformation in nature to achieve a striking variation: the sweet breath of the West Wind, in dispelling winter's cloudy cold, is analogous to the hope dispelling the cares of the fulfilled lover. Parallels in thought and expression with *Dum Diane vitrea* (no. 5) raise the intriguing possibility of composition by the same poet, or at any rate of flattering and talented imitation.

1. **Saturni**: Saturn was in antiquity regarded as the most distant and cold of the planets (so Cicero *Div.* 2.91; Virgil G. 1.336, etc.) and hence the most hostile to humanity (see Horace *Carm.* 2.17.20ff.). The theme of Saturn's hostility is a commonplace in ML; so, e.g., Alan of Lille *Anticlaudianus* 4.465ff., *furaturque decus pratis et sidera florum*, etc.
   Mercurio micante: Here an evening star, observed close to the sun in March and April.
   risum Iovis: Heaven's smile is a cliché in these lyrics. See, e.g., 13.1a.
   coma rutilante: The phrase, evocative of the Gauls' red hair (Suetonius *Cal.* 47), personifies spring by reference to its flowers or more probably its red sky; see 13.1b.

2. **lascive**: So Bischoff for *lascivia* in the manuscript; cf. 25.2, *lascive canunt volucres*.

delinitur: = CL *delenitur*.

spina pungit, flos blanditur: For ML variations on this perennial *sententia* see Walther s.v. *spina*.

3. **dulcia stipendia:** Venus is accorded a kindly role in this poem by contrast to her cruelty in others; see especially 13.8b.

4. **dulcis aura Zephyri:** Cf. 5.1, *dulcis aura Zephyri / spirans.* . . .
   Iovis sideri: Cf. Cicero *Rep.* 6.17, *prosperus et salutaris fulgor qui dicitur Iovis*; *Nat. D.* 2.119, etc.
   Aquilonem . . . deputans: For the role of Aeolus as king of the winds see Virgil *Aen.* 1.51ff. and Ovid *Met.* 14.224.
   sole Taurum tenente: The sun enters Taurus on 14 April.

5. **beati:** Schumann emends to *beat*, but the genitive is apt enough. Vollmann's reading, *sic beat Tispes* [= *Thisbes*] *alitus*, is ingenious, but at 10.1 the name appears as Thisbe and not in this outlandish form.
   halitus flagrans: I punctuate to take this as the subject of *acclinat* in the *dum* clause. The verb *acclinare* is not found transitively used in CL.
   scindit . . . curarum: Cf. 5.3, *quot curarum tempestates sedat.* . . .
   avelli nescit: Supply *nubes* from *nubem*.

6. **sopiuntur:** This further parallel in thought with 5.2–4 is notable.

9 (69)

1. Estas in exsilium
       iam peregrinatur,
   leto nemus avium
       cantu viduatur;
   pallet viror frondium,
       campus defloratur.
               exaruit
               quod floruit,
   quia felicem statum nemoris
               vis frigoris
       sinistra denudavit,
       et ethera silentio
               turbavit,
               exsilio
       dum aves relegavit.

2.   Sed amorem
            qui calorem
nutrit, nulla vis frigoris valet attenuare,
                 sed ea reformare
studet, que corruperat brume torpor. amare
                      crucior,
                      morior,
            vulnere, quo glorior.
        eia, si me sanare
            uno vellet osculo,
            que cor felici iaculo
        gaudet vulnerare!

3. Lasciva, blandi risus,
   omnes in se trahit visus.
                labia
                Veneria
                tumentia
—sed castigate—dant errorem
                leniorem
                dum dulcorem
   instillant, favum mellis, osculando,
   ut me mortalem negem aliquando.
        leta frons tam nivea,
        lux oculorum aurea,
        caesaries subrubea,
        manus vincentes lilia,
        me trahunt in suspiria.
                rideo
                dum video
        cuncta tam elegantia,
            tam regia,
            tam suavia,
            tam dulcia.

1. Summer now journeys abroad into exile. The grove is widowed of the
   happy songs of the birds. The greenness of the foliage turns gray, and the
   plain loses its virgin blossom. All that sprouted has withered, because the
   malevolent power of cold has stripped away the glade's blessed beauty and
   has confounded the sky with silence by banishing the birds into exile.

32 ✛ 9 (69) *Estas in exsilium*

2. But no power of cold can thin the love which nurtures heat; love is avid to renew what the sluggishness of winter had poisoned. I am bitterly tortured, dying of the wound in which I glory. Oh, if only she who rejoices at wounding my heart with her blessed dart would with a single kiss consent to heal me!

3. That pert lady with her alluring smile draws all eyes to her. Those lips, endowed by Venus, which pout—but not permissively—offer the lesser sin. With their kiss they implant the sweetness of the honeycomb, so that at moments I count myself immortal. That smiling brow so snow-white, the golden light in her eyes, her auburn hair, her hands outdoing the lilies, provoke me to sighs; but I smile when I gaze upon that assemblage of all that is refined and princely, sweet and delightful.

THE COMPOSERS of these lyrics constantly seek variation in the familiar comparison between the renewal of spring and the quickening of love in the hearts of the young. Here the poet boldly reverses the theme: though summer has yielded to winter, the spokesman's love defies the sluggishness of the season. The close verbal parallels in stanza 3 with 7.3b-5b suggest that Peter of Blois may again be the author here, or alternatively that this poem flatters by imitation.

1. The rural desolation is picturesquely emphasized to contrast with the warmth of the stanza that follows.

2. **studet:** Supply *amor* as subject from *amorem* above.
   amare: Adverb from *amarus*: there is a constant play in these lyrics on the two possible senses of *amare,* with their suggestion of the connection between bitterness and love.

3. **castigate:** So Heraeus; B has *castigantes,* Vollmann *castiganter.* The parallel with 7.4b is striking.
   dulciorem, favum mellis: Cf. Ps. 18:11, *dulciora super mel et favum.*
   leta frons . . . lilia: For such catalogues of feminine beauty see comments at 7.3–5. *Frons nivea* appears in 7.3a; with *cesaries subrubea* compare Matthew of Vendôme *Ars Versificatoria* 1.56.7, *auro respondet coma.*

1. Estatis florigero tempore
   sub umbrosa residens arbore,
   avibus canentibus in nemore,
   sibilante serotino frigore,
   mee Thisbes adoptato fruebar eloquio,
   colloquens de Veneris blandissimo commercio.

2. Eius vultus,
   forma, cultus
   pre puellis,
   ut sol stellis,
   sic prelucet.
   O, inducet
   hanc nostra ratio
   ut dignetur suo nos beare consortio?

3. Nil ergo restat satius
   quam cecam mentis flammam denudare diffusius.
   audaces fortuna iuvat penitus;
   his ergo sit introitus:

4a. "Ignem cecum sub pectore
   longo depasco tempore,
   qui vires miro robore
   toto diffundit corpore.

4b. Quem tu sola, percipere
   si vis, potes extinguere,
   sic mecum semivivere
   felici ligans federe."

4c. "Amoris spes est dubia,
   aut verax aut contraria.
   amanti necessaria
   virtutis est constantia.

5a. Pre ceteris virtutibus est patientia,
   amoris famulantia.
5b. Sed et ignem, qui discurrit per precordia,
   fac extinguat alia!
5c. Noster amor non furtiva, non fragilia
   amplexatur gaudia!"

6a. "Ignis, quo crucior,
   immo, quo glorior,
   ignis est invisibilis.

6b. Si non extinguitur
   a qua succenditur,
   manet inextinguibilis.

7a. Est ergo tuo munere
me mori vel me vivere."

7b. "Quid refert pro re pendula
vite pati pericula?

8a. Est pater, est mater,
est frater, qui quater
die me pro te corripiunt,

8b. et vetulas per cellulas
et iuvenes per speculas
deputantes nos custodiunt,

9. Argumque centioculum
plus tremo quam patibulum.

10. Est ergo dignum
virum benignum
vitare signum,
unde malignum
murmur cursitat per populum."

11a. "Times in vanum!
tam est arcanum
quod nec Vulcanum
curo cum sophisticis catenis.

11b. Stilbontis more
Letheo rore
Argum sopore
premam, oculis clausis centenis."

12a. In trutina mentis dubia
fluctuant contraria
lascivus amor et pudicitia.

12b. Sed eligo quod video;
collum iugo prebeo,
ad iugum tamen suave transeo.

13. "Non benedixeris
iugum secretum Veneris,
quo nil liberius,
nil dulcius, nil melius?

14a. O, quam dulcia
sunt hec gaudia!
Veneris furta sunt pia!

14b. Ergo propera
ad hec munera!
carent laude dona sera."

15. "Dulcissime!
totam subdo tibi me!"

1. In the flower-laden season of summer I sat beneath a shady tree, and as the birds sang in the glade, and the cool of the evening whispered near, I was enjoying that conversation with my Thisbe that I had longed for, chatting about the most enticing interchange of love.

2. Her features, beauty, and cultivation outshine other girls as the sun the stars; I wonder, will my argument persuade her to deign to be my partner and bring me happiness?

3. No better course remains, then, than to reveal at greater length the fire hidden in my heart. Fortune wholly favors the brave, so let my exordium be this:

4a. "For a long time I have nurtured a hidden fire in my breast, a fire which with wondrous force spreads its strength through my whole frame.
4b. If you are willing to take notice of this fire, you alone can extinguish it, thus binding in blessed compact with me a life half-fulfilled."

4c. "The hope of love is uncertain; it may prove true or the opposite. For a lover, constancy in virtue is essential.
5a. But patience before all other virtues serves as the handmaid of love.
5b. As for the fire coursing through your breast, you must allow another maid to quench it.
5c. Our love embraces no secret or frail joys."

6a. "The fire with which I am tortured, or rather in which I boast, is a fire invisible.
6b. If it is not quenched by the maiden who kindles it, it remains impossible to extinguish.
7a. So it is in your gift whether I die or live."

7b. "What is the point of your suffering mortal hazards for an issue so uncertain?
8a. I have a father, mother, [and] brother who chide me four times daily because of you.
8b. They mount guard over me, placing duennas in our rooms and youths at lookout points.
9. I fear hundred-eyed Argus more than the gibbet.
10. So it is right that one who is well-disposed should avoid any sign which causes spiteful murmuring to race through the crowd."

11a. "Your fear is groundless! Our secret is such that I fear not even Vulcan with his wily bonds.
11b. After the fashion of Mercury I shall close the hundred eyes of Argus, and subdue him with sleep and the water of Lethe."

12a. In the wavering scales of my mind, opposing elements of wanton love and chastity rise and fall.
12b. But I choose what is before my eyes. I offer my neck to the yoke, but it is a sweet yoke under which I pass.

13. "Will you not bless the secret yoke of Venus, than which nothing is freer, nothing sweeter, nothing better?

14a. How sweet are these joys! Holy are the stolen gifts of Venus.

14b. So hasten to these gifts. Presents offered too late forfeit praise."

15. "Sweetest one! I submit my whole person to you!"

THIS COMPOSITION presents an imaginary love dialogue between boy and girl in a *locus amoenus*; many of the motifs of courtly love prominent in the treatise of Andreas Capellanus are observable. Dronke well summarizes: "The lover's hope for condescension, which he sees as the bestowing of blessedness, his putting himself entirely at the lady's mercy, the lady's insistence on love as a school of virtue, the recognition by both of the need for absolute secrecy . . . the praise of secret love as the fount of goodness and *pietas* . . . all these elements go to make this song a celebration as well as an analysis of the ways of *courtoisie*" (*Medieval Latin and the Rise of European Love-Lyric*, 255).

The poem opens with the lovers ensconced under a shady tree; the boy ruminates on whether he can persuade the girl to yield. His opening address is a conventional exordium, not unlike those prescribed in the *De Amore* of Andreas. The girl counsels him that constancy in virtue and patience are essential in wooing; she has no intention of offering frail or furtive joys. He responds by claiming that she alone can extinguish the fire that consumes him and that his continuing life depends on her. The girl counters with the practicalities: her family keeps constant watch over her, and she urges avoidance of affectionate gestures which could publicize the liaison. The boy reassures her that the affair is secret, and he presses her further. Mentally weighing wantonness and chaste behavior in the balance, he opts for love's yoke and urges the girl to hasten to Venus' stolen gifts. She at last complies. This conclusion, together with the parallels with no. 23, makes Peter of Blois an attractive candidate for authorship of this poem.

Like other commentators I allot stanzas 4a–4b to the boy, 4c–5c to the girl, 6a–7a to the boy, 7b–10 to the girl, 11a–11b to the boy, 13–14b again to the boy, and 15 to the girl. But I differ from Schumann, Dronke, and Vollmann in refusing to allot 12a–12b to the lady, because the sentiment in 12a seems too indelicate to be uttered by either, and especially by the lady. I prefer to regard these stanzas as the boy's silent cogitation, after which he resumes the conversation at 13a.

1. **sibilante frigore serotino:** *Serotinus* commonly refers to the late season of the year, but the sense "late in the day" is found in Biblical Latin at Joel 2:23.

Thisbes: So Schmeller for *Tysben* in B; the name is taken over from Ovid *Met.* 4.55ff.

Veneris . . . commercio: For the phrase cf. 5.5; if that stanza is a later addition, and not part of the original poem, this passage could be the source of the phrase.

3. **satius:** This is Patzig's emendation of *saucius* in B.
   audaces fortuna iuvat: Cf. Terence *Phormio* 203, Cicero *Tusc.* 2.11, Virgil *Aen.* 10.284, etc.

4b. In the manuscript lines 3–4 appear before 1–2. The *sic mecum* is Bischoff's improvement on B's *que mecum*; Vollmann has *hoc meum*.

4c. **amoris spes, etc.:** For *spes* in courtly love theory see 4.7, 26.7, and introductory comments at no. 53.

5a. **pre:** So Bischoff, for *sed* in B, following upon Spanke's *nam pre*.
   famulantia: ML, a neologism for *famula*.

5b. **ignem . . . fac extinguat alia:** I prefer to retain B's *fac* against *fax* (Spanke, Bischoff), on the grounds that the mixed metaphor of quenching by a torch is more obtrusively violent than the image of a girl achieving this.

8b. **vetulas:** The word is familiar in both CL (Horace *Carm.* 3.15.16, etc.) and ML (see 21.4).

9. **Argum centioculum:** Hundred-eyed Argus was set by Juno to keep watch on Io-turned-heifer (Ovid *Met.* 1.624ff.) and here symbolizes the prying gaze of a peeping Tom.

10. **signum:** Cf. Boncompagno's *Rota Veneris* (ca. 1200) (ed. Purkart), *nutus, indicium, signum, suspirium. . . .*

11a. **quod nec . . . curo:** = CL *ut non curem.*
   Vulcanum: Vulcan trapped his wife Venus and her lover Mars in bonds *quae lumina fallere possent* (Ovid *Met.* 4.177); hence the description of the chains here as "wily."

11b. **Stilbontis:** "The shining one" is commonly used as a title for Mercury because of the planet's brightness. Mercury drugged and slew Argus (Ovid *Met.* 1.713ff.); hence *sopore* denotes the drugging, *Letheo rore* the consigning of Argus to Hades.

12a. **in trutina:** This recalls the celebrated image at 33.1. For the tentative ascription of that poem to Peter of Blois see introductory comments there.

12b. **iugum suave:** Cf. Matt. 11:30, *iugum enim meum suave est.*

13. **non benedixeris:** (Always + dative in CL, but later + accusative by natural development of language.) Dronke (*Medieval Latin and the Rise of European Love-Lyric*, 255) does well to revert to the manuscript reading *non benedixeris* (Schumann has *non bene dixeris*), but his rendering "Are you not blessed?" does violence to the Latin, which means "Will you not bless?" For the colloquial future perfect cf. 14.12.

14a. **pia:** A quasi-religious status is claimed for such loving, as often in contexts of courtly love.

11 (71)

1a. Axe Phebus aureo
    celsiora lustrat,
    et nitore roseo
    radios illustrat.

1b. Venustata Cybele
    facie florente
    florem nato Semele
    dat Phebo favente.

2a. Aurarum suavium
    gratia iuvante,
    sonat nemus avium
    voce modulante.

2b. Philomena querule
    Terea retractat,
    dum canendo merule
    carmina coaptat.

3a. Iam Dionea
    Leta chorea
    sedulo resonat cantibus horum;

3b. Iamque Dione
    iocis, agone
    relevat cruciat corda suorum.

4a. Me quoque subtrahit illa sopori,
    invigilareque cogit amori.

4b. Tela Cupidinis aurea gesto.
    igne cremantia corda molesto.

5a. Quod michi datur,
    expaveo,
    quodque negatur,
    hoc aveo
    mente severa.

5b. Que mihi cedit,
    hanc caveo,
    que non obedit,
    huic faveo,
    sumque revera

6. infelix, seu peream
seu relever per eam.
que cupit, hanc fugio,
que fugit, hanc cupio.
plus renuo debitum,
plus feror in vetitum:
plus licet illibitum,
plus libet illicitum.

7a. O metuenda
Dione decreta!
O fugienda
venena secreta,
fraudeque verenda
doloque repleta!

7b. Docta furoris
in estu punire
quos dat amoris
amara subire,
plena livoris
urentis et ire!

8a. Hinc michi metus
abundat,
hinc ora fletus
inundat.

8b. Hinc michi pallor
in ore,
est, quia fallor
amore.

1a. Phoebus in his golden car makes his rounds on a higher path and causes his rays to gleam with rosy brightness.
1b. Cybele, her blooming face enhanced with beauty, bestows blossoms on Semele's son with the approval of Phoebus.

2a. With the conspiring favor of sweet breezes, the grove resounds with the tuneful song of birds.
2b. The nightingale with lament repeats the name of Tereus, as in her singing she harmonizes her tunes with the lark's.

3a. The glad dance inspired by Venus now busily responds to the songs of the birds.
3b. And now Venus with both pleasantries and torments relieves and tortures the hearts of her followers.

4a. Me too she deprives of sleep and forces to lie awake, waiting on love.
4b. I endure the golden weapons of Cupid, which burn men's hearts with nagging fire.

5a. I tremble with fear at what is granted me, and long austerely for what is denied me.

5b. I am on my guard against the girl who yields to me, and favor her who does not incline to me. For I am truly

6. unhappy, whether I am undone or comforted through her. I evade the desirous one, am eager for the evasive one. The more I reject what is destined for me, the more I rush to what is forbidden me. The more available the unpleasing, the more pleasing the unavailable.

7a. How awesome are the decrees of Venus! We should shun her secret poisons filled with fearsome deceit and guile.

7b. How skilled she is at punishing with the heat of madness those whom she allows to approach the bitter experiences of love! She is full of scorching malice and anger.

8a. This is why I have fears in plenty, why tears course over my face.

8b. This is why my complexion is ghastly, because I am beguiled by love.

THIS POEM is found in one other manuscript besides B: Erfurt Amplon. Oct. 32 (E).

In this poem, the theme of which is the sorrows of love, the conventional structure is observable: the joys of nature qualified by the grief of the nightingale are paralleled by the happy song of the maidens overshadowed by the spokesman's unhappy emotions. An original touch centers on the availability of unwanted love and the unavailability of that which is desired. The irony of this situation is underlined by antithesis achieved by skillful wordplay, word-sound, and rhyme (note especially stanzas 6–7a). Venus is here presented in her hostile persona, as in 13.8.

1a. **axe . . . aureo:** The golden car of Phoebus, aptly descriptive of the sun, is paralleled by Cupid's "golden" weapons at 4b; the adjective helps to link together the renewal in nature and the onset of human love.
   celsiora lustrat: The higher path indicates the approach of summer.

1b. **venustata Cybele:** The earth goddess Cybele stands by metonymy for *terra*; she is "visited by Venus" and hence "enhanced in beauty" (the verb is not in CL).
   nato Semele: Semele is genitive like Dione in stanza 7a, the form being dictated by the rhyme (Vollmann reads *Cibeles . . . Semeles*). The poet is familiar with the story of the birth of Bacchus from Semele told by Ovid *Met.* 3.310ff.; the mythological formulation merely conveys the prosaic fact that the earth bestows blossom on the vine through the heat of the sun.

2b. **Philomena:** See comments at 3.1.

querule: The adverb is not found in CL.

merule . . . coaptat: The verb appears first in Ecclesiastical Latin (Augustine, Prudentius); *merule* (dative) = *carmini merulae*, a *comparatio compendiaria*.

3a. **Dionea . . . chorea:** We are to imagine a band of maidens dancing in the woodland; their happy song contrasts with the spokesman's pain.

3b. **agone:** The Greek word earlier in Latin retains its sense of "contest," but this meaning of "pain" or "grief" then develops out of the contest sustained by Christian martyrs in witnessing to Christ.

4b. **tela aurea:** See comments to stanza 1a above. For the phrase cf. 18.3; Cupid himself is *aureus* at 42.4.

5a. **aveo:** Haupt's emendation of *faveo* (B) and *deo* (E).

6. **infelix:** This suggestion of Bischoff's for *felix* in B and E is preferable to Schumann's *fidelis*, not only on grounds of paleography; the lover is *infelix* whether he pines away in unrequited love or, through Venus (*per eam*), seeks relief from the wrong girl.

que cupit . . . hanc cupio: These lines are clearly inspired by Ovid *Am.* 2.29.3, *quod licet, ingratum est; quod non licet, acrius urit,* and 2.19.36, *quod sequitur, fugio; quod fugit, ipse sequor.* These neuter forms of the relative, clearly referring to ladies, are imitated here in stanza 5a above.

feror in vetitum: Note again the reminiscence from Ovid: *Am.* 3.4.17, *nitimur in vetitum semper, cupimusque negata.*

7a. **Dione:** Genitive like *Semele* in stanza 1b.

7b. **amoris amara:** The paronomasia appears earlier, in Virgil *Ecl.* 3.109–10, *et quisquis amores / aut metuat dulces aut experietur amaros.*

1–b. For the hostile Venus see the introductory comments above.

12 (72)

1a. Grates ago Veneri,	1b. Dudum militaveram,
que prosperi	nec poteram
michi risus numine	hoc frui stipendio;
de virgine	nunc sentio
mea gratum	me beari,
et optatum	serenari
contulit tropheum.	vultum Dioneum.

2a. Visu, colloquio,
    contactu, basio
    frui virgo dederat;
      sed aberat
    linea posterior
      et melior
        amori.
    quam nisi transiero
      de cetero
    sunt que dantur alia
      materia
        furori.

2b. Ad metam propero,
    sed fletu tenero
    mea me sollicitat,
      dum dubitat
    solvere virguncula
      repagula
        pudoris.
    flentis bibo lacrimas
      dulcissimas;
    sic me plus inebrio,
      plus haurio
        fervoris.

3a. Delibuta lacrimis
    oscula plus sapiunt,
    blandimentis intimis
    mentem plus alliciunt.
    ergo magis capior,
      et acrior
    vis flamme recalescit.
    sed dolor Coronidis
      se tumidis
    exerit singultibus
      nec precibus
        mitescit.

3b. Preces addo precibus
    basiaque basiis;
    fletus illa fletibus,
    iurgia conviciis,
    meque cernit oculo
      nunc emulo
    nunc quasi supplicanti.
    nam nunc lite dimicat,
      nunc supplicat;
    dumque prece blandior,
      fit surdior
        precanti.

4a. Vim nimis audax infero;
    hec ungue sevit aspero,
      comas vellit,
      vim repellit
        strenua,
      sese plicat
      et intricat
        genua,
      ne ianua
    pudoris resolvatur.

4b. Sed tandem ultra milito,
    triumphum do proposito.
      per amplexus
      firmo nexus,
        brachia
      eius ligo
      pressa figo
        basia;
      sic regia
    Diones reseratur.

5a. Res utrique placuit
    et me minus arguit
    mitior amasia,
      dans basia
        mellita,

5b. Et subridens tremulis
    semiclausis oculis
    veluti sub anxio
      suspirio
        sopita.

1a. I give thanks to Venus, for through the power of her favoring smile she has bestowed on me the delightful, much desired victory over my maiden.

1b. My service had been long, yet I still could not enjoy these wages; but now I realize that happiness is mine, that Venus' countenance shines bright.

2a. The maiden had allowed me the enjoyment of beholding, conversing, touching, kissing; but absent from my love was the final and best stage. If I do not attain it, the other rewards for the rest are merely fuel for my madness.

2b. I hasten toward the goal, but the girl entreats me with soft tears; the dear maiden hesitates to loosen the bars of her virginity. As she weeps I drink her tears most sweet, and thus intensify my drunkenness and imbibe a deeper draught of love-heat.

3a. Her kisses tear-smeared taste sweeter, and entice my heart more strongly with their innermost delights. So I am enmeshed more completely, and a keener onset of fire inflames me afresh. But Coronis' grief bursts out in welling sobs and does not soften at my entreaties.

3b. I heap prayers on prayers, kisses on kisses; she pours out tears on tears, rebukes on altercations. She fixes me with an eye now grudging, now almost begging, for at one moment she fights and disputes, at another she entreats. As I seek to soothe her with a prayer, she becomes deafer to my supplication.

4a. With overboldness I use force. She rampages with her sharp nails, tears my hair, forcefully repels my violence. She coils herself and entwines her knees to prevent the door of her maidenhead from being unbarred.

4b. But at last my campaign makes progress; I win a triumph for my battle plan. I tighten by embraces our entwined bodies, I pin her arms, I implant hard kisses. In this way Venus' palace is unbarred.

5a. Both gained satisfaction; my lover grew gentler and reproached me less, bestowing honeyed kisses,

5b. and half-smiling with flickering and half-closed eyes, as though she was drugged beneath the weight of troubled sighs.

THE POEM is also found in another manuscript, London, B.L. Arundel 384, but without stanzas 5a–b.

In a note to her attractive rendering of this poem Adcock comments: "I can scarcely approve of the content of this poem, which describes something suspiciously close to rape, but I was unable to resist the challenge of its intricate form" (*The Virgin and the Nightingale*, 94). The theme of sexual seduction is rare in these lyrics, though contemporary love theory approved such violence in the case of country girls. The reality of course may have been very different, and there is an element of literary fantasy in the advice of Andreas Capellanus (1.11): "But if the love even of peasant women chances to entice you, you should not delay in taking what you seek, gaining it by rough embraces." It is doubtless such comment as this which leads Jackson ("The Medieval Pastourelle") to regard this poem as a pastourelle. But the poet, Peter of Blois, employs the same sobriquet for the girl here as in no. 7; more important, the structure here is in no way comparable with examples of the pastourelle elsewhere. Peter dispenses with the conventional exordium of celebration of the season, proceeding at once to delineate the stages of the conquest. Though the vivid lubricity of the description appears to reflect an actual love encounter, the highly literary texture gives us pause: apart from the mention of the *quinque lineae amoris* in stanza 2a, it is noteworthy that the first two stanzas sustain the imagery of the military campaign (*tropheum . . . militaveram . . . stipendio*) and the second two that of the athlete (*linea . . . ad metam*), with a resumption in 4b of the military metaphor with the storming of the *regia Diones*.

1b. **militaveram . . . stipendio:** The comparison between the pursuit of love and military service is a commonplace in these medieval lyrics as in Augustan love elegy. Ovid is the teacher, and the classic text is *Am.* 1.9, *militat omnis amans, et habet sua castra Cupido.* The extended comparison between lover and soldier which follows in Ovid's poem inspires much of the medieval imagery.

2a. The *quinque lineae amoris* catalogued here are briefly alluded to at Ovid *Met.* 10.342 and detailed by Donatus on Terence *Eun.* 638: *Quinque lineae perfectae sunt ad amorem: prima visus, secunda alloquii, tertia tactus, quarta osculi, quinta coitus.* Cf. Helm, "Quinque linea." The motif appears elsewhere in the collection at 26.8 below (*CB* 88) and *CB* 154.
   que dantur alia materia furori: Cf. Ovid *Ars Am.* 1.669–70, *oscula qui sumpsit si non et cetera sumit, / haec quoque que data sunt perdere dignus erit.*

2b. **ad metam propero:** Cf. Ovid *Ars Am.* 2.727–28, *ad metam properate simul; tum plena voluptas, / cum pariter victi femina virque iacent.*
   virguncula: To be taken with *mea.* The diminutive, and its position next to *repagula pudoris,* emphasizes her maidenhead. McDonough well compares Walter of Châtillon, *St. Omer* 32.7.3: *non frangam castitatis / repagula.*

3a. **Coronidis.** For the sobriquet and its source see comments at 7.5b, where the aptness of the name in this poem is suggested.

4b. **figo basia:** A Virgilian expression; cf. *Aen.* 1.687 (Venus to Cupid), *cum dabit amplexus atque oscula dulcia figet.*
regia Diones: Matthew of Vendôme similarly speaks of the pudenda as *in regno Veneris* (*Ars Versificatoria* 1.57.7).

5a. **amasia:** The masculine forms *amasius* and *amasio* appear earlier in CL and in LL, but the feminine form is not found before the medieval period.

13 (73)

1a. Clauso Cronos et serato
　　　carcere ver exit,
　　risu Iovis reserato
　　　faciem detexit.

1b. Coma celum rutilante
　　　Cynthius emundat,
　　et terrena secundante
　　　aëre fecundat.

2a. Purpurato flore prato
　　　ver tenet primatum,
　　ex argenti renitenti
　　　specie renatum.

2b. Iam odora Rheam Flora
　　　chlamyde vestivit,
　　que ridenti et florenti
　　　specie lascivit.

3a. Vernant veris ad amena
　　　thyma, rose, lilia.

3b. His alludit philomena,
　　　merops et luscinia.

4a. Satyros hoc excitat
　　　et Dryadum choreas,
　　redivivis incitat
　　　hoc ignibus Napeas.

4b. Hoc Cupido concitus,
　　　hoc amor innovatur,
　　hoc ego sollicitus,
　　　hoc michi me furatur.

5. Ignem alo tacitum;
　amo, nec ad placitum
　ut qui contra libitum
　cupio prohibitum.
　votis Venus meritum
　rite facit irritum;
　trudit in interitum
　quem rebar emeritum.

6a. Si quis amans per amare mereri posset amari,
　　posset Amor michi velle mederi dando beari!
6b. Quot faciles michi cerno medelas posse parari,
　　tot steriles ibi perdo querelas absque levari.

7a. Imminet exitus igne vigente,
    morte medullitus ossa tenente.

7b. Quod caro predicat hec macilenta,
    hoc sibi vendicat usque perempta.

8a. Dum mala sentio, summa malorum,
    pectora saucia, plena furorum,
    pellere semina nitor amorum.

8b. Ast Venus artibus usa nefandis,
    dum bene palliat aspera blandis,
    unguibus attrahit omnia pandis.

9. Parce dato pia, Cypris, agone,
   et, quia vincimur, arma repone,
   et quibus es Venus, esto Dione!

1a. Spring emerges from the closed, barred prison of Cronos; it has unlocked heaven's smile and uncovered its face.
1b. The Cynthian god sweeps the sky with crimson locks, and with the favoring breath of the lower air makes fertile the things of the earth.

2a. When the meadow is crimson with flowers, the spring, reborn from the gleaming beauty of silver, holds dominion.
2b. Now fragrant Flora has clothed Rhea with a cloak; she sports with smiling and flowering beauty.

3a. To contribute to spring's attractions, thyme, roses, and lilies bloom.
3b. Among them sport the swallow, bee-eater, nightingale.

4a. Spring rouses the satyrs and bands of dryads; spring stirs the dell nymphs with rekindled fires.
4b. With spring Cupid is roused, with spring love is renewed; with spring I grow restless, and spring steals my heart from me.

5. I nurture a silent flame. I love, but not as I would, for I desire what is forbidden in the face of my wish. What I have duly deserved by prayers Venus renders fruitless; she thrusts me into death when I believed that I had completed my service.

6a. If any lover could by loving deserve to be loved, Cupid could be willing to heal me by granting blessedness.
6b. The number of ready remedies which I see can be afforded me is matched by the number of barren complaints that I fruitlessly expend without relief.

7a. Destruction overhangs me, and the fire burns strong; for death takes hold of my bones deep within.
7b. This wasted flesh of mine proclaims this fate; yet though constantly shattered it demands for itself that fate.

8a. When I experience my ills—the worst of ills, a wounded heart brimming with madness—I strive to expel the seeds of love feelings.

8b. But Venus employs wicked wiles; as she cleverly tempers the harsh with the seductive, with curved claws she draws all things to herself.

9. Cyprian goddess, be kind and spare me after the pain you have imparted; lay aside your arms, for I am vanquished. Show yourself a Dione to those to whom you are a Venus!

THIS POEM appears in St. Gall Stiftsbibl. 383 (G) and in Paris B.N. lat. 1139 (P), as well as in B. The Paris manuscript originated from St. Martial at Limoges, an important quarry for music codices.

The poet here parades an impressive learning in the conventional exordium which celebrates the arrival of spring. The emergence of the new season "from the prison of Cronos" is the sole reference to that deity in the *Carmina Burana*; *Cynthius* used as variant for *Phoebus* is likewise unparalleled elsewhere in the collection. There is a learned evocation from Martianus Capella in stanza 2a (see below). *Rhea* for *Terra* (stanza 2b) is another learned touch, and the reference to the Napeae (stanza 4a) is also unique in the *Carmina Burana*. In the final stanza the distinction made between the spiteful Venus and the kindlier persona of the goddess (Dione) may originate from the false etymology found in Remigius of Auxerre's *Commentary on Martianus Capella* 479.22 (in Migne, PL 131): *Dione dicitur quasi "dianoia," id est sensus delectatio, ideoque mater Veneris fingitur quia omnis libido ex delectatione carnalium sensuum nascitur.*

An original variation in the standard parallelism between the year's renewal and the burgeoning of human love is introduced in the spokesman's despair that his love is illicit. Two unspoken possibilities present themselves. The first is that the lady is already claimed, perhaps as the spouse of a nobleman, so that the spokesman appears in the troubadour's role; the second is that the object of his affection is a consecrated virgin. Such a courtship is formally condemned by Andreas Capellanus 1.8: "My view is that the consolations of nuns are to be utterly avoided as a plague of the soul. They are the cause of our heavenly Father's severest anger; the laws of the state wield strong powers and threaten the severest punishment against such conduct; and from it springs the infamy which kills one's whole reputation in society." Cf. Boncompagno's *Rota Veneris* (ca. 1200) (ed. Purkart), chapter 3. It is important to stress that such exotic variations on the love theme may represent fantasies rather than actual love encounters.

1a. Cronos: Cronos as an indeclinable form, here genitive, is bizarre, but this interpretation of the line fits best with the traditional role of Cronos, whom the Romans equated with Saturn and who in one version of the myth is imprisoned by Zeus/Jupiter in Tartarus. By the time of Aristotle he had already merged with Chronos, god of time; thus by the Middle Ages the story was that he was imprisoned to ensure the regular order of the seasons. Cf. *Mythographus Vaticanus* 3.1.8 (ed. G. H. Bode, Cellis, 1834), *ideo a Iove vinctum, ne immoderatos cursus habeat, atque ut stellarum, per quas disponitur tempus, vinculis alligetur.* A possible alternative to solve the grammatical difficulty is to read *excit* with Cronos as subject, but this does not accord so well with the mythological role of Cronos outlined above.

1b. This stanza is not in B. For *coma rutilante* see comments at 8.1; the Cynthian god (Apollo was born on Mount Cynthus on Delos) sweeps the sky with his rays. Cf. Geoffrey of Vinsauf *Poetria Nova* 809–10, *solis radius . . . emundat caelum.*
secundante aëre: When earth solicits the warmth of fire from the upper region (*aether*), she can obtain it only through the mediation of the lower air (*aër*). Stoic physics (powerfully influenced by Heraclitus) lies behind this concept of the fiery *pneuma* animating all things.

2a. purpurato. See comments at 46.1.
ex argenti renitenti specie: Martianus Capella (1.16–17) lies behind this; of the four urns which hold the seeds in nature, the second, *ex argenti fulgentiore materie, . . . praeferebat serena fulgentia et vernantis caeli temperie renidebat; hanc dicebant risum Iovis.*

2b. Rheam Flora . . . vestivit: Rhea and Flora stand by metonymy for the earth and the flowers (cf. Ovid *Fasti* 4.201, 5.195ff.); such metonymy is a favorite device of learned medieval poets.

3a. thyma: The word is normally neuter in CL, as here, but it is masculine at 22.5 and 47.5.

3b. philomena . . . luscinia: Both these words regularly mean "nightingale." Vollmann reads *melotis lascivia*, "with wantonness of melody," at line 2, adapting B's *melis et lascivia.* But G has *merops et lucinia*, P *meris et lutinia*, and a trinity of birds is required to balance the three flowers in stanza 3a. Schumann suggests that *luscinia* here = German *Grasmücke*, "hedge sparrow." Another possibility is to take *philomena* as "swallow," following Cassiodorus *Variae* 8.31, *mortalium penatibus fiducialis nidos philomela suspendit.*

4a. **Satyros . . . Dryadum . . . Napeas:** Satyrs and dryads are often paired in CL (e.g., Ovid *Met.* 1.690ff.) and reappear together in this collection at 14.3. For *Napeae*, dell nymphs, see Virgil *G.* 4.535.

5. **ignem alo tacitum:** Dido's lovesickness is often evoked in these poems; cf. Virgil *Aen.* 4.2, *vulnus alit venis, et caeco carpitur igni.*
trudit . . . emeritum: In the theory of courtly love, once the suitor has served his probation, he hopes to win acceptance from the lady.

6a. **per amare . . . dando beari:** The infinitive is often used as substantive in ML.

6b. **absque levari:** See the previous note.

7a. **exitus . . . morte:** The theme of rejection in love as living death is a frequent motif in these lyrics.

9. **Cypris . . . Venus . . . Dione:** For Cypris see comments at 3.1. For Venus/Dione see the introductory comments just above.

14 (74)

1. Letabundus rediit
     avium concentus;
   ver iocundum prodiit;
     gaudeat iuventus
   nova ferens gaudia;
   modo vernant omnia.
     Phebus serenatur
   redolens temperiem;
   novo flore faciem
     Flora renovatur.

2. Risu Iovis pellitur
     torpor hiemalis;
   altius extollitur
     cursus estivalis
   solis, beneficio
   ⟨cuius omnis regio⟩
     recipit teporem.
   sic ad instar temporis,
   nostri Venus pectoris
     reficit ardorem.

3. Estivantur Dryades
     colle sub umbroso;
   prodeunt Oreades
     cetu glorioso;
   Satyrorum contio
   psallit cum tripudio
     Tempe per amena;
   his alludens concinit
   cum iocundi meminit
     veris philomena.

4. Estas ab exsilio
     redit exoptata,
   picto ridet gremio
     tellus purpurata.
   miti cum susurrio
   suo domicilio
     gryllus delectatur;
   hoc canore, iubilo,
   multiformi sibilo
     nemus gloriatur.

5. Applaudamus igitur
      rerum novitati;
   felix, qui diligitur
      voti compos grati,
   dono letus Veneris,
   cuius ara teneris
      floribus odorat.
   miser e contrario
   qui sublato bravio
      sine spe laborat.

1. The harmony of the birds has returned, bringing delight. The pleasant spring has come forth. Young people should rejoice as they gain new joys. Now all is green, and Phoebus waxes bright, diffusing pleasant warmth. Flora's complexion is renewed with fresh blossoms.

2. The sluggishness of winter is dispelled by the smile of heaven. The sun's summer course rises higher, and through his kindness every region obtains warmth. In this same way Venus renews the heat of our hearts, like that of the season.

3. The wood nymphs enjoy the summer under a shady hill, the mountain nymphs emerge in exultant throng. The gathering of satyrs sings and dances through the pleasant vale. The nightingale sports and sings in harmony with them, as it recalls the pleasant spring.

4. The summer much-desired returns from exile; the bright earth with dappled bosom smiles. The cricket with its soft buzz takes pleasure in its lodging. The grove exults in this song, this gladness, this whistling of many tunes.

5. So let us show our gladness at the newness in creation. Happy the man who obtains his dear wish, and is loved! He is joyous through the gift of Venus, whose altar is fragrant with young blossoms. Wretched at the other extreme is he who is deprived of his prize, and toils on without hope.

IN THIS SIMPLE but elegant lyric the poet hymns the return of spring with a conventional acknowledgment of the corresponding pulse of love in young hearts (stanzas 2, 5). But this is expressed in general terms. The spokesman does not recount personal joys or sorrows.

1. **avium concentus . . . ver iocundum:** Both phrases are found in CL (Cicero *Leg.* 1.21; Catullus 68.16).

Flora: For Flora as goddess of flowers, and therefore as harbinger of summer, see comments at 13.2b. Her festival in ancient Rome fell on 28 April.

2. **cuius omnis regio:** This is Schumann's suggested supplement. The manuscript has *qui sublato bravio,* which is clearly a contamination from stanza 5.

3. **Dryades . . . Oreades . . . Satyrorum:** Nymphs and satyrs are often associated in these lyrics (e.g., 13.4a, 29.69) as in CL (Horace *Carm.* 1.1.31, 2.19.4, etc.).
Tempe: This neuter plural, initially the name of a valley in Thessaly, is frequently used in CL to denote a picturesque valley generally; cf. Horace *Carm.* 3.1.24, Virgil *G.* 2.469, etc.

4. **purpurata:** In CL *purpureus* is the regular adjective descriptive of flowers, *purpuratus* being used for persons of high estate; clearly rhythm and rhyme recommend its use here.
susurrio: *Susurrium* is a postclassical form. Virgil *Ecl.* 1.56 has *levis susurrus* for the buzzing of the bee.
gryllus: The word is found in the Elder Pliny, but CL generally prefers *cicada,* a symbol of summer at Ovid *Ars Am.* 1.271.
iubilo: Though *iubilum* is occasionally found in CL in the sense of "rustic cry," the inspiration for its common use in ML is probably the use of its cognate verb *iubilare* in the Latin Vulgate (Ps. 99:4, *Iubilate Deo, omnis terra,* etc.).

5. **bravium:** A Graecism for "prize," taken over from Paul at 1 Cor. 9:24.
sine spe: Cf. comments at 4.7.

15 (75)

1. Omittamus studia,
   dulce est desipere,
   et carpamus dulcia
   iuventutis tenere!
   res est apta senectuti
   seriis intendere,
   ⟨res est apta iuventuti
   leta mente ludere.⟩

Refl. Velox etas preterit
   studio detenta,
   lascivire suggerit
   tenera iuventa.

2. Ver etatis labitur,
     hiems nostra properat;
   vita damnum patitur,
     cura carnem macerat.
   sanguis aret, hebet pectus,
     minuuntur gaudia,
   nos deterret iam senectus
     morborum familia.

   Refl.

3. Imitemur superos!
     digna est sententia,
   et amores teneros
     iam venentur retia.
   voto nostro serviamus!
     mos est iste numinum.
   ad plateas descendamus
     et choreas virginum!

   Refl.

4. Ibi, que fit facilis,
     est videndi copia,
   ibi fulget mobilis
     membrorum lascivia.
   dum puelle se movendo
     gestibus lasciviunt,
   asto videns, et videndo
     me michi subripiunt.

   Refl.

1. Let us forsake our studies; it is sweet to play the fool. Let us enjoy the delights of innocent youth. Devotion to serious things is appropriate for old age, but sport with a glad heart is the right course for youth.

   Refrain. Life absorbed by studies passes all too quickly; our innocent youth prompts us to frolic.

2. The spring of life slips away, and our winter hastens in. Our lives suffer damage, and anxiety wastes away the flesh. The blood runs dry, the heart grows sluggish, our joys diminish; and soon old age with its retinue of diseases disheartens us.

   Refrain.

3. Let us imitate the gods above; this is a worthy principle. Let our nets now be deployed to hunt an innocent love. Let us be slaves to our desires; this is the way the gods behave. Let us go down to the streets and watch the dancing of the maidens.

   Refrain.

4. There is free scope there to feast the eyes. Their limbs are there agleam in frisky motion. As the girls sway their bodies and playfully gesture, I stand by and witness them, and as I witness them they steal my heart away.

   Refrain.

THIS POEM barely qualifies as a love lyric; it is more aptly assigned to that category of student songs to which *Gaudeamus igitur* later belongs. But in its conventional contrast between youth and old age, the "Gather ye rosebuds" theme articulates in stanza 3 the spokesman's aspirations for love and in stanza 4 the stirrings of sexual desire. In its emended form the poem reflects a circular pattern of Classical evocations, moving from Horace (stanza 1) to Juvenal (stanza 2), then to Ovid (stanza 3), and finally back to Horace (stanza 4). Behind these more explicit borrowings lie more muted scriptural echoes (stanza 3), which are translated, so to speak, into the secular frame of polytheism. The learning is carried with effortless elegance.

1. **omittamus studia . . . dulce est desipere:** Cf. Horace *Carm.* 4.12.25, 28, *verum pone moras et studium lucri / . . . dulce est desipere in loco.*
seriis intendere: Cf. Horace *Sat.* 1.1.27, *amoto quaeramus seria ludo.*
res est, etc.: The final two lines of the stanza are Herkenrath's; there is a lacuna in the manuscript.

2. **ver etatis:** The metaphor is drawn from CL. Cf. Ovid *Met.* 10.85, *aetatis breve ver*; Catullus 68.16, *iucundum cum aetas florida ver ageret.*
sanguis aret . . . morborum familia: Juvenal's celebrated portrayal of old age is surely in the poet's mind; cf. *Sat.* 10.217–19, *minimus gelido iam in corpore sanguis / . . . circumsilit agmine facto / morborum omne genus.* Vollmann retains *membrorum* for *morborum* and emends *familia* to *famelia* (= *fame*), but this is to lose the sustained reminiscence of Juvenal. There may be a further echo of this passage of Juvenal's earlier in the stanza, where *vita damnum patitur* recalls *Sat.* 10.209–10, *aspice partis / nunc damnum alterius.*

3. **imitemur superos:** Doubtless with jocose recollection of Paul, *Eph.* 5:1, *estote igitur imitatores Dei* (Vollmann).
venentur retia: The subjunctive *venentur* (Peiper) is to be preferred to *venantur* because the entire stanza is hortatory. *Retia* is likewise preferable to *ocia* (B); the poet may have had in mind Ovid *Ars Am.* 1.45, *scit bene venator cervis ubi retia tendat.*
ad plateas descendamus: Perhaps recalling Song of Sol. 3:2, *surgam et circumibo civitatem; per vicos et plateas quaeram quem diligit anima mea* (so Vollmann).

4. **me michi subripiunt:** Cf. Horace *Carm.* 4.13.20, *quae me surpuerat mihi.*

16 (76)

1. Dum caupona verterem   vino debachatus,
   secus templum Veneris   eram hospitatus.
   solus ibam, prospere   vestibus ornatus,
   plenum ferens loculum   ad sinistrum latus.

2. Almi templi ianua   servabatur plene;
   ingredi non poteram,   ut optati, bene.
   intus erat sonitus   dulcis cantilene;
   estimabam plurime   quod essent Sirene.

3. Cum custode ianue   parum requievi;
   erat virgo nobilis   pulchra, statu brevi.
   secum dans colloquia   in sermone levi
   tandem desiderium   intrandi explevi.

4. In ingressu ianue   sedens invitatus
   ab hac pulchra virgine   sum interrogatus:
   "unde es, o iuvenis,   hucce applicatus?"
   cui dixi: "domina,   vestri comitatus."

5. "Que est causa, dicito,   huc tui adventus?
   qualis ad hec litora   appulit te ventus?
   duxit te necessitas,   et tua iuventus?"
   dixi: "necessario   venio detentus.

6. Intus et exterius   asto vulneratus
   a sagitta Veneris;   ex quo fui natus
   telum fero pectore   nondum medicatus.
   cursu veni tacito   quo sim liberatus.

7. Incessanter rogo te,   virgo ter beata,
   ut hec verba Veneri   nunties legata."
   ipsa, mota precibus,   fortiter rogata,
   nuntiavit Veneri   verba destinata:

8. "Sauciorum omnium   salus o divina,
   que es dulcis, prepotens   amoris regina,
   egrum quendam iuvenem   tua medicina
   procurare studeas;   obsecro, festina!"

9. Iussu sacre Veneris ductus in conclavi,
cernens eius speciem, fortiter expavi.
flexis tandem genibus ipsam salutavi,
"salve," dicens "inclita Venus, quam optavi!"

10. "Quis es," inquit "iuvenis, qui tam bene faris?
quid venisti, dicito. quomodo vocaris?
es tu forte iuvenis ille dictus Paris?
ista de quo retulit cur sic infirmaris?"

11. "Venus clementissima, felix creatura,
cerno quod preterita noscis et futura.
ipse sum miserrimus —res iam peritura—
quem sanare poteris tua leni cura."

12. "Bene" inquit "veneris, noster o dilecte
iuvenis! aptissime cedes nostre secte.
si tu das denarios monete electe,
dabitur consilium salutis perfecte."

13. "Ecce," dixi, 'loculus extat nummis plenus,
totum quippe tribuam tibi, sacra Venus.
si tu das consilium ut sat sim serenus,
tuum in perpetuum venerabor genus."

14. Ambo iunctis manibus ivimus mature,
ubi stabant plurime belle creature.
omnes erant similes, unius nature
et unius habitus atque vestiture.

15. Nobis propinquantibus omnes surrexere,
quas ut salutavimus, responsum dedere:
"bene vos veneritis! velitis sedere!"
Venus inquit: "aliud volumus explere."

16. Innuens his omnibus iubet ire cito.
pariter remansimus in loco munito;
aliis quiescentibus strato redimito
plura pertractavimus sermone polito.

17. Exuit se vestibus genitrix Amoris,
carnes ut ostenderet nivei decoris.
sternens eam lectulo fere decem horis
mitigavi rabiem febrici doloris.

18. Postmodum transivimus   ire balneatum
    in hortanum balneum   Iovi consecratum.
    huius aqua balnei   me sensi purgatum
    omnibus languoribus   beneque piatum.

19. Ultra modum debilis,   balneo afflictus,
    fame validissima   steteram astrictus.
    versus contra Venerem   quasi derelictus
    dixi: "vellem edere,   si quis inest victus."

20. Perdices et anseres   ducte sunt coquine,
    plura volatilia,   grues et galline;
    pro placentis ductus est   modius farine;
    preparatis omnibus   pransus sum festine.

21. Tribus, reor, mensibus   secum sum moratus,
    plenum ferens loculum   vixi vir ornatus;
    recedens a Venere   sum nunc allevatus
    nummis atque ⟨vestibus⟩;   sum sic pauperatus.

22. Terreat vos, iuvenes,   istud quod auditis;
    dum sagittam Veneris   penes vos sentitis,
    mei este memores.   vos, quocumque itis,
    liberi poteritis   esse, si velitis.

1. On turning away from a tavern, reeling with the effects of wine, I had taken a lodging close to the shrine of Venus. I was journeying alone, smartly dressed, and carrying a bulging wallet at my left side.

2. The door of that bountiful temple was closely guarded. I could not easily enter there, though it was my keen desire. Within was the sound of sweet music. I reckoned that numerous sirens were in attendance there.

3. I relaxed a little with the guardian on the door. She was a high-born and beautiful girl, diminutive in size. After exchanging pleasantries with her, I finally attained my longing to enter.

4. As I sat by the entrance to the door on being invited in, I was questioned by this lovely girl: "Young sir, why have you made your way here?" I said to her: "To be part of your escort, my lady."

5. "Tell me the reason for your coming here. What wind has driven you to these shores? Has need and your youth brought you here?" I said: "Out of necessity I come and linger here.

6. I stand here wounded within and without by Venus' arrow. Since the day of my birth I have endured her dart in my heart, and am not yet healed. I have come with silent speed to win my freedom.

7. Maiden thrice-blessed, I unremittingly beg you to announce to Venus these words deputed to you." Moved by my prayers, since my plea was so forceful, she reported these words addressed to Venus:

8. "Heavenly salvation of all wounded mortals, sweet and supremely powerful queen of love, be zealous to cure with your healing a youth who is sick. Hasten, I beg you."

9. By the command of holy Venus I was led into her chamber. When I beheld her beauty I was considerably afraid. At last, after genuflecting I greeted her, saying: "Hail, famed Venus, for whom I have longed!"

10. "Young man," she asked, "who are you who speak such fair words? Tell me why you have come. What is your name? Are you perhaps the famous youth named Paris? And why are you sick, as this maiden has recounted?"

11. "Most merciful Venus, blessed creature, I observe that you know what has been and what will be. I am most wretched—my plight will soon be fatal—but with your gentle attentions you will be able to heal me."

12. "Welcome, beloved youth of ours!" said she. "You will be a most suitable addition to our band. If you pay over some coins of approved currency, the counsel which brings total salvation will be accorded you."

13. "See," I said, "my purse is still full of coins. Indeed, I shall offer it in entirety to you, sacred Venus. If you give me counsel to make me happily content, I shall worship your family forever."

14. We both linked hands, and together hastened to where numerous beautiful creatures stood. All alike were of the same nature, appearance, and raiment.

15. As we drew near, they all rose. On our greeting them, they answered: "Welcome to you! Do sit down." Venus said: "It is another purpose which we wish to fulfill."

16. She nodded to all of them and bade them quickly leave. We remained together in this place firmly barred. While other occupants slept, on a couch wreathed with flowers we discussed several matters in elegant talk.

17. Cupid's mother slipped off her garments to reveal the snow-white beauty of her flesh. I laid her on the couch, and for about ten hours quietened the madness of my feverish passion.

18. Later we walked over to a bathhouse dedicated to Jupiter in the garden, to take a bath. I felt myself cleansed by the water of this bath and well rid of my languors.

19. Feeling faint beyond limit and tired from the bath, I stood there, gripped with the most powerful hunger. Like a soul abandoned, I turned to Venus and said: "I should like to eat if there is any food within."

20. From the kitchen partridges and geese were brought, and several birds, cranes, and hens, and a measure of wholemeal to make rolls. When all was ready, I hastily tucked in.

21. For three months, I suppose, I lingered there with her, and as long as my purse was full I lived as a man of distinction. But now on leaving Venus, I have been relieved of money and clothing, and so I am a pauper.

22. Young men, let this story which you hear deter you. Keep me in mind when you feel the arrow of Venus piercing you. Wherever you go, you can remain free, if you wish to be so.

THIS ARCH, not to say titillating, composition demands no detailed exegesis. The account of the spokesman's visit to, and extended stay in, a high-class bordello depicted as the home of Venus culminates in the exemplary warning, but the tone is anything but repentant. The deployment of the four-line "goliardic" rhyming stanza prepares us for a playful narrative composition.

It is possible to exploit the poem to throw light on the tone of *Si linguis angelicis* (no. 17 [77]), a composition written in the same meter which follows next in the collection. Comparison between the structures of the two poems suggests that they may stem from the same pen. Verbal correspondences are not sufficiently close to suggest that one is a parody of the other, and the themes of the two are different; rather the two varying arguments are handled in a similar way. So here, after the setting of the scene (stanzas 1–3), the action is initiated with a comely doorkeeper, beginning in midstanza (stanzas 4–7); similarly in the next poem, after the description of the *locus amoenus*, the spokesman's soliloquy begins in midstanza. In this poem the youth on entering Venus' chamber genuflects and greets her (stanza 9); likewise in no. 17 the lover draws near to Rose, genuflects, and greets her. In this poem the lady asks if the gallant is Paris (stanza 10); in the next, the spokesman greets Rose as Helen. In both poems the boy next asks the lady to heal him, and in their different ways the ladies promise to comply. The ensuing dialogue in no. 17 is much more extended and includes a description of Rose's beauty which is not paralleled here in no. 16. But the night of pleasure here is balanced by the "joys of paradise" in no. 17. Finally, the dutiful warning against such adventures which concludes this poem is paralleled by a similarly generalized exhortation in no. 17, which urges the suitor never to lose hope, however gloomy the prospect.

1. **dum . . . verterem:** = CL *cum . . . verterer.*
ornatus, plenum . . . loculum: The repetition of these expressions in stanza 21 indicates that they serve as a mock moral frame to the narrative.

2. **optati:** This is my suggested reading for *optatu* in B (*optavi* Manitius); construe with *templi.*
cantilene: The word is often found in the Fathers, and subsequently in ML, for "singing."
estimabam plurime: So Sedgwick for B's *estimabant plurimi:* "I reckoned that there were numerous Sirens there." In the Fathers, the sirens are frequently deployed as images of sexual temptation; see Rahner, *Greek Myths and Christian Mystery,* chap. 7.

3. **parum:** = *paulum,* as often in ML.
statu: = *statura* (so also occasionally in CL).
secum: "With her." What would be a solecism in CL is common in ML; *secum* is Schumann's suggested emendation for *secundans* in B.

4. **unde:** In view of the spokesman's reply in the next line, "To belong to your retinue, my lady," *unde* here must mean "why" rather than "whence."
applicatus: The image here and in stanza 5 is of a craft putting in to harbor. Perhaps there is a hint of the Dido-Aeneas meeting.
vestri: The deferential plural had become a common feature of polite address by the twelfth century.

5. **dicito:** Future imperative for a polite instruction.

6. **asto:** So Schumann for the *asta* of B (*hasta* Schmeller).
ex quo fui natus telum fero, etc.: The jocose double entendre in *telum,* denoting the precocious sexual development of the youth, perhaps strengthens the case for reading *hasta* in the previous line, as both words are found in CL for the penis (see Adams, *Latin Sexual Vocabulary,* 17, 19–20).

8. **sauciorum:** So Sedgwick for *secretorum* in B.
salus divina: The language of courtly love frequently appropriates such expressions of Christian commitment; cf. 17.10.

9. **ductus in conclavi:** Cf. 60.5.
flexis genibus. Cf. 17.7, *poplite flexo.*

10. **Paris** frequently appears in these lyrics as the sobriquet of the courtly lover; his Greek role of adulterer perhaps signals a preference for *amor mixtus*.
ista: = *custos ianuae*. The query in this line by Venus is similar to that by Rose in 17.11.

11. **noscis**: So Hilka for *nescis* in B.
leni: Schumann's clearly correct emendation of *levi* in B.

12. **veneris**: The colloquial future perfect (cf. *veneritis* in stanza 15): "Your arrival is welcome."
cedes: This is my suggestion for *sedes* in B; Strecker proposed *sodes* (= *sodalis*); Vollmann *sedis*.

14. **unius nature et unius habitus**: Likewise Phyllis and Flora, at 29.5, *sunt unius habitus et unius moris*.

15. **velitis**: Schumann's emendation of *vultis* in B (*vultus hic* Schmeller).
veneritis: See comments to stanza 12 above.

16. **iubet ire cito**: So Schumann for *abire cito* in B (*dat abire cito* Patzig).
aliis: This is my proposal for *solis* in B.

17. **exuit**: So Schmeller for *et ut* in B.
carnes: For the plural in CL see Ovid *Met.* 2.769, 14.208, etc.

18. **hortanum**: First in ML.
purgatum . . . piatum: Though the bath is "consecrated to Jupiter," these words have a Christian ring. *Balneum* is often used of the baptismal font, and these participles enhance the sense of sacramental cleansing. The usage need not be sacrilegious; these are the words which a twelfth-century cleric would instinctively use.

19. **quasi**: So Bischoff for *quamvis* in B.

20. **coquine**: Dative; from LL onwards a dative of disadvantage approaches close to the sense of an ablative of separation.
modius farine: The phrase suggests lavish provision. In Petronius (*Sat.* 37) Trimalchio's wife Fortunata "measures her money by the peck [*modio*]."

21. **secum**: See comments at stanza 3 above.
vixi: My emendation of *ubi* in B (*fui* Bischoff).
recedens: So Schumann for *residens* in B.
vestibus: Peiper's supplement based on stanza 1 above.
pauperatus: Schumann's emendation of *preparatus* in B.

22. For the closing exhortation see the introductory comments above.
penes: "Wortspiel mit *penis*" (Vollmann).

17 (77)

1. Si linguis angelicis   loquar et humanis,
   non valeret exprimi   palma, nec inanis
   per quam recte preferor   cunctis Christianis,
   tamen invidentibus   emulis profanis.

2. Pange, lingua, igitur   causas et causatum!
   nomen tamen domine   serva palliatum,
   ut non sit in populo   illud divulgatum
   quod secretum gentibus   extat et celatum.

3. In virgultu florido   stabam et ameno,
   vertens hec in pectore: "Quid facturus ero?
   dubito, quod semina   in harena sero;
   mundi florem diligens   ecce iam despero.

4. Si despero merito,   nullus admiretur;
   nam per quandam vetulam   rosa prohibetur
   ut non amet aliquem   atque non ametur.
   quam Pluto subripere,   flagito, dignetur!"

5. Cumque meo animo   verterem predicta,
   optans anum raperet   fulminis sagitta,
   ecce, retrospiciens   loca post relicta,
   audias quid viderim,   dum morarer ita.

6. Vidi florem floridum,   vidi florum florem,
   vidi rosam Madii   cunctis pulchriorem,
   vidi stellam splendidam   cunctis clariorem,
   per quam ego degeram   sentiens amorem.

7. Cum vidissem itaque   quod semper optavi,
   tunc ineffabiliter   mecum exultavi,
   surgensque velociter   ad hanc properavi,
   hisque retro poplite   flexo salutavi:

8. "Ave, formosissima,   gemma pretiosa,
   ave, decus virginum,   virgo gloriosa,
   ave, lumen luminum,   ave, mundi rosa,
   Blanziflor et Helena,   Venus generosa!"

9. Tunc respondit inquiens stella matutina:
   "Ille, qui terrestria regit et divina,
   dans in herba violas et rosas in spina,
   tibi salus, gloria sit et medicina!"

10. Cui dixi: "Dulcissima, cor michi fatetur
    quod meus fert animus, ut per te salvetur.
    nam a quodam didici, sicut perhibetur.
    quod ille qui percutit melius medetur."

11. "Mea sic ledentia iam fuisse tela
    dicis? nego; sed tamen posita querela
    vulnus atque vulneris causas nunc revela,
    ut te sanem postmodum gracili medela."

12. "Vulnera cur detegam que sunt manifesta?
    estas quinta periit, properat en sexta,
    quod te in tripudio quadam die festa
    vidi; cunctis speculum eras et fenestra.

13. Cum vidissem itaque, cepi tunc mirari,
    dicens: 'Ecce mulier digna venerari!
    hec excedit virgines cunctas absque pari,
    hec est clara facie, hec est vultus clari!'

14. Visus tuus splendidus erat et amenus,
    tamquam aër lucidus nitens et serenus.
    unde dixi sepius 'Deus, Deus meus,
    estne illa Helena vel est dea Venus?'

15. Aurea mirifice coma dependebat,
    tamquam massa nivea gula candescebat,
    pectus erat gracile, cunctis innuebat
    quod super aromata cuncta redolebat.

16. In iocunda facie stelle radiabant,
    eboris materiam dentes vendicabant;
    plus quam dicam speciem membra geminabant.
    quidni si hec omnium mentem alligabant?

17. Forma tua fulgida tunc me catenavit,
    michi mentem, animum et cor immutavit.
    tibi loqui spiritus ilico speravit;
    posse spem veruntamen numquam roboravit.

18. Ergo meus animus   recte vulneratur.
    ecce, ⟨Venus⟩ graviter   michi novercatur.
    quis umquam, quis aliquo   tantum molestatur
    quam qui sperat aliquid   et spe defraudatur?

19. Telum semper pectore   clausum portitavi,
    milies et milies   inde suspiravi,
    dicens: 'Rerum conditor,   quid in te peccavi?'
    omnium amantium   pondera portavi.

20. Fugit a me bibere   cibus et dormire,
    medicinam nequeo   malis invenire.
    Christe, non me desinas   taliter perire,
    sed dignare misero   digne subvenire!

21. Has et plures numero   pertuli iacturas,
    nec ullum solacium   munit meas curas,
    ni quod sepe sepius   per noctes obscuras
    per imaginarias   tecum sum figuras.

22. Rosa, videns igitur   quam sim vulneratus,
    quot et quantos tulerim   per te cruciatus,
    ⟨nunc⟩ si placet, itaque   fac ut sim sanatus,
    per te sim incolumis   et vivificatus!

23. Quod quidem si feceris,   in te gloriabor,
    tamquam cedrus Libani   florens exaltabor.
    sed si, quod non vereor,   in te defraudabor,
    patiar naufragium   et periclitabor."

24. Inquit rosa fulgida   "Multa subportasti,
    nec ignota penitus   michi revelasti.
    sed que pro te tulerim   nunquam somniasti;
    plura sunt que sustuli   quam que recitasti.

25. Sed omitto penitus   recitationem,
    volens talem sumere   satisfactionem
    que prestabit gaudium   et sanationem
    et medelam conferet   melle dulciorem.

26. Dicas ergo, iuvenis,   quod in mente geris;
    an argentum postulas   per quod tu diteris,
    pretioso lapide   an quod tu orneris?
    nam si esse poterit,   dabo quidquid queris."

27. "Non est id quod postulo lapis nec argentum,
    immo prebens omnibus maius nutrimentum,
    dans impossibilibus facilem eventum
    et quod mestis gaudium donat luculentum."

28. "Quicquid velis, talia nequeo prescire,
    tuis tamen precibus opto consentire.
    ergo quicquid habeo sedulus inquire,
    sumens si quod appetis potes invenire."

29. Quid plus? collo virginis brachia iactavi,
    mille dedi basia, mille reportavi,
    atque sepe sepius dicens affirmavi:
    "Certe, certe istud est id quod anhelavi!"

30. Quis ignorat, amodo cuncta que secuntur?
    dolor et suspiria procul repelluntur,
    paradisi gaudia nobis inducuntur,
    cuncteque delicie simul apponuntur.

31. Hic amplexus gaudium est centuplicatum,
    hic mecum et domine pullulat optatum,
    hic amantum bravium est a me portatum,
    hic est meum igitur nomen exaltatum.

32. Quisquis amat itaque mei recordetur,
    nec diffidat, illico licet amaretur.
    illi nempe aliqua dies ostendetur
    qui penarum gloriam post adipiscetur.

33. Ex amaris equidem grata generantur;
    non sine laboribus maxima parantur.
    dulce mel qui appetunt sepe stimulantur;
    sperent ergo melius qui plus amarantur!

1. Even if I were to speak with the tongues of angels and men, I could not describe the prize—no trifling one, for by it I am rightly set above all Christians, while jealous noninitiates envy me.
2. So sing, my tongue, of the causes and the effect, but keep the name of the lady cloaked, so that what is kept apart and hidden from the nations may not be revealed among the common folk.

3. I stood in a flowering, beautiful copse, pondering in my heart what I was to do. I was exercised that I was sowing seed in sand. In my love for the world's fairest blossom, I was now in despair.

4. None should be surprised at my justifiable despair, for the rose was prevented by a certain crone from loving any man, and from being loved. Oh, that Pluto might deign to bear off that hag, was my insistent cry!

5. As I turned these aforesaid matters over in my mind, and hoped that a bolt of lightning would bear off the old woman, hear now what I saw when I looked back, as I made to quit that region but still lingered there.

6. I saw a blossoming flower, blossom of blossoms, a May rose more beautiful than all others. I saw a shining star brighter than the rest, the girl through whom my life had become a love experience.

7. So when I beheld what I ever longed for, I then rejoiced at heart more than words can describe. I rose and swiftly hastened to her, and with these words hailed her on bended knee:

8. "Greetings, most beautiful one, precious jewel! Greetings, glory of maidens, maiden of fair fame! Greetings, light of lights! Greetings, rose of the world, a Blanchefleur, a Helen, a noble Venus!"

9. Then that morning star said to me: "May He who rules over the regions of earth and heaven, who implants violets in the grass and roses on the thorn, be your salvation, glory, and healing!"

10. To her I said: "Sweetest one, my heart confesses what my mind conveys, that its salvation comes through you; for I have learnt from some source the proverbial saying that the striker makes the better healer."

11. "Do you claim that my darts have already harmed you in this way? I do not accept this. But abandon your complaint, and now reveal your wound and the reasons for it, so that I may later heal you with a simple remedy."

12. "Why need I uncover wounds so conspicuous? A fifth summer has passed and, see, a sixth draws near since I first saw you dancing on some feast day. You were a mirror and a window for all.

13. So when I laid eyes on you, at that moment I began to admire you. I said: 'Here is a woman worthy of reverence. She excels all maidens; she has no equal. How bright is her countenance, how bright her features!'

14. Your appearance was radiant and beautiful, shining and gleaming like the bright air. So I said again and again: 'My God, is she Helen, or is she the goddess Venus?'

15. Your golden hair was a picture as it hung down, and your throat gleamed white like an expanse of snow. Your bosom was slender, intimating to all that its fragrance excelled all spices.

16. In your charming face twin stars shone. Your teeth claimed the stuff of ivory as their own. Your limbs redoubled your beauty more than I can describe. So it is not surprising that these qualities captivated the minds of all.

17. Your gleaming beauty there and then enchained me. It transformed my mind, disposition, and heart. My spirit at once aspired to address you, but practicality never strengthened that hope.

18. So my heart is genuinely wounded: see how Venus heavily oppresses me. What man is ever caused so much trouble by anything as he who entertains some hope and is then cheated of it?

19. I have constantly borne this dart enclosed in my breast. A thousand and yet another thousand sighs have I breathed because of it, saying: 'Creator of the world, what sin did I commit against You?' I have borne the burdens of all lovers.

20. Drink, food, sleep have deserted me; I can find no healing for my ills. Christ, do not allow me to perish thus, but deign to lend worthy aid to this wretched soul!

21. These privations and more than these have I endured. No consolation shuts out my cares, except that repeatedly in the darkness of night I am with you in forms shaped by the imagination.

22. So, rose, seeing the extent of my wounds, the number and severity of the tortures which I have endured because of you, if now you approve, grant that I may be healed, [made] safe, and restored to life through you.

23. If indeed you act in this way, I shall glory in you, and I shall be exalted and flourish like the cedar of Lebanon. But if—a fate I do not fear—I am cheated of my hope of you, I shall suffer shipwreck and mortal danger."

24. The gleaming rose said: "Many things have you endured, and you have revealed things not wholly unknown to me. But you have never dreamt of what I have borne for you. My sufferings have been more numerous than those which you have recounted.

25. But I abandon the recital of them wholly, for I wish to obtain from them the satisfaction which will afford joy and healing, and which will bestow a remedy sweeter than honey.

26. So tell me, young sir, what you have in mind. Do you ask for silver to enrich yourself, or to adorn yourself with precious stones? If it proves possible, I will give you whatever you seek."

27. "I do not ask for stones or silver, but what offers greater nourishment to all, brings a ready outcome to a hopeless situation, and proffers bright joy to those who are sorrowful."

28. "I cannot have foreknowledge of what it is you wish, but I long to fall in with your entreaties. So diligently investigate all that I have, and take what you seek if you can find it!"

29. Need I say more? I threw my arms around the maiden's neck, gave her a thousand kisses, and took a thousand in return. Repeatedly I made this claim: "Yes, yes, this is what I longed for!"

30. Who does not know all that now ensued? Griefs and sighs were now driven far off. The joys of paradise were ushered in to us, and all delights set before us simultaneously.

31. Now the joy of the embrace is reenacted a hundred times, now my lady's desire bursts out in harmony with mine, now I carry off the prize of lovers, and now my name is accordingly raised on high.

32. So let every lover be mindful of me. He must not lose heart, though at that point his lot is bitter. For certainly some day will dawn upon him at which he will later triumph over his troubles.

33. Indeed it is from bitterness that pleasant joys are sprung; the greatest gains are not won without toils. Those who seek sweet honey often feel the sting, so those whose lot is more bitter should maintain the stronger hope.

As I indicate in "Amor Clericalis," this poem has attracted wholly contrasting interpretations. Dronke (*Medieval Latin and the Rise of European Love-Lyric*, 318–31) portrays it as a serious and lyrical exposition of the aspirations of the courtly lover. By contrast, Robertson ("Two Poems from the *Carmina Burana*") regards it as essentially ironical and humorous. Others seek a via media: so Parlett in his Penguin translation writes, "I do find the expression humorous, but am in no doubt about the sincerity of the emotion." Vollmann similarly speaks of a genuine love lyric beneath the mask of wit. The alternatives of "serious" and "ironical" are too crude and constricting. The poem is serious insofar as the poet enthusiastically associates himself with the courtly experience, but the theme is handled wittily as a literary mode rather than with deep emotional involvement. In short, the composition is a stylized exercise: the scriptural exordium, the description of the *locus amoenus*, the physiognomy of feminine beauty on conventional lines punctuated with biblical and liturgical evocation, the rhetorical supplication of the lover, the succession of courtly love motifs—all point to a studied artificiality. The use of the four-line "goliardic" stanza underlines the poem's status of playful rather than ironical commentary; this meter is regularly (though not invariably) deployed in medieval lyric for satirical or jocular purposes. Obvious parallels in this collection are no. 29; the Archpoet's *Confession* (CB 191; *Thirty Poems*, no. 2); *Cum in orbem universum* (CB 211; *Thirty Poems*, no. 1), and above all no. 16 above. See the introductory comments to no. 16 for indications of parallel techniques of presentation.

1. **Si linguis angelicis ...** : In medieval devotional poetry the exordium frequently cites scripture; the poem itself forms an extended meditation of the passage. The reminiscence of 1 Cor. 13:1 here (*si linguis hominum loquar et angelorum, charitatem autem non habeam, factus sum velut aes sonans aut cymbalum tinniens*) encourages the reader to anticipate a meditation on love, but the love which emerges is not the theological virtue but courtly *amor*. The humorous tone is thus established at the outset.

palma: Perhaps in evocation of Ovid *Am.* 3.2.82, where the spokesman and his girl are at the races. The boy points to the victorious charioteer and says: *ille tenet palmam; palma petenda mea est.* (The girl responds to the witticism: *risit, et argutis quiddam promisit ocellis: "hoc satis est; alio cetera redde loco."*)

cunctis Christianis: The pursuit of courtly love is often depicted as analogous to a vocation to the religious life; hence the contrast here between Christian initiates and the *profani* (on whom see comments at 2.8) not admitted to the sacred rites. In stanza 31 the prize is denoted by the Pauline word *bravium*; see the note there.

2. **pange, lingua**: The scriptural evocation in stanza 1 is here reinforced by an echo of Venantius Fortunatus' celebrated hymn commemorating the arrival of the True Cross at Poitiers: *Pange, lingua, gloriosi proelium certaminis* ... (2.2). That *certamen* was the victorious struggle of Christ with Satan, won on the wood of the Cross. We are promised here the story of another famous victory. The parody in these first stanzas (cf. Lehmann, *Die Parodie*, 102ff.) sets the witty tone for what follows.

causas et causatum: This scholastic language (cf. Boethius *Anal. Post.* 2.17, *si vera causa sit et causatum simul*; and Albertus Magnus *Metaph.* 5.2.8) adds a further jocose touch.

serva palliatum: The victory but not the identity of the lady can be proclaimed. This plea for confidentiality is conventional in courtly love theory; we are not to regard this as exhortation to protect an actual relationship.

3. **in virgultu florido**: Robertson suggests that we regard this as a metaphor for the spokesman's state of mind, but that is too metaphysical a conceit for this jocular composition; it is essential to preserve the literal sense of the *locus amoenus* so that the lady's sobriquet (*Rosa*) may emerge from the appropriate background. But see further at *audias quid viderim* below in stanza 5.

   semina in harena sero: The crudity of this double entendre is lightened by the literary reminiscence; cf. Ovid *Her.* 5.115, *quid harenae semina mandas?*

4. **si despero merito, nullus admiretur**: This punctuation is preferable to placing the comma after *despero*.

   rosa: For the possible influence of this poem on *The Romance of the Rose* see Langlois, *Les origines et les sources de la roman de la rose*; and Dronke, *Medieval Latin and the Rise of European Love-Lyric*, who speculates that there is a gap of more than a generation between the appearances of the two works.

5. **optans . . . raperet**: The paratactic construction, a survival from early Latin, is frequent in CL. The combination here of Pluto and thunderbolt as prospective agents of destruction lends a further touch of humor.

   loca: This is Bischoff's emendation of *lata* in B (*laeta* B[1]; *laete* Dronke).

   audias quid viderim: Robertson, in his eagerness to present the love experience as imaginary, renders this as "Hear what I may have seen"; the Latin means "Hear what I saw." Nonetheless, as the old hag abruptly disappears from the scene, the spokesman appears to describe a mystical experience rather than an actual one.

5–8. The description of the girl with Hebraic idiom (*florum florem*) and in the imagery of blossoms and stars helps to invest her with the persona of the Virgin; see especially stanzas 8–9. Boncompagno remarks in *Rota Veneris*, chap. 4: "Sometimes a woman is likened to the sun, sometimes to a star . . . sometimes to a rose."

6. **rosam Madii**: For *Madius = Maius mensis* see Du Cange s.v.

   sentiens: My suggestion for *semp in* in B; *lapsus in* (Heraeus) is paleographically less likely.

7. **poplite flexo**: Biblical; see Judges 7:6.

8–9. The combination of biblical and secular evocation is characteristic of twelfth-century lyric. *Formosissima* recalls Song of Sol. 1:4, *nigra sum sed formosa*, a phrase often applied to the Virgin. *Stella matutina* appears in the Litany of Loreto to the Blessed Virgin, as does *rosa mystica*, which would be an apt title for the poem. Though the Litany is of later date, it is based on earlier litanies dating from the twelfth century. Other phrases evoke the Magnificat (stanza 7, *exultavi / surgensque*; cf. Luke 1:39, 47) and traditional Marian hymns (stanza 8, *virgo gloriosa*). *Blanziflor et Helena, Venus generosa* translates us to the other world of secular literature. Blancheflor is the heroine of the romance *Floire et Blancheflor,* the earliest known version of which appeared in 1167 (ed. Wirtz, Frankfurt, 1937). The identification of the loved one with Helen need not have embarrassed Dronke (*Medieval Latin and the Rise of European Love Lyric,* 326: "Helen signifies the true, innocent Helen of Egypt"), for in these lyrics Helen is the symbol of peerless beauty without animadversion on morals; see e.g., *CB* 61.5.

8. **mundi rosa**: Bischoff speculates on the possibility of a punning reference to Rosamund, favorite of Henry II of England.

9. **Ille qui terrestria, etc.**: The piety of the lady is a conventional feature of these courtly exchanges; see, e.g., Andreas Capellanus 1.6.115.
   rosas in spina: Perhaps a jocular reference to her own name and to the prickly experience of the spokesman.

10. The spokesman's response to the girl's pious wish that God be his salvation is to express the conviction that such salvation can come only through her; cf. Andreas 1.6.40, *non enim est spes ulla salutis, si de tuo me desperes amore.*
    a quodam didici: The teacher is inevitably Ovid, the *magister amoris.* Cf. Ovid *Rem. Am.* 44, *una manus vobis vulnus opemque feret*; Henderson's edition (Edinburgh, 1979) notes ad loc. that the sentiment goes back through Propertius to the Greeks.

11. **ut te**: So Schumann for *vis te* in B (retained by Schmeller).
    gracili medela: The strange adjective may be attributable to its juxtaposition with *rosa* in Horace's well-known *Quis multa gracilis te puer in rosa* (*Carm.* 1.5.1).

12. Robertson rightly draws attention to the lengthy period of the spokesman's speechless yearning. It is tempting to regard this as ironical humor directed at the "unapproachable maiden" motif in courtly love theory.
    speculum et fenestra: Dronke (*Medieval Latin and the Rise of European Love-Lyric,* 326) refers these images to the status of angels, with their insight into the divine. Robertson well cites Wisd. of Sol. 7:26, where Sapientia is *speculum sine macula Dei maiestatis,* an apt designation for the

maiden implicitly envisaged as a second Virgin Mary. Robertson's further suggestion of an allusion to Ambrose *Comm. Ps.* 118.37 (*si videris mulierem ad concupiscendam eam, intravit mors per fenestram . . . claude ergo hanc fenestram*), implying that the spokesman condemns the relationship, seems to me academic fantasy.

13. **excedit:** So Strecker for *extendit* in B (*exscendit* Schmeller).

–16. For the conventional nature of this description of feminine beauty see comments at 7.3ff. We are reminded of similarly gushing passages in sentimental novels of the eighteenth and nineteenth centuries. Such elaboration of the lady's charms need not reflect soulful passion, and may even contain an element of parody (cf. 7.3, 9.3, 10.2).

14. **Helena . . . Venus.** See general comments for stanzas 8–9 above.

15. **aurea . . . coma, etc.:** Golden hair, snowy throat, and slender bosom are all recommended for mention by Matthew of Vendôme's *Ars Versificatoria* 56–57.

16. **vendicabant:** The alternative form of *vindicabant*.
    geminabant: So Schmeller, rightly, for *gemmabant* in B.

17. **posse:** Here used substantivally as subject of *roboravit*.

18. **vulneratur:** Perhaps recalling Song of Sol. 4:9, *vulnerasti cor meum. . . .*
    Venus: This supplement of Schumann's is the best of all the suggestions to fill the lacuna; *vita, fatum,* and *deus* have all been proposed, but *Venus* fits best with *novercatur*, "plays the stepmother with" = "treats harshly."

19. **telum . . . portitavi:** Cf. *Pamphilus* 1 (ed. Bate, who dates the comedy before 1174), *vulneror, et clausum porto sub pectore telum.*
    peccavi: Cf. Luke 15:18, *Pater, peccavi in caelum et coram te.*

20. **desinas:** This reading of B is defended by N. Fickermann (*Festschrift A. Hofmeister,* Halle, 1955, 60) as = *sinas*; Schumann proposed *destines.*

22. **nunc si:** Dronke's suggested supplement is preferable to *dicens* (Schumann).

23. **in te gloriabor:** Cf. Rom. 5:11, *gloriamur in Deo.*
    cedrus Libani: Cf. Ecclus. 24:17, *quasi cedrus exaltata sum in Libano.* The lofty cedars of Lebanon are a cliché in the Fathers as symbols of outstanding virtue.

24. **nunquam somniasti:** Referring to the consoling dreams mentioned in stanza 21.

25. **melle dulciorem**: Cf. Ps. 18:11, *dulciora super mel et favum.*

26. The lady makes gentle sport of the suitor, pretending that she does not understand his needs, though she has just stated that his passion is reciprocated.
pretioso lapide an quod tu orneris: (So Schumann; *pretiosos lapides . . ameris* B, Dronke.) In Schumann's emendation the first part of the double question contains a final relative (*per quod tu diteris*), the second part an indirect command with ML *quod* replacing CL *ut* (*quod tu orneris*).

28. **si**: Schumann's emendation of *id* in B (retained by Dronke).

29. **quid plus?**: The denouement evokes Ovid *Am.* 1.5.23–24, *singula quid referam . . . cetera quis nescit?*
mille dedi basia: The echo of Catullus 5.7 (*da mihi basia mille*) need not be a direct reminiscence; see Introduction, section 11.
sepe sepius. The repetition from stanza 21 underlines the realization of the dream.

31. **amplexus**: Genitive.
bravium: The Graecism (*bravium = brabeion*) is taken over from Paul (1 Cor. 9:24, the letter which also provides the exordium of this poem): *omnes quidem currunt, sed unus accipit bravium.*
exaltatum: Cf. Ps. 148:13, *exaltatum est nomen eius solius.*

32. **amaretur**: From *amarare.*

33. **grata**: So Patzig. In B the scribe has inserted *amara* above the line, and Robertson retains this. But the sense of the whole stanza clearly demands a contrasting word like *grata* or *leta.*

18 (78)

1. Anni novi redit novitas,
   hiemis cedit asperitas;
   breves dies prolongantur,
   elementa temperantur
   subintrante Ianuario.
   mens estu languet vario
   propter puellam, quam diligo.

2. Prudens est, multumque formosa,
   pulchrior lilio vel rosa;
   gracili coartatur statura,
   prestantior omni creatura;
   placet plus Francie regina.
   michi mors est iam vicina
   nisi sanet me flos de spina.

3. Venus me telo vulneravit
   aureo, quod cor penetravit.
   Cupido faces instillavit,
   Amor amorem inspiravit
   iuvencule, pro qua volo mori.
   non iungar ⟨puelle⟩ cariori,
   licet accrescat dolor dolori.

4. Illius captus sum amore,
   cuius flos adhuc est in flore.
   dulcis fit labor in hoc labore,
   osculum si sumat os ab ore.
   non tactu sanabor labiorum,
   nisi cor unum fiat duorum
   et idem velle. vale, flos florum!

1. The newness of the new year is back again; the harshness of winter gives place. The short days are lengthened, the elements gain warmth as January tiptoes in. My heart faints with vacillating heat because of the girl whom I love.

2. She is circumspect and very lovely, more beautiful than the lily or the rose. Her build is slight and slender. She surpasses all other creatures, wins more approval than the queen of France. Unless the blossom on the thorn heals me, my death is now close at hand.

3. Venus has wounded me with her golden dart, which pierced my heart. Cupid implanted torches, Love has breathed into me love for this young maiden, for whom I am willing to die. Though pain is heaped on pain, I would not be joined to a soul more dear than her.

4. I am enthralled by the love of the maiden whose blossom is still in bloom. Sweet becomes the toil expended in this toil, if my mouth wins a kiss from that mouth. I shall not be healed by the touch of our lips unless the hearts of both become one, and our wishes unite. Farewell, blossom of blossoms!

AT FIRST SIGHT this is a wholly conventional love lyric; the passing from winter into spring is paralleled by the increasing ardor of the lover. It is clearly a scholastic exercise rather than an expression of emotions deeply felt. But the unusual stanza structure, the subtlety of the rhyme scheme, and above all the experimentation with sound patterns and word repetition (especially in stanza 4) conspire to accentuate the harmony between burgeoning nature and burgeoning human love but simultaneously underscore the painful alienation which results if such love is not reciprocated.

1. **redit**: So Patzig for *rediit* in B, aligning the tense to that of the other verbs in the stanza.
   prolongantur: The verb becomes frequent in Ecclesiastical Latin.
   subintrante Ianuario: The turn of the year is visualized as the harbinger of spring; cf. 2.1, where February brings warm weather.

2. **Francie regina:** Perhaps with reference to the celebrated beauty of Eleanor of Aquitaine, whose marriage to Louis VII of France ended in divorce and remarriage to Henry II of England in May 1152. See Duby, *The Knight, the Lady and the Priest*. If the reference is to Eleanor, the poem will have been composed before or in 1152.

3. **Cupido . . . Amor:** There is a medieval tradition in which Cupid and Amor are regarded as a duo; see Stephen of Tournai's *In Commune Theatrum* 65 (in Migne, *PL* 211), *duo dee filii, matrem subsecuti* (on which see L. Auvray in *Mélanges P. Fabre*, Paris, 1902, 286). But it is hardly necessary to posit twin personalities here.

   faces instillavit: A curious image; the poet may have visualized burning pitch dripping from Cupid's torch into the suitor's wound.

   inspiravit: So Heraeus for *superavit* in B.

   puelle: My supplement; in the other three stanzas, lines 6 and 7 have an identical number of syllables.

4. **flos in flore / labor in hoc labore / os ab ore:** The word repetitions recall *anni novi . . . novitas* in stanza 1 and help to establish the correspondence between the season and the lover's emotion.

   idem velle: Doubtless Sallust, the most popular of the Classical historians at this time, was in the poet's mind. Cf. Sallust *Cat.* 20.4, *idem velle atque idem nolle, ea demum firma amicitia est.*

19 (79)

1. Estivali sub fervore
   quando cuncta sunt in flore,
   totus eram in ardore.
   sub olive me decore,
   estu fessum et sudore,
   detinebat mora.

2. Erat arbor hec in prato
   quovis flore picturato,
   herba, fonte, situ grato,
   sed et umbra, flatu dato.
   stilo non pinxisset Plato
   loca gratiora.

3. Subest fons vivacis vene
   adest cantus philomene
   Naiadumque cantilene.
   paradisus hic est pene;
   non sunt loca, scio plene,
   his iocundiora.

4. Hic dum placet delectari
   delectatque iocundari
   et ab estu relevari,
   cerno forma singulari
   pastorellam sine pari
   colligentem mora.

5. In amorem vise cedo;
fecit Venus hoc, ut credo.
"ades," inquam "non sum predo,
nichil tollo, nichil ledo.
me meaque tibi dedo,
   pulchrior quam Flora!"

6. Que respondit verbo brevi:
"ludos viri non assuevi.
sunt parentes michi sevi:
mater longioris evi
irascetur pro re levi.
   parce nunc in hora."

1. At the onset of the summer's heat, a time when all things are in flower, I felt hot from head to toe. Wearied with the heat and sweat, I lingered under a handsome olive tree.

2. This tree was in a meadow dappled with every kind of flower. There was grass, a spring, a charming situation, and shade, with the addition of a breeze. Plato with his pen could not have painted a more idyllic region.

3. Close by ran the water of a living stream; near at hand a nightingale sang, and the songs of the water nymphs were heard. It was almost a paradise. No region, I know full well, is more pleasant than this.

4. Whilst I resolved to sit here in delight, and was taking joy in happy relaxation and relief from the heat, I saw a shepherdess unsurpassed in beauty, gathering blackberries.

5. I fell in love with her at first sight, the doing of Venus, I believe. "Come close," I said, "I am no robber. I do not plunder or harm. I commit myself and all I have to you; you are more beautiful than Flora!"

6. She answered in few words: "I am not used to a man's games. My parents are harsh to me; my mother, who is getting on in years, will get very angry even for a trifling reason. So spare me at this present time!"

THIS IS THE FIRST example of the pastourelle, or shepherdess poem, in this selection. (For the development of the genre see Introduction, section 6.) In this composition the poet has sought a careful balance between the charming description of the *locus amoenus* (stanzas 1–3) and the narrative of encounter (stanzas 5–6). The rejection motif, by which the shepherdess refuses the gallant's advances, represents the most basic formula of the genre, but it is presented with consummate elegance. The witty rhyme scheme is particularly effective.

1. **sub olive . . . decore**: Indicating the southern mise-en-scène.

2. **Plato**: In *Phaedrus* 230B Plato describes just such a scene, with a tree, a spring, shade, and a pleasant breeze. We are not, however, to imagine that this is a direct evocation. Cicero in his dialogues imitates Plato's techniques of presentation (see, e.g., *De Or.* 1.28), and the *locus amoenus* was already a stylized feature in CL (cf. Horace *Ars P.* 17). As Curtius demonstrates (chap. 10), the stock motifs are repeatedly found in ML in the poetry of Alan of Lille, Matthew of Vendôme, Peter Riga, and many others.

3. **philomene**: = CL *philomelae* (see comments at 3.1).
   paradisus: Christian writers naturally visualize paradise in terms of the *locus amoenus*; see Curtius, chap. 10 n. 31.

4. **iocundari**: Biblical Latin; cf. Rev. 11:10, etc.
   pastorellam: The word which lends its name to the genre of the pastourelle first appeared in the twelfth century.
   mora: The indifference to quantity in this rhythmical rhyming poetry can be measured by the appearance of *mŏra* in stanza 1 and *mōra* here at the identical point of the stanza.

5. **Flora**: For the description of the feast of the goddess Flora see Ovid *Fasti* 5.183ff.

6. **sevi**: Spanke's emendation from *Suevi* in B (retained by Hilka and Schumann) seems certain. Compare the similar ending to no. 51, where the shepherdess has been forcibly taken.

20 (80)

1a. Estivali gaudio
    tellus renovatur,
militandi studio
    Venus excitatur.
gaudet chorus iuvenum,
dum turba frequens avium
    garritu modulatur.

Refl. Quanta sunt gaudia
    amanti et amato,
    sine fellis macula
    dilecte sociato!
    iam revernant omnia
    nobis delectabilia,
    hiems eradicatur.

1b. Ornantur prata floribus
    varii coloris,
quorum delectatio
    causa fit amoris.
gaudet chorus iuvenum,
dum turba frequens avium
    garritu modulatur.

Refl.

2a. In calore vivido
      nunc reformantur omnia,
    hiemali tedio
      que viluere languida.
    tellus ferens gramina
      decoratur floribus,
    et vestiuntur nemora
      frondosis arboribus.

    Refl.

2b. Amorum officiis
      hec arrident tempora,
    geminatis sociis
      restaurantur federa.
    festa colit Veneris
      puellaris curia,
    propinat Amor teneris
      amaris miscens dulcia.

    Refl.

1a. The earth is renewed with the joy of summer; love is aroused by our keen-ness to campaign. The band of the young is joyful, while the dense crowd of birds tunefully chatters.

Refrain. How great are the joys of the lover who is loved, when he is joined to his dear one without disfiguring bile! Now all the things which delight us grow green again, and winter is uprooted.

1b. The meadows are adorned with flowers of different color, and our delight in them causes love's prompting. The band of young men is joyful, while the dense crowd of birds tunefully chatters.

Refrain.

2a. In the enlivening heat are now renewed all things which were enervated and worthless through the weariness of winter. The earth bears grass and is adorned with flowers; the groves are clothed with trees bearing full leaf.

Refrain.

2b. This season smiles on duties devoted to affairs of love. Compacts are re-newed between comrades who are united. The court of maidens celebrates Venus' feast time; Cupid attends on the young, proffering his mixture of the bitter and the sweet.

Refrain.

THIS IS CLEARLY a dance lyric (see Spanke's review of *CB*, 39). There is the conventional correspondence between nature's renewal and the growth of amorous feeling in the young, here expressed as generalities rather than as personal confession by the spokesman. As always, the nice balance achieved between the two by structural technique is to be noted. The themes are intermingled in stanzas 1a and 1b, but 2a is devoted wholly to the transformation in nature, and this is set against the love theme in stanza 2b.

1b. **delectatio causa fit**: As often elsewhere, it is the observation of the change in the world of nature which awakens love feelings.

2b. **amorum officiis**: It is better to take *amorum* as lower case (= "love affairs") rather than as a personification ("Cupids"), as *Amor* personified appears later in the stanza. Vollmann retains *annorum* from B, but Du Méril's *amorum* seems certain.

puellaris curia: No evidence exists for such a court of love in the real world before the reign of Charles VI, ca. 1400 (see Benton, "Clio and Venus," 19ff.). But such courts obtain frequent mention in the fantasy world of literature, as evidenced in these lyrics and in Andreas Capellanus' *De Amore* (see the introduction to my edition, p. 5).

propinat: The image is that of Cupid as wine steward, serving his mixture of sweetness and bitterness; this sense of *propinare* had already occurred in LL.

21 (81)

1. Solis iubar nituit
     nuntians in mundum
   quod nobis emicuit
     tempus letabundum.
   ver, quod nunc apparuit
     dans solum fecundum,
   salutari meruit
     per carmen iocundum.

   Refl. Ergo nostra contio
     psallat cum tripudio
       dulci melodia!

2. Fugiente penitus
     hiemis algore,
   spirat ether tacitus
     estu gratiore.
   descendente celitus
     salutari rore,
   fecundatur funditus
     tellus ex humore.

   Refl.

3. Sol extinctus fuerat,
     modo renitescit;
   frigus invaluerat,
     sed modo tepescit.
   nix, que nos obruerat
     ex estu liquescit,
   qui prius aruerat
     campus revirescit.

   Refl.

4. Philomena stridula
     voce modulatur;
   floridum alaudula
     tempus salutatur.
   anus, licet vetula,
     mire petulatur;
   lascivit iuvencula
     cum sic recreatur.

   Refl.

1. The radiance of the sun has shone forth, announcing to the world that the season of joy has gleamed on us. The spring, which has now made its appearance, rendering the soil fruitful, deserves an accolade in happy song.

Refrain. So our gathering must sing and dance with sweet melody!

2. The cold of winter is utterly fled, and the air's breath is silent with the more welcome heat. As the health-giving dew comes down from heaven, its moisture makes the earth wholly fruitful.

Refrain.

3. The sun had earlier been blotted out, but now it shines again. The cold had hardened but is now dissolving in warmth. The snow which had overwhelmed us melts with the heat; the plain, earlier arid, grows green again.

Refrain.

4. The nightingale sings in hoarse tones; the flowering season is greeted by the fond lark. In spite of her years the old hag becomes strangely saucy, while the young girl frolics in this time of new life.

IN THIS FURTHER example of a dance lyric, the poet's eye is concentrated solely on the manifestations of nature in the spring. Only in the final four lines is there mention of the human participation in this annual recreation of the world.

1. **quod nobis emicuit**: This alternative construction to the accusative and infinitive, already a feature of colloquial expression in CL, is especially frequent in ML and foreshadows the regular construction in the Romance languages.
   ver: Patzig's emendation of *per* in B.
   salutari: Present infinitive passive.

   Ref. **psallat cum tripudio**: Sempronia, female counterpart in degeneracy to Catiline in Sallust *Cat.* 25.2, could *psallere, saltare elegantius*.

2. **spirat . . . gratiore**: This suggests the warmth of a cloudless, windless sky; the *aether* is the upper air as opposed to *aër*, and *tacitus* indicates its stillness.

salutari rore: The dew is "health-giving" because it brings a blessed cool-ness to men and women as well as moisture to plants; but the literate Christian reader would at once connect the phrase with the dew which de-scended on Gideon's fleece, and subsequently on the earth around, the sign that the Israelites would win salvation from Midian (Judges 3:36ff.); hence the aptness of the adjective *salutaris*.

3. **frigus . . . tepescit:** *Frigus* is Meyer's emendation of *prius*, and is clearly right. Schumann then proposed *tepescit* for *tabescit*, which can stand if taken with the following *nix*. But throughout the poem the couplets are self-contained in sense, as is more natural in a dancing lyric.

4. **stridula:** "Hoarse" suggests that the nightingale recalls her sad history (see comments at 3.1); her voice is more regularly described as harmonious.
mire petulatur: *Petulans* as adjective is well attested in CL, but the verb is not found there. For participation in the dance by the elderly cf. 49.3.
iuvencula: The word is used of a young girl in Biblical Latin (e.g., Ps. 68:26). Cf. 18.3.

22 (82)

1. Frigus hinc est horridum,
   tempus adest floridum.
   veris ab instantia
   tellus iam fit gravida;
   in partum inde solvitur,
   dum florere cernitur.

   Refl. O o o a i a e !
   amoris solamine
   clerus scit diligere
   virginem plus milite!

2. Sol tellurem recreat
   ne fetus eius pereat.
   ab aëris temperantia
   rerum fit materia,
   unde multiplicia
   generantur semina.

   Refl.

3. Mons vestitur floribus
   et sonat a volucribus;
   in silvis aves concinunt
   dulciterque garriunt;
   nec philomena desinit;
   iacturam suam meminit.

   Refl.

4. Ridet terre facies
   colores per multiplices.
   nunc audite, virgines:
   non amant recte milites!
   miles caret viribus
   nature et virtutibus.

   Refl.

5. Thymus et Lapathium
   inierunt hoc consilium:
   "Propter formam milites
   nobis sunt amabiles."
   "De quibus stulta ratio,
   suspensa est solutio."

   Refl.

6. "Sed in cursibus milites
   depingunt nostras facies,
   cum serico in palliis,
   colore et in clipeis."
   "Quid prosunt nobis talia,
   cum forma perit propria?

   Refl.

7. Clerici in frigore
   observant nos in semine,
   pannorum in velamine,
   deinde et in pyxide.
   mox de omni clerico
   amoris fit conclusio."

   Refl.

1. The grisly cold is departed, and the blossom time is here. The earth now becomes pregnant at the prompting of spring; then it parts to give birth when it is seen to flower.

   Refrain. O, o, o, aiae! The cleric knows better than the knight how to court a maiden with love's consolation!

2. The sun renews the earth to rescue her offspring from death. From the air's warmth emerges the stuff of creation, from which are begotten seeds of many kinds.

   Refrain.

3. The mountain is clothed with flowers and is loud with winged creatures. In the woods birds sing in harmony and chatter sweetly. The nightingale harps on unceasingly, recalling the loss which she suffered.

   Refrain.

4. The face of the earth smiles with manifold colors. Now, maidens, listen: Knights are not proper lovers; a knight lacks the powers and virtues which nature bestows.

   Refrain.

5. Thyme and Sorrel began this matter for debate: "Knights are lovable in our eyes because of their handsome appearance."—"On issues foolishly considered, no solution can be reached."

Refrain.

6. "But knights bear our portraits on their journeyings, in silk on their cloaks, and in color on their shields."—"What use to us are such things, when our own beauty is wasting away?

Refrain.

7. Clerics when the world is cold lay eyes on us at our conception, and when we are swathed in swaddling clothes, and later in the cradle. Thereafter love's consummation is gained from every cleric."

Refrain.

THE COMPOSER of this poem treats in brief compass the disputation whether the cleric or the knight should be preferred as lover, a topic handled at greater length and more humorously in no. 29. But here the controversy is introduced curiously and artificially following the conventional exordium of the renewal of nature, to which it has less relevance than has the more usual theme of the joys or sorrows of lovelorn youth. The deliberate emphasis in the first part of the poem on the sexual union of spring and the receptive earth (note *instantia, gravida, partum* in stanza 1, *fetus, semina* in stanza 2) seems to be preparing us for a recommendation to maidens likewise to participate willingly in this scene of cosmic regeneration, but this teasing prospect is disappointed. The careful structural balance between the two themes (with three and one-half stanzas allotted to each), with the concept of *vires naturae* uniting them (see comments to stanza 4) argues against the possibility mooted in Schumann's commentary that the end of the poem may be lost. Some difficulty of interpretation is manifest in the final stanza; my solution can be regarded as only tentative.

1. **instantia**: So B¹ (*absentia* B). The word, suggesting the pressure of the suitor, pleasingly extends the metaphor of sexual union in *gravida* and *partum*.

Ref. **solamine**: This is my suggestion for *insolabilis* in B, obelized by Schumann. Cf. the refrain to no. 26, *amoris solamine / virgino cum virgine.*
clerus scit diligere: The claim is indicative of the nature of author and audience; these lyrics are written by and for clerics. Cf. 29.41, *quid Dione valeat et amoris deus, / primus novit clericus et instruxit meus.*

2. **ab aëris ... materia**: Contemporary philosophers were familiar with this notion of heat-inspired creation, which goes back to Heraclitus; see comments at 13.1b.

3. **philomena . . . iacturam suam meminit:** The mythological story of Philomela (the regular form in CL; *philomena* is the usual form in ML) repeatedly recurs in these lyrics. See, e.g., 3.1 (and comments there).

4. **viribus nature et virtutibus:** At 29.25 Flora contrasts the emaciated physique of the knight with the healthier-looking cleric, whose *virtutes* lie especially in his intellectual superiority (29.40–41).

5. **Thymus et Lapathium:** Like Flora and Phyllis in no. 29, Thyme and Sorrel are apposite names for disputants in a rustic setting, the one supporting the knight as the better lover, the other the cleric.
   de quibus, etc.: We are to infer that this scholastic tag is the riposte of Sorrel to the thesis proposed by Thyme.

6. **in cursibus:** This is my tentative suggestion for *in cordibus* in B; Schumann prints *in cortinis* ("on their curtains") and suggests alternatively *in curtibus* ("in their manors"). But the implication of the final two lines of the stanza is that the knights are crusading abroad.
   forma propria: "Our own beauty" in contrast to the handsome bearing of the knights in stanza 5. Underlying the argument is the idea that while clerics are available for courtship at home, knights are constantly away.

7. **in frigore:** The reading is not only dubiously relevant, but also a poor rhyme; perhaps *in limine*.
   in pyxide: The sense ("in a box") is uncertain. It can scarcely have the liturgical sense of the container for the Sacred Host in the Eucharist, or again refer to a box of cosmetics. I assume a sense similar to that described at Christ's nativity in Luke 2:7, *et pannis eum involvit, et reclinavit eum in presepio.*
   amoris: I prefer not to personify *amoris* here, and I assign these last two lines with the previous six, to the spokeswoman Lapathium; the sense then conveys that the cleric is on hand from the cradle to maturity, in contrast to the absent knight. If *Amoris* is read, the two lines are not part of the dialogue but represent the poet's own commentary; the dispute is referred to Cupid as in no. 29 below, and "Cupid's conclusion concerns every cleric"—meaning, "is in every cleric's favor"?—but this entails a violence to the Latin.

23 (83)

1. Sevit aure spiritus,
    et arborum
come fluunt penitus
    vi frigorum;
silent cantus nemorum.
nunc torpescit, vere solo
    fervens, amor pecorum;
semper amans sequi nolo
    novas vices temporum
        bestiali more.

Refl. Quam dulcia
    stipendia
    et gaudia
    felicia
    sunt decore
    nostre Flore!

2. Nec de longo conqueror
        obsequio;
nobili remuneror
        stipendio.
leto letor premio.
dum salutat me loquaci
    Flora supercilio,
mente satis non capaci
    gaudia concipio,
        glorior labore.

Refl.

3. Michi sors obsequitur
        non aspera;
dum secreta luditur
        in camera,
favet Venus prospera.
nudam fovet Floram lectus
    caro candet tenera;
virginale lucet pectus,
    parum surgunt ubera
        modico tumore.

Refl.

4. Hominem transgredior
    et superum
sublimari glorior
    ad numerum,
sinum tractans tenerum,
cursu vago dum beata
    manus it, et uberum
regionem pervagata
    descendit ad uterum
        tactu leviore.

Refl.

5. A tenello tenera
        pectusculo
distenduntur latera
        pro modulo;
caro carens scrupulo
levem tactum non offendit.
    gracilis sub cingulo
umbilicum preextendit
    paululum ventriculo
        tumescentiore.

Refl.

6. Vota blando stimulat
        lenimine
pubes, que vix pullulat
        in virgine
tenui lanugine.
crus vestitum moderata
    tenerum pinguedine,
levigatur occultata
    nervorum compagine,
        radians candore.

Refl.

7. O, si forte Iupiter
      hanc videat,
   timeo ne pariter
      incaleat
   et ad fraudes redeat;
   si vel Danes pluens aurum
      imbre dulci mulceat,
   vel Europes intret taurum,
      vel Ledeo candeat
         rursus in olore.

   Refl.

1. The wind's breath is harsh, and the foliage of the trees is totally disappearing under the violence of the cold. The songs in the groves are silent. Now love between cattle grows sluggish, for it is in heat only in spring. But I am always in love, and I refuse to follow the new changes of the seasons as beasts are wont to do.

   Refrain. How sweet are the wages and blessed joys bestowed by my lovely Flora!

2. I do not complain of my long service, for I am recompensed with notable payment. I rejoice in my happy reward. As Flora greets me with eyebrows that speak volumes, I cannot take in the joy, for my mind cannot contain it, and I glory in the toil.

   Refrain.

3. It is no harsh lot that attends me. As we sport in our sequestered room, Venus is well-disposed and favorable. The couch hugs my naked Flora. Her youthful flesh gleams white, her maiden's bosom is aglow, her breasts rise slightly with modest swelling.

   Refrain.

4. I transcend mere humanity and boast that I am raised to the number of the gods as I fondle her soft bosom, and as my blessed hand in wandering course roams over the region of her breasts, and with lighter touch reaches down to her belly.

   Refrain.

5. From her small, soft bosom her delicate flanks harmoniously extend. Her unblemished flesh does not irritate the gentle touch. Beneath her girdle her slender form makes her navel project just slightly, with her small belly's modest swelling.

Refrain.

6. Her lower parts, barely sprouting with a maiden's soft hair, fire my desire with their alluring softness. Her soft limbs with their restrained covering of flesh feel smooth as they conceal the line of her sinews, and shine with their whiteness.

Refrain.

7. If Jupiter happened to lay eyes on her, I fear that he would become as passionate as I, and return to his deceits; for he would either rain down Danaë's gold and soften her with that sweet shower, or masquerade as Europa's bull, or turn white once more as Leda's swan.

Refrain.

THE POEM APPEARS in full in Arundel 384. Verses 1, 2, 5, 4 in that order appear in Vat. Reg. Christ. 344 (V). B contains only 1–3, 5, 7 in that order.

In this composition Peter of Blois (on his authorship see Introduction, section 2) exploits the reversal of the conventional exordium, as he does earlier, in no. 9. Instead of the celebration of spring, he describes the onset of winter to emphasize that human love transcends the sexual urges of animals, which are in heat with the onset of summer. The description of nature is perfunctory; after one stanza he turns to the intimate joys of the love encounter. The almost clinical description of Flora's physiognomy, so characteristic of the author, bears a close resemblance to Matthew of Vendôme's prescription for the *deliciosus auditor* in *Ars Versificatoria* 1.57.

Ref. This appears only in B.
decore: Schumann's emendation of *hec hore*.

2. **de longo obsequio**: The stylized reference to the courtly love procedure (by which the lady dominates the relationship, and the suitor offers his obedient service in performing labors in her name) perhaps suggests that Peter, like Ovid before him, was a theorist rather than a practitioner of love-sport.

loquaci . . . supercilio: The classic text for modes of silent communication between lovers is Ovid *Am.* 1.4; for the use of the eyebrows see 1.4.19, *verba superciliis sine voce loquentia dicam.*

Flora: As noted earlier (see no. 3), Flora is often the sobriquet of the chaste maiden courted by the cleric. Here she is a more permissive lady, though in Andreas Capellanus *amor purus* can advance *ad oris osculum lacertique amplexum et verecundum amantis nudae contactum, extremo praetermisso solacio* (1.6H.471). Note that her *pectus* is *virginale*, that she is a *virgo* (stanzas 3, 6).

glorior labore: For this feature of courtly love McDonough well compares Arundel 11.1–2, *In laborem sponte labor / nec invitus patior, / . . . O quam felix ille labor, / illa patientia.*

3. **obsequitur:** So the spokesman's *obsequium* to the lady (stanza 2) is nicely matched by the happy fortune which in turn attends on him.
fovet . . . lectus: Wordplay in Peter's poems is so ubiquitous that one wonders is there is an ambivalence here between "couch" and "chosen one."
candet: The word is used of bare flesh in Horace *Carm.* 1.2.31 (Apollo's shoulders) and Tibullus 1.8.33 (arms).
parum: = *paulum*, as often in ML.

4. **hominem transgredior:** The use of the verb in this sense is postclassical.
superum: Genitive plural, as often in CL (Virgil *Aen.* 1.4, etc.).

5–6. In this uninhibited description of the girl's physical attributes, Ovid *Am.* 1.5.17ff. is doubtless in Peter's mind: *ut stetit ante oculos posito velamine nostros, / in toto nusquam corpore menda fuit. / . . . quam castigato planus sub pectore venter! / quantum et quale latus! quam iuvenale femur!*

5. **a tenello modulo, etc.:** The sustained sequence of diminutives underlines the girl's youthfulness. Matthew of Vendôme's *Ars Versificatoria* similarly has *artatur laterum descensus ad ilia, donec / surgat ventriculo luxuriante tumor* (1.57.3–4).

6. **lanugine:** Used of the hair of the head in Ovid's comic account of Corinna's disastrous experiment with hair dye (*Am.* 1.14.23).
crus . . . tenerum: Peter proceeds remorselessly downward. *Crus* (in CL the leg below the knee, as distinct from *femur* or thigh) seems here to denote the leg as a whole.
vestitum moderata pinguetudine: In this overelaboration of Matthew of Vendôme's *carnea crura* (1.57.9; Maximian 1.86 has *carnea membra*) Peter approaches perilously close to bathos.
lēvigatur . . . compagine: The spokesman waxes lyrical about Flora's knees.

7. **Danes pluens aurum**: (*Danes* must be genitive, balancing *Europes* two lines below.) The story of how Jupiter breached the bronze tower which enclosed Danaë by assuming the form of a golden shower became a parable for the victory of money over virtue. See especially Ovid *Met.* 4.697ff. and Horace *Carm.* 3.16.1ff.

Europes taurum: Jupiter took the form of a bull to bear Europa off to Crete. See esp. Ovid *Met.* 2.836ff. and Horace *Carm.* 3.27.25ff.

vel Ledeo . . . in olore: This story of Jupiter's impersonating a swan to achieve intimacy with Leda is combined with the other stories, of Danaë and Europa, in Ovid's description of Arachne's embroidery at *Met.* 6.103ff. and again at *Am.* 3.12.33–34.

24 (84)

1.   Dum prius inculta
coleret virgulta
estas iam adulta,
hieme sepulta,
    vidi viridi
Phyllidem sub tilia,
    vidi Phyllidi
quevis arridentia.
invideo, dum video.
sic capi cogit sedulus
me laqueo virgineo
cordis venator oculus,
    visa captus virgine.

Refl.   Ha, morior!
sed quavis dulcedine
    mors dulcior.
sic amanti vivitur,
dum sic amans moritur.

2.   Fronte explicata
exiit in prata,
ceu Dione nata
venerit legata.
    videns, invidens
huc spe duce rapior;
    ridens, residens
residenti blandior.
sed tremula virguncula
frondis in modum tremule
ut primula discipula
nondum subiecta ferule,
    tremit ad blanditias.

Refl.   Ha, morior!
sed quavis dulcedine
    mors dulcior.
sic amanti vivitur,
dum sic amans moritur.

3.   Respondendi metus
trahit hanc ad fletus.
sed rapina letus
Amor indiscretus
    meam in eam,
ut pudoris tangere
    queam lineam,
manum mittit propere.
dum propero, vim infero
posti minante machina;
nec supero; nam aspero
defendens ungue limina
    obserat introitus.

Refl.   Ha, morior!
    sed hec michi penitus
        mors dulcior.
    sic amanti vivitur,
    dum sic amans moritur.

4.   Tantalus admotum
non amitto potum.
sed, ne tamen totum
frustret illa votum,
    suo denuo
iungens collo brachium,
    ruo, diruo
tricaturas crurium.
ut virginem devirginem,
me toti totum insero;
cardinem, ⟨ut⟩ determinem
duellum istud, resero.
    sic in castris milito.

Refl.   Ha, morior!
    sed hec michi penitus
        mors dulcior.
    sic amanti vivitur,
    dum sic amans moritur.

---

1. When the summer now full-grown made its dwelling in thickets earlier un-
clothed, and winter was now buried, I saw Phyllis under a green lime tree. I
saw every facet of nature smiling on Phyllis. As I gazed on her, I coveted
her; so the eye, the heart's unwearying hunter, forced me to be trapped in
the maiden's noose, trapped by the sight of that maiden.

Refrain. Oh, death is upon me, but a death sweeter than any sweetness.
This is what life is for the lover, experiencing death through such loving.

2. She walked out into the fields with unfurrowed brow, as if she had come as
the ambassadress of Dione's daughter. Seeing her and coveting her, I was
drawn there, guided by hope. As she sat there I took my place smilingly beside her and paid her compliments. But the young maiden, trembling like
the trembling foliage, like a youthful pupil not yet schooled to the cane,
trembled at my flattery.

Refrain. [As in stanza 1.]

3. Fear of making reply brought her to tears. But Cupid, who takes joy in
plundering and knows no discretion, swiftly guided my hand toward her, so
that I could touch the line of her maidenhead. In my haste I applied force,
my engine threatening her portal. But I did not prevail, for she defended her
threshold with her sharp nails and blocked the entrance.

Refrain. Oh, death is upon me, but for me this death is utterly sweeter. This is what life is for the lover, experiencing death through such loving.

4. I was a Tantalus who did not lose the drink placed before him. But so that she should not deny me my full longing, I put my arm again around her neck, brought her down, and forced apart her interlocking thighs. I thrust all of me all the way in to deflower her virgin flower; I loosed the hinge to bring this duel to a close. This is my manner of campaigning in warfare.

Refrain. [As in stanza 3.]

THIS POEM is also found in Vat. Reg. Christ. 344 (V), with the heading *De virginis rapta virginitate.*

The speculative attribution to Peter of Blois (see Introduction, section 2) can be supported on the basis of style and message; the clinical and sadistic description of what can only be called rape (cf. no. 12) is characteristic. In one letter in which he alludes to his youthful compositions Peter labels them *lasciviores cantilenae*; in another he laments what he calls *amores illicitos canere, et se corruptorem virginum iactitare* (*Epp.* 57, 76 in *Opera*, ed. Giles, 1:169, 225; cf. Raby, *SLP* 2:323–24). In spite of this unsavory and disavowed treatment, it has seemed desirable to include this composition with the other lyrics tentatively ascribed to Peter, as he is the only identifiable author of love poems in this collection and his technical skill is incontrovertible.

The setting of the poem, in which the spokesman approaches Phyllis as she sits under a lime tree, has prompted some critics to ascribe it to the genre of the pastourelle (see Introduction, section 6). But Phyllis (a name deployed elsewhere for a courtly partner; see nos. 4, 29, and *CB* 156) is no shepherdess; more important, there is no stylized dialogue, which is the staple of that genre.

1. **Dum prius inculta, etc.:** The conventional exordium greeting the arrival of summer is confined to four lines; Peter characteristically concentrates on the love encounter.

    cordis venator oculus: Twelfth-century love theory, following the lead of the love literature of antiquity (especially the romances) and the condemnation of *concupiscentia oculorum* (1 John 2:16) in Christian literature, lays great emphasis on the eye as the initiator of love feeling. Cf. Andreas Capellanus 1.1.8, *Ex sola cogitatione quam concipit animus ex eo quod vidit passio illa procedit. Nam quum aliquis videt aliquam aptam amori. . . .* For the phrase *cordis venator* cf. *CB* 110.2, *cepit puellam / oculus / cordis hanc preambulus / venari.*

Ref. This is the reading of V; B has *sed hec michi penitus*, as after stanza 3.

2. **venerit**: So Heraeus, emending Veneris in B (*Venere* V). Bischoff and Vollmann retain *Veneris*, but can she be simultaneously the daughter of Dione
(= Venus) and the messenger of Venus?

   subiecta: So V; *seducte* B. There is a case for reading *subducta* as an evocation of Juvenal 1.15, *et nos ergo manum ferulae subduximus*. But the *primula discipula* is "not yet subject (*subiecta*) to the cane," as Phyllis is not
yet subjected to male domination; *subducere* in Juvenal means "withdraw
from," hardly apt here.

   Ref. V does not repeat the refrain, and there is a lacuna in B, which has
merely *sed . . . ias*. I presume that V intends us to understand the same refrain as after stanza 1.

3. **respondendi**: Perhaps of responding physically, as at Propertius 4.8.88
(Vollmann).

   rapina: So V (*natura* B). Schumann's *raptura* is hardly an improvement; cf.
Ovid *Ars Am.* 1.675, *quaecumque est Veneris subito violata rapina, / gaudet*.

   posti minante machina: Schumann's emendation (*minanti postimachina* V;
post imminentem machinam B) well captures the image of storming a
threshold, which is sustained to the end of the stanza, and resumed at the
end of stanza 4.

   Ref. So B; the refrain is absent in V.

4. **Tantalus . . . non amitto**: Cf. Ovid *Am.* 2.2.43–44, *quaerit aquas in aquis,
et poma fugacia captat / Tantalus. Amitto* is Schmeller's emendation of *ad-
mitto* in B (*admittit* V).

   tricaturas: First in ML.

   cardinem ⟨ut⟩ . . . resero: V has *ut cardinem . . . resero*; B omits *ut*. I follow Vollmann's punctuation but transpose V's *ut*, which he bafflingly
omits; this makes more satisfactory sense than Schumann's *ut cardinem determinem, duellum istud refero*.

   sic in castris milito: So V; B's *glorior victoria* has the ring of an unimagina-
tive "improvement" by a later contributor.

   Ref. Once again line 2 in B is defective, reading *sed . . . ito*; I assume that
ito is a corruption of *-itus* in *penitus* and posit the same refrain as after
stanza 3.

25 (85)

1. Veris dulcis in tempore
   florenti stat sub arbore
   Iuliana cum sorore.

   Refl.   Dulcis amor!
          qui te caret hoc tempore,
                 fit vilior.

2. Ecce florescunt arbores,
   lascive canunt volucres;
   inde tepescunt virgines.

   Refl.

3. Ecce, florescunt lilia,
   et virginum dant agmina
   summo deorum carmina.

   Refl.

4. Si tenerem quam cupio
   in nemore sub folio,
   oscularer cum gaudio.

   Refl.

1. In the season of the sweet spring, Juliana stands with her sister, under a blossoming tree.

   Refrain. How sweet is love! He who forgoes you at this season becomes more tawdry.

2. See, the trees are in blossom, and the birds sing their wanton song. This is the source of maidens' warm stirrings.

   Refrain.

3. See, the lilies are in bloom, and the bands of maidens sing their songs to the highest of the gods.

   Refrain.

4. If I held the girl of my desire, in the glade beneath the foliage, I would kiss her with rapture.

   Refrain.

THE POEM APPEARS in Escorial Z II 2, and at two different places in B. This is the simplest of compositions, incorporating the design of the medieval love lyric at its most basic: first, the joyful renewal of nature in the springtime and, second, the effect of the change of season on the hearts of young girls. The ethos is that of Classical antiquity (hence *summo deorum* in stanza 3). The name of the girl, Juliana, makes its sole appearance here in the lyrics of the *Carmina Burana*.

2. **inde tepescunt**: Note that the sight of the budding trees and the singing of the birds are the cause of the stirrings of emotion in the girls.

3. **virginum . . . agmina**: So Schmeller for *virgines . . . agmina*; Schumann prints *virgines dant gemina*, an improbable suggestion.
summo deorum: This is Cupid, because he exercises sway over all the deities. Cf. no. 26, *Amor habet superos*. *Summo* is Schmeller's emendation for *summa* in B, which Vollmann retains.

26 (88)

1. Amor habet superos;
   Iovem amat Iuno;
   motus premens efferos
   imperat Neptuno;
   Pluto tenens inferos
   mitis est hoc uno.

   Refl. amoris solamine
   virgino cum virgine;
   aro non in semine,
   pecco sine crimine.

2. Amor trahit teneros
   molliori nexu,
   rigidos et asperos
   duro frangit flexu;
   capitur rhinoceros
   virginis amplexu.

   Refl.

3. Virgo cum virginibus
   horreo corruptas,
   et cum meretricibus
   simul odi nuptas;
   nam in istis talibus
   turpis est voluptas.

   Refl.

4. Virginis egregie
   ignibus calesco,
   et eius cotidie
   in amore cresco;
   sol est in meridie,
   nec ego tepesco.

   Refl.

5. Gratus super omnia
   ludus est puelle,
   et eius precordia
   omni carent felle;
   sunt que prestat basia
   dulciora melle.

   Refl.

6. Ludo cum Cecilia,
   nichil timeatis!
   sum quasi custodia
   fragilis etatis,
   ne marcescant lilia
   sue castitatis.

   Refl.

7. Flos est; florem tangere
   non est res secura.
   uvam sino crescere
   donec sit matura;
   spes me facit vivere
   letum re ventura.

   Refl.

8. Volo tantum ludere,
   id est, contemplari,
   presens loqui, tangere,
   tandem osculari;
   quintum, quod est agere,
   noli suspicari!

   Refl.

9. Quicquid agant ceteri,
   virgo, sic agamus
   ut, quem decet fieri
   ludum faciamus;
   ambo sumus teneri;
   tenere ludamus!

---

1. Love controls the gods above. Juno loves Jupiter; Love lords it over Neptune, restraining his fierce motions; Pluto, who confines the spirits below, becomes gentle through Love alone.

   Refrain. In the consolation of love I play the virgin with a virgin. I plow without sowing, my erring excludes serious sinning.

2. Love constrains the innocent with a gentler bond, but the unbending and truculent with his harsh yoke. Even the rhinoceros is captured by a maiden's embrace.

   Refrain.

3. I am a virgin among virgins, and am repelled by shop-soiled women. I loathe the married no less than the harlots, for with such as these the pleasure is base.

   Refrain.

4. I am hot with flaming desire for an outstanding maiden, and every day my love for her grows. The sun is at its zenith, and I too feel the heat.

   Refrain.

5. Sporting with this girl of mine is more pleasing than all else; there is no bile whatever in her heart. The kisses which she offers are sweeter than honey.

   Refrain.

6. I sport with Cecilia, but you need have no fear. I am, so to say, on sentry-go over her tender years, to ensure that the lilies of her chastity do not wither.

Refrain.

7. She is a virgin blossom, and it is not safe to handle a virgin blossom. I let the grape swell until it becomes ripe; hope makes me live in joy at the future prospect.

Refrain.

8. My one wish is for innocent sport—to gaze, to talk face to face, to touch, and finally to kiss. The fifth stage of intercourse you must not suspect!

Refrain.

9. However the rest of the world behaves, dear maiden, let *our* intercourse be such that we sport with propriety. We are both innocent, so let us sport innocently!

Refrain.

THE POEM IS FOUND in one other manuscript, Florence Laur. Edili 197 (F), of the thirteenth century, in a much superior version. In B this and the next composition (no. 27 [88a]) are conflated, and the order of stanzas (6, 8, 7, 5, 2, 1, 3, 9) is hopelessly confused. In F the order is 1–2, 4–7, 7a, 3, 9, 8; 7a is a clearly spurious supplement, defective in rhyme and irrelevant in content, so that there is no need to print it here. The refrain appears in F but not in B.

The theme is the universal sway of Cupid and the two forms of love that he inspires, which Andreas Capellanus labels *amor purus* and *amor mixtus.* The poet expresses his loathing for *amor mixtus,* the love which goes as far as intercourse and is *turpis voluptas* (see stanza 3). His love is the *amor purus* which advances as far as kissing (stanza 8) but goes no further. The distinction between the two forms of love may owe much to Avicenna's treatise (trans. Fackenheim, "A Treatise of Love by Ibn Sina"), which owes its inspiration to Plato, notably the *Phaedrus.*

1. **Amor habet superos**: Ovid *Met.* 5.369ff. is the inspiration: *tu* [Cupid] *superos ipsumque Iovem, tu numina ponti / victa domas, ipsumque regit qui numina ponti: Tartara quid cessant?* . . . (so Vollmann).

Ref. **virgino**: The word appears in Ecclesiastical Latin as a deponent (Tertullian *De Virginibus Velandis* 12).

aro non in semine: The biblical image of Ecclus. 6:19 (*qui arat et seminat*) is humorously deployed to distinguish between *amor purus* and *amor mixtus*.

pecco sine crimine: *Pecco* implies venial sinning, and *crimen* here suggests fornication, as at Ovid *Met.* 9.24.

2. **rhinoceros:** The popular belief that the unicorn (identified with the rhinoceros; see White, *Book of Beasts*, 20–21) could be captured through the charms of a pretty girl goes back to *Physiologus* 1000–1001: "it sits in her lap, enjoys her breasts and suckles them like a child." Isidore *Etym.* 12.2.13 shows acquaintance with the tradition: *tantae autem esse fortitudinis ut nulla venantium virtute capiatur; sed sicut asserunt qui naturas animalium scripserunt, virgo puella praeponitur quae venienti sinum aperit, in quo ille omni ferocitate deposita caput ponit, sicque soporatus velut inermis capitur.* The motif is also found in no. 30 (see comments there).

3. **corruptas . . . turpis voluptas:** The adjectives condemn *amor mixtus*.

4. **calesco:** An Ovidian word: cf. *Met.* 3.272, *Her.* 18.177, etc.

5. **ludus:** For the limits of such love play see stanza 8 below.
   precordia . . . felle: Such expressions are often used to denote the human temperament. Physiologically the *praecordia* is the breast and the *fel* the gallbladder. See Celsus 4.1, *iecur a dextra parte sub praecordiis; ex inferiore parte ei fel inhaeret.*

6. **Cecilia:** The name does not appear elsewhere in the *Carmina Burana* (except with dubious authority in the refrain to *CB* 86), but the fame of the third-century martyr and patroness of church music (her feast day is 22 November) made it a popular one.

7. **flos:** The word is a symbol of virginity from Classical times; see, e.g., Catullus 62.46.
   spes: For the technical sense in courtly love theory see comments at 4.7.

8. **id est, contemplari, etc.:** *ludere* is equated in these lyrics with the *amor purus* which embraces only the first four stages of the *quinque lineae amoris* (on which see 12.2a and comments there).

9. **agant . . . agamus:** The jocose repetition of the verb from stanza 8 should be noted.
   quem decet . . . ludum: A vehement defense of the ideals of *amor purus*.

27 (88a)

1. Iove cum Mercurio   Geminos tenente
   et a Libra Venere   Martem expellente,
   virgo nostra nascitur,   Tauro tunc latente.

2. natus ego pariter   sub eisdem signis,
   pari par coniunctus sum   legibus benignis;
   paribus est ignibus   par accensus ignis.

3. solus solam diligo   sic me sola solum,
   nec est cui liceat   immiscere dolum;
   non in vanum variant   signa nostra polum.

4. obicit "ab alio"   forsitan "amatur,"
   ut quod "solus" dixerim,   ita refellatur;
   sed ut dictum maneat,   sic determinatur.

1. My maiden was born when Jupiter and Mercury were in Gemini, and when Venus was driving Mars out of Libra. Taurus at that time lay hidden.

2. I too was born under the same signs, and so we are alike, joined under nature's kindly laws. A like fire is kindled in both because of the like fires of our birth.

3. I alone love her alone, and likewise she alone loves me alone, and there is no one who can infiltrate his guile. It is not for nothing that our stars spangle the heavens.

4. Perhaps the crafty one objects: "She is loved by another," so that my claim to be her only lover may be refuted. But it is predestined that my claim abides.

THE POEM APPEARS also in Paris B.N. lat. 3719, where it is confined to the four stanzas printed here. B, in which this poem is joined to no. 26, has two further stanzas inserted between 2 and 3, but they are clearly irrelevant to the theme of the poem; for further detail see *Thirty Poems*, comments at no. 17.

The astrological exordium is a variation from the theme of the coming of spring (see no. 8). The lovers' compatibility is introduced by the claim that they were were born under the same stars. Such astrological concerns were a prominent feature in the medieval schools: "Astrologers were not 'false magicians' but people who measured nature; for them the real practitioners of 'false magic' were people who busied themselves with religion" (Heer, *The Medieval World*, 299). As natural scientists preaching a doctrine of determinism, they encountered the opposition of Christian thinkers espousing the opposing tenet of free will. Hence the topicality of the astrological treatment. Because the names of planets and signs of the zodiac were familiar to readers of the poems, they could be exploited to make witty connections with the love theme. Stanza 1 makes perfect sense astronomically (for details see *Thirty Poems*, no. 17); the birth of the lovers is assigned to some evening in March or April, when Mercury was an evening star and Venus in Libra a morning star.

1. **Iove cum Mercurio, etc.**: Jupiter and Mercury are favorable stars, and their presence in Gemini suggests an auspicious future for the twin souls.
Venere Martem expellente: Venus driving out the god of war indicates a harmonious relationship.
Tauro . . . latente: The absence of the Bull excludes brutality from the love exchanges.

2. The notion that persons born under the same star would share the same destiny had provoked controversy from antiquity onward. Cicero's counterargument (*Div.* 2.90) that twins often follow different fortunes was taken up by Augustine (*Conf.* 7.6.8ff., *Civ. Dei* 5.1–6), but the idea obstinately persisted.
ignibus . . . ignis: Note the play on the two senses "star" and "fire of passion."

3. **cui liceat immiscere dolum**: The gossip-monger who disturbs a relationship by malicious suggestions frequently appears in courtly love literature. See no. 37.

4. **obicit**: The subject is to be supplied from *cui liceat* in stanza 3.
determinatur: The word epitomizes the spokesman's claim that the course of his love is predestined by the stars.

28 (90)

1. Exiit diluculo
   rustica puella
cum grege, cum baculo
   cum lana novella.

2. Sunt in grege parvulo
     ovis et asella,
   vitula cum vitulo,
     caper et capella.

[3. Conspexit in cespite
     scolarem sedere:
   "quid tu facis, domine?
     veni mecum ludere."]

1. A country girl went out at daybreak with her flock and staff, wearing a lamb's-wool scarf.

2. In her tiny flock are a sheep and a she-ass, a cow-calf and a bull-calf, a billy-goat and a nanny-goat.

[3. She spotted a student sitting on the turf: "What are you doing there, sir? Come and play games with me."]

THE POEM APPEARS in one other manuscript, from Diessen (Clm. 5529, fourteenth century).

I include this brief fragment in this selection because of the interesting literary controversy which it has provoked. Schumann, noting that the third stanza was absent in the Diessen manuscript and, more important, that the rhymes and rhythms were defective (*caespite/domine*; *sedēre/ludĕre*; an extra syllable in the final line), suggested that the poem is the fragmentary beginning of a pastourelle, to which a later contributor has added the third stanza. Von den Steinen (cited in Dronke, "Poetic Meaning") signals cautious agreement but adds that the addition shows a spark of genius. Dronke in his article goes further; in a splendid analysis he shows how artistically fitting it is for the shepherdess, as she leads her paired charges, to long for a companion for herself, and he argues that it is part of the original composition. Both he and Von den Steinen make the valid literary point that the third stanza offers a climax and a close to the poem. Dronke claims that there is an element of textual pedantry in Schumann's exclusion of it. He goes on to observe that the musical score for the song, extant in the Diessen manuscript, also appears in a famous Spanish music manuscript, the Codex de las Huelgas, where it is attached to a hymn of the Resurrection, and where the musical notation indicates the existence of three stanzas and not two.

However much one is tempted by these arguments, Schumann's critique is valid: our poet in the first two stanzas exhibits exemplary control in a rhyme scheme carried over from the first stanza into the second. The third stanza not only departs from that scheme but betrays a technique rudimentary by comparison with the earlier lines. It can also be argued that the shepherdess reveals an uncharacteristic forwardness in issuing such an invitation; more normally in the pastourelle if the girl speaks first, it is to issue an appeal in distress. The argument from the musical score on the Spanish manuscript is quite inconclusive; the original melody could have been extended for its new purpose.

1. **cum lana novella:** Even in CL *lana* is sometimes found in the sense of a woolen garment; see *OLD* s.v. An alternative rendering might be "with the new-shorn wool," which the girl would card or spin while herding.

2. **ovis et asella:** "The sheep and the little she-ass may be an incongruous twosome, yet still they are companions, they are together" (Dronke, "Poetic Meaning")—but not of course as companions in love, which weakens to some extent the argument for incorporating the third stanza in the original poem.

29 (92)

1. 1. Anni parte florida,   celo puriore,
       picto terre gremio   vario colore,
       dum fugaret sidera   nuntius Aurore
       liquit somnus oculos   Phyllidis et Flore.

    2. Placuit virginibus   ire spatiatum,
       nam soporem reicit   pectus sauciatum;
       equis ergo passibus   exeunt in pratum,
       ut et locus faciat   ludum esse gratum.

    3. Eunt ambe virgines   et ambe regine,
       Phyllis coma libera,   Flora compto crine.
       non sunt forme virginum,   sed forme divine,
       et respondent facies   luci matutine.

    4. Nec stirpe nec facie   nec ornatu viles
       et annos et animos   habent iuveniles;
       sed sunt parum impares   et parum hostiles,
       nam huic placet clericus   et huic placet miles.

5. Non eis distantia   corporis aut oris,
    omnia communia   sunt intus et foris,
    sunt unius habitus   et unius moris;
    sola differentia   modus est amoris.

6. Susurrabat modicum   ventus tempestivus,
    locus erat viridi   gramine festivus,
    et in ipso gramine   defluebat rivus
    vivus atque garrulo   murmure lascivus.

7. Ad augmentum decoris   et caloris minus
    fuit secus rivulum   spatiosa pinus,
    venustata folio,   late pandens sinus,
    nec intrare poterat   calor peregrinus.

8. Consedere virgines;   herba sedem dedit.
    Phyllis iuxta rivulum,   Flora longe sedit.
    et dum sedet utraque,   dum in sese redit,
    amor corda vulnerat   et utramque ledit.

9. Amor est interius   latens et occultus,
    et corde certissimos   elicit singultus;
    pallor genas inficit,   alternantur vultus,
    sed in verecundia   furor est sepultus.

10. Phyllis in suspirio   Floram deprehendit,
    et hanc de consimili   Flora reprehendit;
    altera sic alteri   mutuo rependit;
    tandem morbum detegit   et vulnus ostendit.

11. Ille sermo mutuus   multum habet more,
    et est quidem series   tota de amore;
    amor est in animis,   amor est in ore.
    tandem Phyllis incipit   et arridet Flore.

12. "Miles" inquit "inclite,   mea cura, Paris,
    ubi modo militas   et ubi moraris?
    o vita militie,   vita singularis,
    sola digna gaudio   Dionei laris!"

13. Dum puella militem   recolit amicum,
    Flora ridens oculos   iacit in obliquum,
    et in risu loquitur   verbum inimicum:
    "Amas," inquit "poteras   dicere, mendicum.

14. Sed quid Alcibiades   facit, mea cura,
     res creata dignior   omni creatura,
     quem beavit omnibus   gratiis Natura?
     o sola felicia   clericorum iura!"

15. Floram Phyllis arguit   de sermone duro,
     et sermone loquitur   Floram commoturo;
     nam "ecce virgunculam"   inquit "corde puro,
     cuius pectus nobile   servit Epicuro!

16. Surge, surge, misera,   de furore fedo!
     solum esse clericum   Epicurum credo;
     nichil elegantie   clerico concedo,
     cuius implet latera   moles et pinguedo.

17. A castris Cupidinis   cor habet remotum
     qui somnum desiderat   et cibum et potum.
     o puella nobilis,   omnibus est notum,
     quod est longe militis   ab hoc voto votum.

18. Solis necessariis   miles est contentus,
     somno, cibo, potui   non vivit intentus;
     amor illi prohibet   ne sit somnolentus,
     cibus, potus militis   amor et iuventus.

19. Quis amicos copulet   nostros loro pari?
     lex, natura sineret   illos copulari?
     meus novit ludere,   tuus epulari;
     meo semper proprium   dare, tuo dari."

20. Haurit Flora sanguinem   vultu verecundo,
     et apparet pulchrior   in risu secundo,
     et tandem eloquio   reserat facundo,
     quod corde conceperat   artibus fecundo.

21. "Satis" inquit "libere,   Phyllis, es locuta,
     multum es eloquio   velox et acuta,
     sed non efficaciter   verum prosecuta,
     ut per te prevaleat   lilio cicuta.

22. Dixisti de clerico   quod indulget sibi,
     servum somni nominas   et potus et cibi.
     sic solet ab invido   probitas describi;
     ecce, parum patere,   respondebo tibi.

23. Tot et tanta, fateor, sunt amici mei
  quod nunquam incogitat aliene rei.
  celle mellis, olei, Cereris, Lyei,
  aurum, gemme, pocula famulantur ei.

24. In tam dulci copia vite clericalis,
  quod non potest aliqua pingi voce talis,
  volat et duplicibus Amor plaudit alis,
  Amor indeficiens, Amor immortalis.

25. Sentit tela Veneris et Amoris ictus;
  non est tamen clericus macer aut afflictus,
  quippe nulla gaudii parte derelictus;
  cui respondet animus domine non fictus.

26. Macer est et pallidus tuus preelectus,
  pauper et vix pallio sine pelle tectus,
  non sunt artus validi nec robustum pectus;
  nam cum causa deficit, deest et effectus.

27. Turpis est pauperies imminens amanti.
  quid prestare poterit miles postulanti?
  sed dat multa clericus et ex abundanti;
  tante sunt divitie reditusque tanti."

28. Flore Phyllis obicit: "multum es perita
  in utrisque studiis et utraque vita,
  satis probabiliter et pulchre mentita;
  sed hec altercatio non quiescet ita.

29. Cum orbem letificat hora lucis feste,
  tunc apparet clericus satis inhoneste,
  in tonsura capitis et in atra veste
  portans testimonium voluptatis meste.

30. Non est ullus adeo fatuus aut cecus
  cui non appareat militare decus.
  tuus est in otio quasi brutum pecus;
  meum terit galea, meum portat equus.

31. Meus armis dissipat inimicas sedes.
  et si forte prelium solus init pedes,
  dum tenet Bucephalam suus Ganymedes,
  ille me commemorat inter ipsas cedes.

32. Redit fusis hostibus   et pugna confecta,
    et me sepe respicit   galea reiecta.
    ex his et ex aliis   ratione recta
    est vita militie   michi preelecta."

33. Novit iram Phyllidis   et pectus anhelum,
    et remittit multiplex   illi Flora telum.
    "frustra" dixi "loqueris   os ponens in celum
    et per acum niteris   figere camelum.

34. Mel pro felle deseris   et pro falso verum
    que probas militiam   reprobando clerum.
    facit amor militem   strenuum et ferum?
    non! immo, pauperies   et defectus rerum.

35. Pulchra Phyllis, utinam   sapienter ames,
    nec veris sententiis   amplius reclames!
    tuum domat militem   et sitis et fames,
    quibus mortis petitur   et inferni trames.

36. Multum est calamitas   militis attrita,
    sors illius dura est   et in arto sita,
    cuius est in pendulo   dubioque vita,
    ut habere valeat   vite requisita.

37. Non dicas opprobrium,   si cognoscas morem,
    vestem nigram clerici,   comam breviorem;
    habet ista clericus   ad summum honorem,
    ut sese significet   omnibus maiorem.

38. Vniversa clerico   constat esse prona,
    et signum imperii   portat in corona.
    imperat militibus   et largitur dona;
    famulante maior est   imperans persona.

39. Otiosum clericum   semper esse iuras;
    viles spernit operas,   fateor, et duras;
    sed cum eius animus   evolat ad curas,
    celi vias dividit   et rerum naturas.

40. Meus est in purpura,   tuus in lorica;
    tuus est in prelio,   meus in lectica,
    ubi gesta principum   relegit antiqua,
    scribit, querit, cogitat   totum de amica.

41. Quid Dione valeat et amoris deus,
    primus novit clericus et instruxit meus;
    factus est per clericum miles Cythereus;
    his est et huiusmodi tuus sermo reus."

42. Liquit Flora pariter vocem et certamen,
    et sibi Cupidinis exigit examen,
    Phyllis primum obstrepit, acquiescit tamen,
    et probato iudice redeunt per gramen.

43. Totum in Cupidine certamen est situm;
    suum dicunt iudicem verum et peritum,
    quia vite noverit utriusque ritum;
    et iam sese preparant ut eant auditum.

44. Pari forma virgines et pari pudore,
    pari voto militant et pari colore;
    Phyllis veste candida, Flora bicolore;
    mulus vector Phyllidis erat, equus Flore.

45. Mulus quidem Phyllidis mulus erat unus
    quem creavit, aluit, domuit Neptunus.
    hunc post apri rabiem, post Adonis funus
    misit pro solacio Cytheree munus.

46. Pulchre matri Phyllidis et probe regine
    illum tandem prebuit Venus Hiberine,
    eo quod indulserat opere divine;
    ecce, Phyllis possidet illum leto fine.

47. Faciebat nimium virginis persone;
    pulcher erat, habilis et stature bone,
    qualem esse decuit quem a regione
    tam longinqua miserat Nereus Dione.

48. Qui de superpositis et de freno querunt,
    quod totum argenteum dentes muli terunt,
    sciant quod hec omnia talia fuerunt
    qualia Neptunium munus decuerunt.

49. Non decore caruit illa Phyllis hora,
    sed multum apparuit dives et decora;
    et non minus habuit utriusque Flora;
    nam equi predivitis freno domat ora.

50. Equus ille, domitus   Pegaseis loris,
     multum pulchritudinis   habet et valoris,
     pictus artificio   varii coloris;
     nam mixtus nigredini   color est oloris.

51. Forme fuit habilis,   etatis primeve,
     et respexit paululum   tumide, non seve;
     cervix fuit ardua,   coma sparsa leve,
     auris parva, prominens   pectus, caput breve.

52. Dorso pando iacuit   virgini sessure
     spina, que non senserat   aliquid pressure;
     pede cavo, tibia   recta, largo crure.
     totum fuit sonipes   studium Nature.

53. Equo superposita   radiabat sella;
     ebur enim medium   clausit auri cella,
     et, cum essent quattuor   selle capitella,
     venustavit singulum   gemma quasi stella.

54. Multa de preteritis   rebus et ignotis
     erant mirabilibus   ibi sculpta notis;
     nuptie Mercurii   superis admotis,
     fedus, matrimonium,   plenitudo dotis.

55. Nullus ibi locus est   vacuus aut planus;
     habet plus quam capiat   animus humanus.
     solus illa sculpserat,   que spectans Vulcanus
     vix hoc suas credidit   potuisse manus.

56. Pretermisso clipeo   Mulciber Achillis
     laboravit phaleras   et indulsit illis;
     ferraturam pedibus   et frenum maxillis
     et habenas addidit   de sponse capillis.

57. Sellam texit purpura   subinsuta bysso,
     quam Minerva, reliquo   studio dimisso,
     acantho texuerat   et flore narcisso,
     et per tenas margine   fimbriavit scisso.

58. Volant equis pariter   due domicelle;
     vultus verecundi sunt   et gene tenelle.
     sic emergunt lilia,   sic rose novelle,
     sic decurrunt pariter   due celo stelle.

59. Ad Amoris destinant   ire paradisum.
     dulcis ira commovet   utriusque visum;
     Phyllis Flore, Phyllidi   Flora movet risum.
     fert Phyllis accipitrem   manu, Flora nisum.

60. Parvo tractu temporis   nemus est inventum.
     ad ingressum nemoris   murmurat fluentum;
     ventus inde redolet   myrrham et pigmentum;
     audiuntur tympana   citharaeque centum.

61. Quicquid potest hominum   comprehendi mente,
     totum ibi virgines   audiunt repente;
     vocum differentie   sunt illic invente,
     sonat diatessaron,   sonat diapente.

62. Sonant et mirabili   plaudunt harmonia
     tympanum, psalterium,   lyra, symphonia;
     sonant ibi phiale   voce valde pia,
     et buxus multiplici   cantum prodit via.

63. Sonant omnes avium   lingue voce plena;
     vox auditur merule   dulcis et amena,
     corydalus, graculus   atque philomena,
     que non cessat conqueri   de transacta pena.

64. Instrumento musico,   vocibus canoris,
     tunc diversi specie   contemplata floris,
     tunc odoris gratia   redundante foris
     coniectatur teneri   thalamus Amoris.

65. Virgines introeunt   modico timore,
     et eundo propius   crescunt in amore.
     sonat queque volucrum   proprio rumore;
     accenduntur animi   vario clamore.

66. Immortalis fieret   ibi manens homo.
     arbor ibi quelibet   suo gaudet pomo,
     vie myrrha, cinnamo   fraglant et amomo;
     coniectari poterat   dominus ex domo.

67. Vident choros iuvenum   et domicellarum,
     singulorum corpora   corpora stellarum.
     capiuntur subito   corda puellarum
     in tanto miraculo   rerum novellarum.

68. Sistunt equos pariter   et descendunt, pene
    oblite propositi   sono cantilene.
    sed auditur iterum   cantus philomene,
    et statim virginee   recalescunt vene.

69. Circa silve medium   locus est occultus,
    ubi viget maxime   suus deo cultus;
    Fauni, Nymphe, Satyri,   comitatus multus
    tympanizant, concinunt   ante dei vultus.

70. Portant vina manibus   et coronas florum;
    Bacchus Nymphas instruit   et choros Faunorum.
    servant pedum ordinem   et instrumentorum;
    sed Silenus titubat   nec psallit in chorum.

71. Somno vergit senior   asino prevectus
    et in risus copiam   solvit dei pectus.
    clamat "vina!"—remanet   clamor imperfectus;
    viam vocis impedit   vinum et senectus.

72. Inter hec aspicitur   Cytheree natus;
    vultus est sidereus,   vertex est pennatus,
    arcum leva possidet   et sagittas latus;
    satis potest conici   potens et elatus.

73. Sceptro puer nititur   floribus perplexo,
    stillat odor nectaris   de capillo nexo.
    tres assistunt Gratie   digito connexo
    et Amoris calicem   tenent genu flexo.

74. Approprinquant virgines   et adorant tute
    deum venerabili   cinctum iuventute;
    gloriantur numinis   in tanta virtute,
    quas deus considerans   prevenit salute.

75. Causam vie postulat;   aperitur causa,
    et laudatur utraque   tantum pondus ausa.
    ad utramque loquitur: "modo parum pausa,
    donec res iudicio   reseretur clausa!"

76. Deus erat; virgines   norunt deum esse;
    retractari singula   non fuit necesse.
    equos suos deserunt   et quiescunt fesse.
    Amor suis imperat   iudicent expresse.

77. Amor habet iudices,   Amor habet iura;
    sunt Amoris iudices   Vsus et Natura.
    istis tota data est   curie censura,
    quoniam preterita   sciunt et futura.

78. Eunt et iustitie   ventilant vigorem,
    ventilatum retrahunt   curie rigorem;
    secundum scientiam   et secundum morem
    ad amorem clericum   dicunt aptiorem.

79. Comprobavit curia   dictionem iuris,
    et teneri voluit   etiam futuris.
    parum ergo precavent   rebus nocituris,
    que sequuntur militem   et fatentur pluris.

1. In the blooming season of the year, as the sky grew clearer and the earth's bosom was dappled with a range of colors, when Dawn's messenger routed the stars, sleep quitted the eyes of Phyllis and Flora.

2. The maidens decided to take a stroll, for their wounded hearts rejected sleep. So step for step they passed into a meadow, so that the setting might lend additional charm to their disputation.

3. Both were maidens, and both high-born. Phyllis let her hair flow free, while Flora's locks were elegantly braided. Their beauty is not that of maidens but of goddesses, and their faces shine like the morning light.

4. They are vulgar neither in birth, nor appearance, nor adornment; they carry the years and spirit of youth. But they are a little at odds, and rather sharp with each other, for one is taken with a cleric, but the other with a knight.

5. There is no contrast between their figures or features; they are identical within and without. They have the same bearing and the same disposition; their only difference is the form of their loving.

6. A seasonal breeze whispered softly. The place was bright with green grass, and through the grass flowed a running stream, sportive with prattling murmur.

7. To increase the beauty of the spot and to moderate its heat, beside the rill was a spreading pine, its charm enhanced by its foliage and spreading wide its bosom, so that no foreign heat could penetrate it.

8. The maidens seated themselves; the grass afforded a couch. Phyllis sat by the stream, Flora further away. As both settled themselves and recovered their breath, love stabbed at their hearts and pierced one and the other.

9. Love lurks hidden within them and draws from their hearts sighs most pronounced. Wanness drains their cheeks, their faces change their color, but their fierce love is buried beneath their modesty.

10. Phyllis detects Flora sighing, but then Flora rebukes Phyllis on the same count. Thus each catches out the other, and at last both uncover their sickness and reveal their wounds.

11. Their conversation is punctuated with much hesitation; it forms a sequence wholly concerned with love. Love is in their hearts and on their lips. At length Phyllis begins, directing a smile at Flora.

12. Says she: "Illustrious knight, my heart-throb Paris, where are you now campaigning, and where are you lodged? The life of soldiering, that life unrivaled, is the only life that deserves the joy of Venus' household!"

13. As the girl calls to mind the knight her love companion, Flora smiles and flashes at her a sideways look; with a laugh she utters an unfriendly word: "You might say that your lover is a beggar.

14. But what is my heart-throb Alcibiades doing, a creation worthier than any creature, whom Nature has endowed with every grace? Sovereign rights of clerics, you alone are blessed."

15. Phyllis rebukes Flora for her harsh comment and speaks in words calculated to rouse her: "Just look at this dear, clean-hearted maid whose noble breast is enslaved to an Epicurus!

16. Rouse yourself, rouse yourself, poor girl, from this foul madness! I account a cleric as nothing but an Epicurus. I grant no elegance to the cleric, with his fat bulk bulging all around him!

17. He keeps his heart far removed from Cupid's camp; he feels the need for sleep and food and drink. My high-minded girl, we all know that the knight's aspiration is a far cry from this.

18. The knight is content with needs alone. He does not concentrate his life on sleep, food, and drink. Love prevents him from nodding off. A knight's love and exultant youth are his food and drink.

19. Who would harness our love partners together? Would law or nature allow them to be associated? My lover's knowledge lies in love-sport, yours in feasting; giving is mine's invariable mark, but receiving is that of yours."

20. Flora drains the blood from her modest face, and her second laugh makes her look more beautiful. At last with eloquent utterance she unbars the thought she had begotten in a heart fertile in rhetorical skills.

21. "You have spoken, Phyllis, quite without inhibition. You are swift and sharp enough in expression, but you have not effectively pursued the truth, so that through you the hemlock prevails over the lily.

22. You have said that the cleric is self-indulgent; you call him the slave of sleep, drink, and food. Such jibes are how true worth is usually described by a jealous person. But grant me a moment; I shall reply to you.

23. I claim that my friend's possessions are so numerous and great that he gives never a thought to other people's property. Store-cupboards full of honey, oil, corn, wine, gold, jewels, and goblets are at his call.

24. In this abundance of the cleric's life, so sweet that no words can depict its nature, Love circles round and beats applause with twofold wings—Love that is unfailing, Love that is immortal.

25. The cleric endures Venus' weapons and Cupid's wounds; but he is not skinny or downtrodden, for he is deprived of none of joy's blessings, and the unfeigned affection of his lady harmonizes with his.

26. But your chosen one is emaciated, pale, and poverty-stricken; he has barely a cloak and no fur to cover him. His limbs are frail, his chest unhealthy, for when the cause is lacking the effect too is wanting.

27. The poverty which looms over your lover is demeaning. What can a knight offer to one who solicits him? But the cleric bestows a great deal, and his store is copious, so great are his riches and his revenues."

28. Phyllis objects to Flora: "You have much experience of the pursuits and lives of both. Your lies have been quite persuasive and beguiling, but this dispute will not be settled on these terms.

29. When the hour of a feast day brings joy to the world, the cleric then makes his quite disreputable appearance. His hair is tonsured, and his clothes are black, and he bears the traces of his gloomy pleasure.

30. No one is so moronic or blind as not to witness the knight's glory. But your lover lives in idleness like a brute beast, whereas mine feels the rubbing of his helmet and sits astride a horse.

31. My lover scatters enemy positions by force of arms, and if he chances to enter battle alone on foot, while his Ganymede holds Bucephalas, he recounts my name in the midst of the slaughter.

32. When he has routed the enemy and ended the fighting, he returns, and pushing back his helmet often gazes on me. So by rightful reasoning based on these and other factors, I put the life of soldiering first."

33. Flora notes Phyllis' anger and panting breast and in return launches many barbs at her. "Your words are vain as you raise your praise to heaven," she said. "You are trying to thrust a camel through the eye of a needle.

34. You are forsaking honey for gall, and truth for falsehood, when you seek to approve soldiering by rebuke of the clergy. Is it love which makes the knight vigorous and spirited? No; it is poverty and lack of possessions which move him.

35. Lovely Phyllis, if only you would love wisely and not contest true opinions in this matter further. Both thirst and hunger bear heavily on your knight, and because of this he seeks the path to death and hell.

36. The knight's disastrous condition is most wearing; his lot is hard and constrained, for his life hangs in the balance, in uncertainty that he can obtain the necessities of life.

37. You would not label the black clothes and shorter hair of the cleric a reproach if you knew the convention. The cleric wears these to denote the greatest distinction, to show that he is greater than all others.

38. Clearly all things are subject to the cleric, and the mark of his authority he bears in his tonsure. He gives commands to knights and bestows gifts upon them. The personage who issues commands is greater than the servant.

39. You swear that the cleric is always idle. I grant that he scorns cheap and grinding occupations, but when his mind rises high to its concerns, he distinguishes the paths of heaven and the elements of the universe.

40. My lover is clad in purple, yours in a breastplate. While your lover joins in battle, mine is in his litter, where he reviews the ancient achievements of princes, and writes, investigates, ponders wholly on his mistress.

41. My cleric is preeminent in knowledge and instruction on the power of Venus and of the god of love. It is through the cleric that the knight has become a follower of Venus. Through these and similar facts your arguments are indictable."

42. Flora abandoned argument and the contest alike, and demanded for herself Cupid's adjudication. Phyllis initially objected but then agreed, and once they had approved the judge they made their way back over the grass.

43. The whole contest is left to the discretion of Cupid; people say that he is a true and experienced judge because he knows the manner of life of both suitors. They now prepare themselves to go to listen to him.

44. The maidens are matched in beauty and modesty. Their aspirations in their warring too are matched, and so is their complexion. Phyllis' robe is white, Flora's two-toned. A mule was Phyllis' steed, a horse was Flora's.

45. Phyllis' mule was the one which Neptune bred, nourished, and trained. After the fury of the boar and the death of Adonis, he sent it as a consoling gift to the Cytherean goddess.

46. Venus finally bestowed it on the beautiful mother of Phyllis, an honest Spanish noblewoman, because she had devoted herself to the work of the goddess. See, then, how by a happy outcome Phyllis came to possess it.

47. The mule did a lot for the maiden's bearing; it was handsome, presentable, and well built, as befitted one which the sea god had sent to Venus from so distant a region.

48. Those who inquire about trappings and bit—for the mule's teeth champed on nothing but silver—should know that all these things were such as befitted a gift of Neptune.

49. Phyllis at that moment was not lacking in beauty, but appeared most opulent and handsome. And Flora showed both qualities no less, for with her bridle she governed the mouth of a horse exceedingly rich.

50. That horse, subdued by the reins of Pegasus, had much beauty and strength and was dappled with a pattern of differing colors, for mingling with black was the color of the swan.

51. It was of presentable beauty and of youthful years; its gaze was somewhat lordly but not savage. Its neck was high, its mane spread smoothly out, its ears short, its chest pronounced, its head small.

52. Along its curved back the spine, without earlier experience of any sagging weight, extended for the maiden to sit upon. Its hooves were hollow; it was straight-shinned, big-shanked. The steed reflected the whole of Nature's skill.

53. The saddle placed upon the horse gleamed bright, for a gold frame enclosed ivory within. As the saddle had four raised corners, a starlike jewel enhanced each of them.

54. On it were many engravings with marvelous markings depicting unknown events of the past—the marriage of Mercury, with the gods introduced there, the compact, the wedding, the abundant dowry.

55. No part of the saddle is unadorned or without relief. It contains more than the human mind can take in. Vulcan alone had engraved these scenes, and when he eyed them he scarcely believed that his hands could have achieved them.

56. Vulcan had neglected the shield of Achilles and had toiled at the trappings and given free scope to them. He nailed shoes on the hooves, affixed a bridle on the jaws, and reins made from his bride's hair.

57. Cloth of purple sewn on with cotton covered the saddle. Minerva had abandoned her other pursuits and had interwoven it with acanthus and narcissus patterns. Along the edges she had worked a tasseled fringe.

58. The two damsels fly along side by side on their mounts, their faces modest and their cheeks glowing with youth. They are like blossoming lilies or new-sprung roses, or like twin stars speeding side by side down from the sky.

59. Their planned destination is the park of Love. Sweet anger lends life to the features of both. Phyllis rouses Flora's laughter, Flora that of Phyllis. Phyllis bears a falcon on her wrist, Flora a sparrow hawk.

60. After a short lapse of time they lighted on a glade. A stream whispers at the entrance to this glade, from which a breeze bears the scent of myrrh and spice. The sound of timbrels and a hundred harps is heard.

61. Of a sudden the maidens hear there all that can be taken in by the minds of men. In that place contrasting melodies are in evidence. Both diatessaron and diapente resound.

62. Timbrel, harp, lyre, and drum resound and beat in marvelous harmony. There viols play most sacred notes, and the boxwood pipe brings forth its tune from many apertures.

63. All the tongues of the birds sing out full-throatedly. The sweet and enchanting voice of the blackbird is heard. So too are the crested lark, the jackdaw, and the nightingale, which never stops lamenting the pains she has endured.

64. The musical instruments, the tuneful voices, then too the appearance of various flowers which they behold, as well as the charming scent wafted abroad, lead them to infer that this is the chamber of the young Cupid.

65. The maidens enter somewhat apprehensively, and as they draw nearer their feelings of love wax greater. Every bird sings out her own melody, and their spirits are fired by the diversity of the cries.

66. Any person remaining there would become immortal. Each and every tree rejoices in its particular fruit. The paths are fragrant with myrrh, cinnamon, and balsam. One could guess from the house who is its master.

67. They behold bands of young men and damsels. The persons of each and all are like so many stars. The hearts of the girls are suddenly entranced with the great wonder of these unprecedented sights.

68. Side by side they rein in their horses and dismount. The sound of harmonious music almost makes them forget their plan. But the song of the nightingale is heard again, and at once the maidens' hearts again wax hot.

69. At the center of the wood is a hidden spot where the god's worship throbs with most intense life. Fauns, nymphs, satyrs, a numerous band of escorts, beat their drums and sing in harmony before the god's presence.

70. In their hands they bear wine and garlands of flowers. Bacchus schools the nymphs and the bands of fauns; so they preserve the due arrangement of the dances and playing of the instruments, except that Silenus staggers and does not sing in harmony.

71. That elder, riding ahead on a donkey, nods off and diverges from his path, causing the god's heart to dissolve in floods of laughter. "Wine!" cries Silenus, but his shout remains slurred, for wine and old age block the progress of his voice.

72. In the midst of this the son of the Cytherean goddess is sighted, his face star-bright and his shoulders winged. His left hand wields his bow, and his arrows hang at his side. One can safely guess at his power and high status.

73. The boy leans on a scepter wreathed with flowers. Sweet-scented nectar drips from his combed locks. The three Graces with fingers interlocked attend him and with bent knee bear Love's cup before him.

74. The girls draw near and with self-assurance worship the god who is invested with revered youth. They delight in the mighty power of his divinity. The god gazes at them, and offers a greeting first.

75. He asks the reason for their journey; the reason is explained, and both are praised for daring to undertake so burdensome a task. He addresses each of them: "Now rest awhile till this unresolved case is clarified by the judgment."

76. He who spoke was divine. The maidens know that he is a god, and it was unnecessary to recount each detail. They leave their horses and wearily take their rest. Love commands his officers to deliver judgment unambiguously.

77. Love possesses judges and has laws. Love's judges are Experience and Nature. The entire judicial process of the court is entrusted to them, for they know both the past and the future.

78. They depart and give free rein to the power of justice, and bring its rigor duly aired back to the court. They pronounce the cleric more suited to love by virtue of his knowledge and by virtue of his way of life.

79. The court approved the pronouncement of the law and decreed that it be observed also for the future. So those who court the knight and claim that he is of greater worth are taking insufficient precautions against things which will do them harm.

THIS POEM, deservedly popular, exists in twelve extant versions in manuscripts or early editions. For details see Schumann ad loc., with Bischoff's addendum in *CB*, vol. 1.3.

The genre of the literary disputation, already exemplified in antiquity with the contest between Aeschylus and Euripides in Aristophanes' *Frogs* and in Ovid's *Amores* 3.1 (Elegy versus Tragedy) and, later, in the Carolingian age with Alcuin's *Conflictus Veris et Hiemis*, became extremely popular in the High Middle Ages with such compositions as *Dialogus inter Aquam et Vinum* and *Altercatio Ganymedis et Helenae* (see Manitius, 3:944ff. for further examples). The theme of cleric versus knight as love-suitors is handled in both Latin and vernacular poetry; as always, Ovid is never far away, though his treatment of *eques* versus *poeta* in *Amores* 3.8 laments the victory of the soldier, whereas in these twelfth-century poems, composed in the *respublica clericorum*, the cleric usually prevails. Of particular interest is the relationship between our poem and *The Love Council of Remiremont*; in 1151 Pope Eugenius III censured this convent community for its licentious ways, and the poem satirically describes how the nuns in council debate the respective merits of clerics and knights as suitors and finally proclaim excommunication for those who opt for the knight. (For older bibliography see Walther, *Das Streitgedicht*; Manitius, 3:565ff.; and

Haller, "The *Altercatio Phyllidis et Florae*.") A decision on which poem was composed first cannot be definitively reached, though Walther's view that the poem presented here, technically more accomplished, is an artistic development of *The Love Council* seems inherently more likely. Another document with transparently close connections with our poem is the *De Amore* of Andreas Capellanus, in which the cleric and the layman are contrasted as lovers (1.6H.487ff.). The *De Amore* was composed in the 1180s, a date not too distant from that at which our poem was composed, though again it is impossible to decide which appeared first.

The poem is clearly and wittily structured. Stanzas 1–11 depict the scene and the disputants; 12–41 the debate, with description of the characters and appearance of knight and cleric; and 42–79 the decision to seek adjudication, dominated by the account of the journey to Cupid's court (44–59) and by description of the court and its inhabitants (60–76).

1. **nuntius Aurore:** Appropriately Venus, the Morning Star.
   Phyllidis et Flore: For "Foliage" and "Flower Goddess" as contestants earlier, see comments at no. 4, where Phyllis is taken over from Virgil (*Ecl.* 3.78) and Horace (*Carm.* 4.11.3); Flora is called after the Roman goddess (Ovid *Fasti* 1.595ff., etc.)

3. **regine:** "Noblewomen," as at Martial 10.64.1, etc.

4. **iuveniles:** Perhaps containing the sense of the vernacular *jovens,* which implies generous courtesy (Lazar, *Amour courtois et fin'amors,* 42) as well as youth.
   parum: = *paulum,* as often in ML.

5. **intus et foris / habitus et moris:** Notice the witty chiasmus.

-7. The description of the *locus amoenus* is on conventional lines, with breeze, grass, stream, spreading pine tree. See comments at 19.2.

9. **furor:** Recalling the celebrated love-madness of Dido at Virgil *Aen.* 4.91, etc.

11. **amor est in animis . . . in ore:** In the *Munda cor meum,* the prayer preceding the Gospel in the *Ordo Missae,* the priest prays, *Dominus sit in corde meo, et in labiis meis.*

12. **Paris:** The Trojan warrior is often the apt exemplar of the lover-knight in these poems. See, e.g., *CB* 65.3b and *CB* 76.10 (= 16.10 above).
    Dionei: As often in CL (cf. Ovid *Am.* 1.14.33, etc.), Dione, mother of Venus, is conflated with her daughter.

13. **mendicum:** The image of the knight as beggar is prominent in Andreas Capellanus 1.6H.

14. **Alcibiades . . . quem beavit . . . natura:** Alcibiades as the sobriquet of the scholar-cleric owes its origin to his presence in Plato's *Symposium*; he is celebrated in antiquity as the epitome of beauty, wealth, and all natural endowments. Cf. Nepos *Alc.* 1, *omnium aetatis suae formosissimus; ad omnes res aptus consiliisque plenus . . . disertus . . . dives.* This tradition is mediated through authors familiar to twelfth-century clerics, such as Augustine (*Civ. Dei* 14.8, *beatus*) and Boethius (*Cons.* 3.8.6, *pulcherrimum corpus*).

15. **Epicuro:** The Epicurus of medieval literature is not the noble philosopher in Lucretius but the caricature in Cicero (e.g., *Tusc.* 5.87, *quem mollem, quem voluptarium dicimus*), who was vehemently critical of the thesis of pleasure as the *summum bonum*. The crude evaluation is reflected in *CB* 211: *alte clamat Epicurus: / "venter satur est securus, / venter deus meus eris."*

16. **fedo:** = CL *foedo*.

17. **a castris Cupidinis:** The image of the pursuit of love as army service goes back to Augustan elegy, notably to Ovid *Am.* 1.9.
    somnum . . . et cibum et potum: Cf. Andreas 1.6H.490, *[clericus] continuo reperitur otio deditus et ventris solummodo mancipatus obsequiis,* and 1.7.4, *otia multa continua et ciborum abundantiam copiosam.*

18. **somno, cibo, potui . . . ne sit somnolentus, cibus, potus, etc.:** Effectively contrasting the knight with the cleric in stanza 17.

19. **meo . . . dare . . . tuo dari:** Cf. Andreas 1.6H.429–30 for the layman's generosity as a facet of his courtly worth, whereas the cleric (1.6H.490) *neminem potest largitatis praemiis adiuvare.* But see stanza 27 below.

20. **in risu secundo:** She was *ridens* earlier, in stanza 13.
    conceperat . . . fecundo: The Classical doctrine of the formulation of eloquence (*inventio, dispositio, elocutio*) is here expressed by the image of conception and fertility.

21. **lilio cicuta:** This does not seem to be a proverbial phrase; as the lily in Christian art is the symbol of innocence and purity, Flora is perhaps indicating that her relationship is one of *amor purus*, with the hemlock denoting the death-dealing nature of *amor mixtus.*

22. **probitas**: This is the courtly quality (Andreas 1.6.1, 1.6.13–14, etc.) which embraces generosity and courage. Cf. Andreas 2.1.8, *omnis namque probitas ex avaritiae admixtione supprimitur . . . plurimum cuiusque probitati detrahitur, si timidus proeliator exsistat.*
    parum: See comments at stanza 4.

23. **quod . . . incogitat**: = CL *ut incogitet*.
    Cereris, Lyei: Similarly combined in metonymy at Terence *Eun.* 732 and Virgil *G.* 2.229.

24. **quod non potest**: See just above, stanza 23.
    plaudit alis: Cf. Ovid *Met.* 8.239, *plausit pennis*.

26. **macer . . . sine pelle**: For the shabby clothing cf. Andreas 1.6H.427.
    causa . . . effectus: For the scholastic tag cf. Andreas 1.6A.50, *cessante . . . causa, eius de necessitate cessat effectus.*

27. **turpis est pauperies**: For the disastrous effects of poverty on a love affair see Ovid *Rem. Am.* 749, *non habet unde suum paupertas pascat amorem*; and Andreas 2.3, *Amator inopia multa detentus, tanta . . . cogitatione quassatur ut amoris non possit actibus servire nec debita sibi incrementa praestare.*
    sed dat multa: Challenging the charge laid in stanza 19.

29. **in tonsura capitis**: As Isidore (*De eccl. offic.* 4) and others explain, the practice of tonsuring clerics to designate their special status originated with the Nazarites of the Old Testament; clerics bore the alternative title of *tonsurari*.
    in atra veste: Cf. Andreas 1.6H.490, *clericus quidem muliebri apparet ornatu vestitus, et capite deformiter incedit abraso.*
    testimonium voluptatis meste: The phrase contains a hint of the condemnation of clerics in illicit unions who perform the liturgy after rising from their shared beds. Cf. *Goliae versus de sacerdotibus* (Wright, *Anglo-Latin Satirical Poets*, 48), *O sacerdos, haec responde, / qui frequenter et iocunde / cum uxore dormis, unde / mane surgens, missam dicis, / corpus Christi benedicis.*

31. **Bucephalam . . . Ganymedes**: Bucephalas was the horse of Alexander the Great, whose career (versified by Walter of Châtillon ca. 1180 in his *Alexandreis*) achieved great popularity at a time when speculation about the perfect man was a favorite topic (cf. Alan of Lille's *Anticlaudianus*). Ganymede, cupbearer of Jupiter, is an apt sobriquet for a squire; the boy-favorite is celebrated in the *Altercatio Ganymedis et Helenae* (see introductory comments above).

33. **per acum . . . camelum:** Matt. 19:24, Mark 10:25.

34. **mel pro felle:** Plautus *Cist.* 69 has *amor et melle et felle est iucundissimus.*
    Subsequently the verbal jingle had a long history in Latin literature; cf.
    Fechter, "Galle und Honig."
    strenuum et ferum: These adjectives proclaim the necessary quality for a
    knight of *animositas.* Cf. Andreas 2.1, *studere debet ut eius cunctis appareat animositas manifesta.*

35. **quibus:** I.e., it is thirst and hunger, not love, which goad him to undertake
    deeds of hazard.

36. **valet:** *Valere* is increasingly found for *posse* in postclassical Latin.

37. **ad summum honorem . . . omnibus maiorem:** In Andreas 1.6.20 and 1.7.1
    the cleric is awarded the status of *nobilissimus*; at 1.6H.493 it is stated that
    the cleric wears his special dress to distinguish him from other men.

38. **in corona:** See comments at stanza 29.

39. **celi vias dividit et rerum naturas:** "At no point is the intellectual revival of
    the twelfth century more marked than in the domain of science. . . . The
    century from ca. 1125 on made available Euclid and Ptolemy, and the
    mathematics and astronomy of the Arabs, the medicine of Galen and Hippocrates and Avicenna" (Haskins, *The Renaissance of the Twelfth Century,*
    303, the exordium of a useful discussion on this subject). It was of course
    the clerics who pursued such research.

40. **in purpura:** The cleric has changed his outfit since stanza 37; doubtless his
    purpura, the dress of princes, refers to his liturgical persona, the black to
    his walking dress.
    gesta principum . . . antiqua: Doubtless a reference to Suetonius' *Lives,*
    much read in the twelfth century (imitated, for example, in William of
    Malmesbury's *Gesta Regum*; see Schütt, "The Literary Form"). See in general the index in Manitius, vol. 3.

41. **Dione:** See comments at stanza 12.
    primus novit clericus: The cleric's superior knowledge in science (stanza
    39) and history (stanza 40) extends particularly to love theory. In Andreas
    1.6H.533ff. the cleric's advice is sought on a problem of love, and repeatedly in these lyrics this superior knowledge is emphasized: see, e.g., the refrain to no. 22, *clerus scit diligere / virginem plus milite.*
    Cythereus: = CL *Cythereius.* The island of Cythera, off Cape Malea in the
    Peloponnese, was a famous shrine of Venus.

42. It is notable that Flora, the *amica* of the cleric, demands the judgment of Cupid.

43. **noverit . . . ut eant auditum**: Correctness of syntax and Classical idiom denote the poet's ready familiarity with Classical usage.

45. **quem . . . Neptunus**: Neptune was said to have created the first horse by a stroke of his trident (Virgil *G*. 1.12ff, Lucan 6.393); in his Greek dress as Poseidon Hippios he was "lord of horses." The suggestion that he bestowed a horse on Venus as consolation for the death of Adonis seems to be the happy invention of our poet.
post Adonis funus: The story of the death of Adonis, favorite of Venus, after being gashed by a boar, is told by Ovid at *Met*. 10.529ff.
Cytheree: See comments at stanza 41.

46. **regine . . . Hiberine**: On *regine* see comments at stanza 3; for *Hiberine* cf. Juvenal 6.53.

47. **Nereus Dione**: Nereus, the old sea god and father of the nereids, is here used as sea god personified and equated with Neptune/Poseidon. Dione (see stanza 12) is dative; Cicero *Nat. D*. 3.59 uses the form *Diona-ae*, as here.

49. **utriusque**: That is, *divitiarum et decoris*.

50. **Pegaseis loris**: Our poet seeks to invest Flora's mount with some equivalent or even superior status in mythology to that of Phyllis (stanzas 45–48); by endowing it with Pegasus' reins he aptly reminds us that the winged horse Pegasus was sired by Neptune (on Medusa, Ovid *Met*. 6.115ff., 4.785–86). For the phrase cf. Claudian *In Ruf*. 1.263, *non Pegaseis adiutus habenis*.

-52. The characteristics of the ideal horse as listed here appear in Xenophon's *Art of Horsemanship* 1.3.12; in CL there are descriptions in Varro *De Agr*. 2.7.5, Columella 6.29.2, Virgil *G*. 3.72ff.; see Vigneron, *Le cheval dans l'antiquité*, 4ff. Our poet has exploited Isidore *Etym*. 12.1.45 for his description.

53. **sella**: Saddles were not unknown in antiquity (see Vigneron, *Le cheval*, 82ff.), but this is a medieval model; see Gay, *Glossaire archéologique*, s.v. selle, for illustrations from contemporary vernacular literature.

54. **multa . . . sculpta**: The poet indulges in description of art motifs, a tradition as old as Homer's shield of Achilles (*Il*. 18.478ff., imitated by Virgil's account of that of Aeneas, *Aen*. 8.626ff.). A contemporary parallel is Alan of Lille's depiction of the motifs on Prudentia's chariot (*Anticlaudianus* 2.486ff.).

nuptie Mercurii: Martianus Capella's *Nuptiae Philologiae et Mercurii* enjoyed a great vogue at this period. Cf. no. 2.

superis admotis . . . plenitudo dotis: The gods attended the marriage, and Philologia's mother Sophia presented the dowry (Martianus Capella 1.97ff., 9.892ff.).

55. **Vulcanus**: Hephaestus/Vulcan crafted the artifacts in Homer and Virgil (see comments at stanza 54).

56. **praetermisso clipeo Mulciber Achillis**: Mulciber ("The Softener"), a frequent epithet for Vulcan in CL, gives the horse's trappings a higher priority than the shield of Achilles (stanza 54).

57. **Minerva . . . acantho texuerat et . . . narcisso**: For Athene/Minerva's fame with the needle see Ovid *Met.* 6.1ff. Acanthus and narcissus are combined at Virgil *G.* 4.123. Such floral decoration on saddles was worked also in metal; cf. Theophilus *De Diversis Artibus* 3.78 (probably twelfth century, ed. Dodwell, Edinburgh, 1961): *potes in auro et argento facere bestias atque aviculas ac flores super sellas equestres matronarum exterius.*
tenas: "Edges," a neologism in ML by extension from the preposition *tenus.*

58. **lilia . . . rose**: Often combined in descriptions of beautiful complexions; see 7.5a, and Alan of Lille *Anticlaudianus* 1.281–82, *sidereum vultus castigavere ruborem / lilia nupta rosis.*

59. **ad Amoris . . . paradisum**: For this visit to Cupid's estate, compare a similar account in Andreas Capellanus 1.6E.229ff., where the spokesman obtains the twelve *Amoris Praecepta.* On *paradisum* see comments at 19.3.
accipitrem . . . nisum: Hawking was one of the requirements of a lady's courtly education. Power (*Medieval Women,* 77–78) quotes the thirteenth-century poet Robert de Blois: "She could carry and fly falcon, tercel and hawk." In Andreas Capellanus 2.8.3ff. the knight who goes to Arthur's court presents the hawk he obtained there to the lady who had dispatched him there. (One is irresistibly reminded of American ladies who jog with their dogs on leads.)

60. **pigmentum**: The sense of "cosmetic" in CL is extended to "spice" in ML.
tympana, etc.: So in Andreas 1.6E.260: *omnia instrumentorum ibi musicae genera resonabant.*

61. **diatesseron . . . diapente:** These Greek technical terms were familiar to twelfth-century writers through Macrobius, Martianus Capella, and Boethius. For *diatesseron* ("using four strings") cf. Macrobius *Comm. in Somn. Scip.* 2.1.25, *constat de duobus tonis et hemitonio . . . et fit ex epitrito* [hence 4:3]; Boethius *De mus.* 1.8. On the *diapente* ("using five strings") Macrobius says, *constat ex tribus tonis et hemitonio, et fit de hemiolo* [hence 3:2]. Alan of Lille *Anticlaudianus* 3.436–47 includes these terms in his discussion of *musica* and its part in the creation of the chariot of Prudentia.

62. **symphonia:** Isidore *Orig.* 3.22 defines this as a species of drum.
    buxus: Cf. Virgil *Aen.* 9.619, Ovid *Met.* 4.30.

63. **graculus:** The jackdaw is not renowned as a great singer, as the old proverb *nihil cum fidibus graculo* (Gellius *Praef.* 19) notes.
    que non cessat conqueri: See comments at 3.1.

64. **contemplata:** The deponent *contemplor* is commoner in CL, but the collateral active form is found in early and late authors.

65. **crescunt in amore:** I.e., under the influence of Cupid's ambience.

66. **fraglant:** I print this alternative form of *fragrant,* frequent in LL and subsequently, for the less apt *flagrant* ("are ablaze"), as it is the aroma rather than the color for which these plants are renowned.

68. **iterum cantus philomene:** Heard earlier (stanza 63), the plaint of the nightingale is of course a traditional call to love.
    vene: Strictly of the veins, or of the blood coursing through them.

69. **Fauni, Nymphe, Satyri:** For nymphs and satyrs see comments at 14.3. For the fauns as sylvan deities accompanying the satyrs see below at stanza 71; also Ovid *Met.* 6.392, etc.

70. **portant vina . . . et coronas:** Cf. Ovid *Fasti* 1.405, *vina dabat Liber; tulerat sibi quisque coronam.*
    Silenus titubat: Cf. Ovid *Met.* 11.89ff., *hunc [Bacchum] assueta cohors Satyri Bacchaeque frequentant; / at Silenus abest. titubantem annisque meroque / ruricolae cepere Phryges.*

71. **vergit . . . asino prevectus:** Our poet effortlessly switches to Ovid's *Ars Am.* 1.543–44: *Ebrius ecce senex pando Silenus asello / vix sedet.* Cf. Ovid *Fasti* 1.399, *Venerat et senior pando Silenus asello,* again in company with pans/fauns, satyrs, and nymphs (397–98).

dei: This must refer to Bacchus, not to Cupid (*pace* Vollmann), for Bacchus is organizing the parade, and Cupid makes his appearance first in stanza 72.

vinum et senectus: See the citation from Ovid *Met.* above at stanza 70.

72. **Cytheree:** See comments at stanza 41.

   sidereus: Used of Bacchus by Seneca (*Oed.* 409).

73. **digito connexo:** The Graces are regularly represented in CL with hands joined; cf. Horace *Carm.* 3.19.16–17, 3.21.22.

74. **venerabili . . . iuventute:** Though Cupid is depicted as a boy, he represents the love that is as old as the world. So in Longus' *Daphnis and Chloe* 2.3ff., "he is older than Saturn, and all that is."

75. **parum pausa:** For *parum* see comments at stanza 4; *pausa* passes into ML through Biblical and Late Latin.

76. **imperat . . . iudicent:** The paratactic construction is frequent in CL as a survival from early Latin, when the two words were both main verbs ("he orders . . . let them judge").

77. **Amor habet iudices . . . iura:** This suggestion that courts of love existed at this period is literary fantasy; see Benton, "Clio and Venus."

   Usus et Natura: The symbolism suggests that love develops through habit as well as natural attraction. For *usus/consuetudo* cf. Lucretius 4.1283, *consuetudo concinnat amorem*; and Ovid *Ars Am.* 2.345, *nil adsuetudine maius.* For *natura* see Cicero *Fin.* 3.62 and Andreas Capellanus 1.1.1, *amor est passio quaedam innata.* . . .

78. **secundum scientiam:** Cf. stanzas 39–41 (esp. comments at 41).

79. As regularly with these jocular compositions in "goliardic" meter, the poem ends with a moral to the story. Cf. the final stanzas of nos. 16 and 17.

30 (93)

1. Hortum habet insula   virgo virginalem;
   hunc ingressus, virginem   unam in sodalem
   spe robustus Veneris   elegi principalem.

2. Letus ergo socia   elegantis forme
   (nil huic laudis defuit,   nil affuit enorme)
   cum hac feci geminum   cor meum uniforme.

3. Est amore dulcius   rerum in natura
   nichil, et amarius   conditione dura;
   dolus et invidia   amoris sunt scissura.

(93a)

1. Cum Fortuna voluit   me vivere beatum,
   forma, bonis moribus   fecit bene gratum
   et in altis sedibus   sedere laureatum.

2. Modo flos preteriit   mee iuventutis,
   in se trahit omnia   tempus senectutis;
   inde sum in gratia   novissime salutis.

3. Rhinoceros virginibus   se solet exhibere;
   sed cuius est virginitas intemerata vere,
   suo potest gremio   hunc sola retinere.

4. Igitur que iuveni   virgo sociatur
   et me senem spreverit, iure defraudatur,
   ut ab hac rhinoceros   se capi patiatur.

5. In tritura virginum   debetur seniori
   pro mercede palea,   frumentum iuniori;
   inde senex aream   relinquo successori.

1. My maiden is an island, her garden untrodden. I have entered this garden, and emboldened with the hope of love I have chosen this maiden alone as my chief companion.

2. Thus overjoyed by an ally with beauty so refined (for she lacks nothing which merits praise, and has nothing unshapely), I have in her company made my solitary heart a twin.

3. Nothing in the created world is sweeter than love, nothing more bitter than a bleak existence; guile and envy cleave love apart.

(93a)

1. When Fortune wished me to live in blessedness, she made me popular, with good looks and worthy manners, and she set me on a lofty seat, crowned with the victor's laurel.

2. But now my youth's bloom is past, and the period of old age arrogates to itself all things. Thus I gain the grace of salvation at the very last.

3. The rhinoceros usually reveals himself to maidens, but only one whose virtue is truly inviolate can keep him in her bosom.

4. So the maiden who associates with a young man and who scorns my advanced years is rightly robbed of the right by which the rhinoceros allows himself to be captured by her.

5. At the threshing season for maidens, the older man is owed the chaff as his reward, but the wheat goes to the younger man. So now in my old age I leave the threshing floor to another to succeed me.

THESE TWO PIECES appear as one in the sole manuscript, but Schumann was certainly right to separate them, for the themes are clearly different. The first is a brief but self-contained celebration of a new love liaison; the second and longer poem introduces a topic incidentally present in many lyrics (e.g., 15.2) but nowhere else forming the main theme of a poem: namely, the lament for the arrival of old age, which forecloses the pursuit of love. Once again, therefore, one notes how the frontiers of the love lyric are further extended to embrace this motif.

93. *Hortum habet insula*

1. **hortum . . . virginalem**: The inspiration is clearly Song of Sol. 4:12, *hortus conclusus soror mea,* a biblical passage regularly interpreted in the Fathers as symbolizing sacred virginity; hence *virginalem.*
   Veneris: This is Herkenrath's emendation of *virginis* in B.

3. **rerum in natura**: The parallel with Lucretius' exordium (esp. 1.21ff., *quae quoniam rerum naturam sola gubernas / .. . neque fit laetum neque amabile quicquam*) is probably coincidental; but for a possible indication of knowledge of Lucretius at this time see comments at 5.1.

93a. *Cum Fortuna voluit*

It is a useful exercise to contrast the imagery of this poem with that of Horace *Carm.* 3.26, *Vixi puellis nuper idoneus.* In the Horatian ode the retiring lover depicts himself in the conventional garb of the lover of Augustan elegy, a *miles* now aging who dedicates his love weapons in the shrine of Venus. By contrast, in this poem the rhinoceros and the separation of wheat and chaff offer distinctively different images (see below on stanzas 3–5) more appropriate to the Christian era. Characteristically Horace's spokesman begs Venus for one last fling (*tange Chloen semel arrogantem*), whereas the *senex* here faces the reality of an old age without love but with the prospect of salvation.

Vollmann usefully draws attention to Maximian's earlier treatment (*Elegies* 1.9ff.) of the lament for past glories.

1. **Fortuna**: The goddess of pagan antiquity (mediated through Boethius *Cons.* 2) frequently appears in twelfth-century literature as the arbitrary controller of wealth, beauty, health, and nobility. She is prominent in the first section of the *Carmina Burana*, where a group of Fortune poems (*CB* 14, 16, 18) is followed by the famous miniature of the Wheel of Fortune. See, in general, Patch, *The Goddess Fortuna*.

   in altis sedibus . . . laureatum: The general message echoes *CB* 16.2, *In Fortunae solio sederam elatus, / prosperitatis vario flore coronatus.* One wonders if the spokesman here alludes to his academic distinction; Maximian writes (*Elegies* 1.9–10): *dum iuvenile decus, dum mens sensusque maneret, / orator toto clarus in orbe fui.*

2. **trahit omnia tempus senectutis**: Cf. 15.2.

   in gratia novissime salutis: The implication is that the spokesman will now be able to gain the grace of final salvation, having renounced the illicit preoccupations of love.

3. **rhinoceros, etc.**: For the tradition, dating back to the *Physiologus*, that the unicorn (identified with the rhinoceros) would lay its head on a virgin's breast, and thus submit to capture, see comments at 26.2. White (*The Book of Beasts*, 20–21) quotes Harl. 4751, in which Christ is identified with the unicorn spiritually on the basis of Ps. 28:6, "He was beloved like the son of unicorns"; this allegorical interpretation, which goes back to Cassiodorus' *Expositio Psalmorum*, allows us to speculate that the rhinoceros symbolizes the cleric as *alter Christus*. The unicorn is in other contexts associated with chastity (e.g., *Analecta Hymnica* 20.276, 20.188), and accordingly the association of rhinoceros with virgin may point to the espousal of *amor purus* (see Introduction, sections 3, 5). It is of some interest that the author of the *Vita Gosvini* (ed. Bouquet) calls Abelard a *rhinoceros indomitus*, and one wonders if the rhinoceros motif in these poems originates from his exploits with Heloïse.

4. **ut rhinoceros**: The self-identification of the spokesman with the animal encourages the speculation at the end of the preceding note.

5. **in tritura virginum, etc.**: The image of separation of wheat and chaff (cf. Matt. 3:12) is curiously and strikingly applied to the harvest of available maidens, from which the young men get the preferential choice.

31 (95)

1. Cur suspectum   me tenet domina?
   cur tam torva   sunt in me lumina?
   testor celum   celique numina:
   que veretur   non novi crimina!

   Refl. Tort a vers mei ma dama!

2. Celum prius   candebit messibus,
   feret aër   ulmos cum vitibus,
   dabit mare   feras venantibus,
   quam Sodome   me iungam civibus!

   Refl.

3. Licet multa   tyrannus spondeat
   et me gravis   paupertas urgeat,
   non sum tamen,   cui plus placeat
   id quod prosit   quam quod conveniat.

   Refl.

4. Naturali   contentus Venere
   non didici   pati, sed agere.
   malo mundus   et pauper vivere
   quam pollutus   dives existere.

   Refl.

5. Pura semper   ab hac infamia
   nostra fuit   ⟨terra⟩ Britannia;
   ha, peream   quam per me patria
   sordis huius   sumat initia!

1. Why does my mistress hold me in suspicion? Why do her eyes frown so upon me? I call heaven and the deities of heaven to witness: I have no knowledge of the sins which she fears!

   Refrain. My lady does me wrong!

2. The sky will whiten with harvests, the lower air will bring forth elms and attendant vines, the sea will provide huntsmen with wild beasts, before I associate with the citizens of Sodom!

Refrain.

3. Even if a king made me lavish promises and grinding poverty oppressed me, I am not the kind of man to let utility influence me more than propriety.

Refrain.

4. I am content with natural love and have learned to take the active, not the passive role. I prefer to live pure and poor rather than be unchaste and wealthy.

Refrain.

5. Britain, our native land, was always unblemished by this notoriety. I pray that I may die before my native land should through me embark on such foulness!

Refrain.

ON THIS POEM see the Introduction, section 7. It seems surprising that the theme of homosexual love appears so infrequently in the Codex Buranus; *CB* 127 is the only clear example other than this poem. The subject was widely aired in the twelfth century. Ovid's influence, as in all aspects of courtly loving, was conspicuous through such stories as that of Narcissus (*Met.* 3.353, *multi illum iuvenes, multae cupiere puellae*) and through the permissive doctrine of the *Amores*, where he claims that Cupid has imposed on him as a love theme *aut puer, aut longas compta puella comas* (1.1.20). In the creative writing of the twelfth century Alan of Lille's *De Planctu Naturae* (ed. Häring, trans. Sheridan) above all lends prominence to the prevalence of the vice. After the spokesman there in Meter 1 laments that "No longer does the Phrygian adulterer pursue Tyndareus' daughter, but Paris performs with Paris unmentionable and monstrous deeds," Nature herself appears in Prose 4 to bewail such sexual disorders in the world. John of Salisbury in the *Policraticus* is another leading figure who draws attention to the prevalence of sodomy. At the more jocular level there is the celebrated *altercatio* between Ganymede and Helen (text in Walther, *Das Streitgedicht*, 141ff.), in which stanzas 30 and 40 brazenly suggest that the love of boys is more apt for clerics. The attraction of boys is also celebrated in the poems of Hilarius (ed. Fuller). For a general review of the treatment of the topic in the Middle Ages see Curtius, 113ff., and the Introduction here, section 7.

The present poem is inspired by an earlier composition on the same theme by Hilarius (*Lingua servi, lingua perfidie*, no. 6 in Fuller; conveniently in *OBMLV*, no. 168), which is addressed to his master Abelard and which likewise has a refrain in Old French, "Tort a vers nos li mestre." Homosexuality was of course condemned by the Church as a serious sin because it entailed the misdirection of the means of propagation. When considered against the code of courtly love, it is still more heinous, as it is claimed to pervert the nature of love: "Love can exist only between persons of different sex. Between two males or females it can claim no place, for two persons of the same sex are in no sense fitted to reciprocate each other's love, or to practise its natural acts. Love blushes to embrace what nature denies" (Andreas Capellanus 1.2.1).

1. **torva . . . lumina:** Evoking Dido in the underworld; Virgil *Aen.* 6.467–68, *talibus Aeneas ardentem et torva tuentem / lenibat dictis animum.*
testor . . . numina: The treatment is reminiscent of *Lingua mendax* (see 38.3): *sciat deus, sciant dei / non sum reus huius rei!*

Ref. The vernacular intrusion ("My lady does me wrong!") sets the poem firmly in the French context.

2. **celum prius:** Again the similarity to *Lingua mendax* (see 38.10–11, *ergo dum nox erit dies, / et dum labor erit quies,* etc.) is notable.
Sodome: For its wickedness and destruction see Gen. 18:16ff.

4. **pati sed agere:** In CL *patior* is the regular term for passive intercourse, but *facio* seems to be more frequent than *ago* for the active role (Adams, *The Latin Sexual Vocabulary,* 189, 204–5). In ML *agere* is more frequent; cf. 26.8, *quintum, quod est agere, / noli suspicari.*

5. This stanza is notoriously corrupt in the one manuscript.
⟨terra⟩ **Britannia:** This is Raby's hesitant because radical solution (see *SLP,* 2: Appendix 2) for *Briciauvia* in B. Less violent emendations have been proposed: *Brisacagawia* = Breisgau (J. Grimm); *Bressa avia* = La Bresse, near Lyon (Du Méril); *Brescia avia* (Giesebrecht); and P. A. Becker, following Raby's lead, suggests ⟨minor⟩ *Britannia* = Brittany. (For these references see Raby's Appendix, and Bischoff's further annotations on the poem in *CB* vol. 1.3.) As Raby diffidently mentions, Hilarius, whose poem was the model for this piece, was an Englishman, so perhaps his imitator was also.
per me: Peiper's emendation of *perimit* in B.
sumat initia: So Grimm for *sumant initia* in B (*sumat indicia* Schmeller).

32 (105)

1. Dum curata vegetarem
   soporique membra darem,
   et langueret animalis
   prevaleret naturalis
      virtutis dominium,

2. En, Cupido pharetratus
   crinali, torque spoliatus,
   manu multa tactis alis,
   mesto vultu, numquam talis,
      visus est per somnium.

3. Quem ut vidi perturbatum
   habituque disturbatum,
   membra stupor ingens pressit.
   qui paulatim ut recessit
      a membris organicis,

4. Causam quero mesti vultus
   et sic deformati cultus,
   cur sint ale contrectate,
   nec ut decet ordinate,
      causam et itineris.

5. Amor, quondam vultu suavis,
   nunc merore gravi gravis,
   ut me vidit percunctari
   responsumque prestolari
      reddit causam singulis:

6.   'Vertitur in luctum organum Amoris,
   canticum subductum absinthio doloris,
   vigor priscus abiit, evanuit iam virtus.
   me vis deseruit, periere Cupidinis arcus!

7.   Artes amatorie iam non instruuntur
   a Nasone tradite passim pervertuntur;
   nam si quis istis utitur, more modernorum
   turpiter †abutitur† hac assuetudine morum.

8. Naso, meis artibus et regulis instructus,
    mundique voluptatibus feliciter subductus,
    ab errore studuit mundum revocare;
    qui sibi notus erat, docuit sapienter amare.

9. Veneris mysteria iam non occultantur
    cistis, sed exposita coram presentantur
    proh dolor! non dedecet palam commisceri?
    precipue Cytherea iubet sua sacra taceri.

10. Amoris ob infamiam moderni gloriantur,
    sine re iactantiam anxii venantur,
    iactantes sacra Veneris corporibus non tactis.
    eheu, nocturnis titulos imponimus actis!

11. Res arcana Veneris virtutibus habenda
    optimisque meritis et moribus emenda,
    prostat in prostibulo, redigitur in pactum;
    tanta meum populo ius est ad damna redactum.'

1. After tending and refreshing my limbs, entrusting them to sleep, when the dominance of my conscious powers was waning, and nature's hold waxed stronger,

2. Behold, Cupid with his quiver, but despoiled of diadem and necklace, his wings crushed with brute force and his features sadder than ever before, appeared to me in a dream.

3. When I saw him in his troubled state, with his appearance in disarray, a monstrous paralysis seized my limbs. When this slowly quitted my faculty of speech,

4. I asked the reason for his sad countenance and his adornment thus befouled—why his wings had been roughly handled and were not suitably ordered, and what was the reason for his journey.

5. When Love (his face, once sweet, oppressed by grim sorrow) saw that I was questioning him and was awaiting his reply, he explained the reason for each circumstance:

6. "The voice of Love is translated into grief. My song has been silenced by the wormwood of sorrow. My former strength has left me, my power is now drained away. Vigor has forsaken me, and Cupid's bow has lost its force!

7. Instruction is not now given in the arts of love handed down by Ovid; those arts are widely debased. For if anyone employs them as present-day men commonly do, he basely misuses them because of this trend in behavior.

8. Naso, schooled by my skills and rules and blessedly withdrawn from the world's base pleasures, was eager to recall the world from the error of its ways. He taught the person acquainted with him to love wisely.

9. Venus' mysteries are not now hidden in boxes, but laid out and made available in public. Good grief, it is surely inappropriate for them to mingle openly with the mob? Venus commands us particularly to be silent about her rites.

10. Men today boast of their notoriety in love. They eagerly pursue the boasting without the actuality, vaunting the rites of Venus when their bodies are virgin. Alas, we advertise our activities of the night!

11. The secret transaction of love, to be performed through virtues and purchased through the most deserving merits and manners, is laid out for sale in the brothel, or reduced to a contract. To such injuries is my law subjected before the people."

THIS LAMENT for the decline of courtly love is described within the framework of a dream, a favorite twelfth-century device for recounting amusing fantasy (compare the *Dialogue between Water and Wine*, cited in the introductory remarks to no. 29). A woebegone Cupid makes his disheveled appearance to lament the decline in suitors' behavior which has caused his influence to wane. In her perceptive article "The Bedraggled Cupid" Elliott rightly regards this as a satirical and humorous treatment in the manner of Ovid himself. Cupid wears the mask or mantle of a suffering Job (see comments at stanza 6); his distinctive dress and instruments are symbolically ruffled. Appreciation of the direction of the satire demands a knowledge of courtly love theory as summarized in the twelve *Praecepta Amoris* and the thirty-one *Regulae Amoris* listed in Andreas Capellanus 1.6E.268–69, 2.8.44ff.; particularly relevant are the injunctions against publication of love affairs (stanza 9 below), lying and dishonesty (stanza 10), and association with women of ill repute or with matrons (stanza 11).

It will be noted that Cupid's reply is couched metrically in the combination of three "goliardic" lines followed by the "authoritative" hexameter which contains a citation or a reminiscence of a Classical author. This idiosyncratic medium was popularized by Walter of Châtillon (see Strecker,

"Walter von Châtillon und seine Schule," 166). Because Walter may be evoked in stanza 6, and because his satirical poetry laments the disappearance of probity in other spheres, it is possible that our poet is parodying him here in this sententious *cri de coeur* for the decline of courtly love. As Elliott observes, the quotations in stanzas 8–10 are all taken from the same section of Ovid's *Ars Amatoria* (2.493–640).

1. **dum curata . . . darem:** The exordium is a learned evocation of Horace *Sat.* 2.2.80–81: *alter, ubi dicto citius curata sopori / membra dedit, vegetus praescripta ad munia surgit.* The theme of praise of the simple life is not, however, significant in the context of the present poem.
   animalis . . . naturalis virtutis: Vollmann well cites the influential twelfth-century intellectual William of St. Thierry's *De Natura Corporis et Animae* (in Migne, *PL,* 180:700ff.), where the distinction is drawn between *virtus naturalis,* housed in the liver, and *virtus animalis,* situated in the brain. The *virtus animalis* controls feeling and emotion, which are suspended in sleep, *virtus naturalis* the vegetative functions nurturing the body. The use of *vegetare* in this stanza points to this description of the powers of the *virtus naturalis.*

2. **pharetratus:** Used of Cupid by Ovid at *Am.* 2.5.1, *Met.* 10.525.
   crinali, torque: I abandon my suggestion (in *Thirty Poems*) of taking these words as "curly locks"; Rossi (284) observes that Cupid in his medieval garb wears a diadem as headband (*crinale*) at Andreas 1.6E.242.

6. **vertitur in luctum organum Amoris:** Laistner pointed to the parallel with Walter of Châtillon, *Versa est in luctum / cithara Waltheri* (ed. Strecker, *Moralisch-satirische Gedichte,* no. 17), where Walter is evoking Job 30:31, *versa est in luctum cithara mea, et organum meum in vocem flentium*; here Cupid is thus comically depicted as a Job-like suffering figure.
   absinthio: Walter's use of this word (ed. Strecker, *Lieder von St. Omer* 351, 22) encourages the speculation that he is being parodied.
   me vis deseruit, etc.: The poet has adapted Ovid *Rem. Am.* 139 to the situation: *otia si tollas, periere Cupidinis arcus.*

7. **artes amatorie . . . a Nasone tradite:** Ovid's *Ars Amatoria,* the bible of courtly love, was translated by Chrétien de Troyes (see the beginning of his *Cligès*) and is repeatedly cited by Andreas and evoked by writers of love lyrics in this era.
   modernorum: First in LL, an extension of *modo.*
   turpiter abutitur, etc.: The line does not scan as a hexameter; hence Sedgwick's *abiicitur.* Schumann considered the possibility of excising the whole stanza to bring numerical balance to the stanzas in each half of the poem.

8. **mundique voluptatibus . . . subductus:** This characterization is so flagrantly at odds with the Ovid of the *Amores* and *Ars Amatoria* that one must suspect an ironical purpose here; the poet directs his wit at the idealization of the Latin poet as *magister amoris curialis*.

qui sibi, etc.: Cf. Ovid *Ars Am.* 2.501, *qui sibi notus erit, solus sapienter amabit. Sapienter* indicates the discretion in loving which is at the heart of courtly love theory.

9. **Veneris mysteria . . . cistis:** The fundamental tenet of the need for secrecy in love goes back to Ovid's *Ars Am.* 2.607ff.: *praecipue Cytherea iubet sua sacra taceri: / admoneo veniat ne quis ad illa loquax, / condita si non sunt Veneris mysteria cistis.* The image of the casket containing Venus' secrets is adopted from the practice of the mystery religions; see Griffiths's learned note on *cista* in his edition of Apuleius' *Metamorphoses* 11 (*Apuleius of Madauros: The Isis Book*, London, 1975, 222).

precipue, etc.: For the direct citation of *Ars Am.* 2.607 see the note immediately above.

10. **iactantes . . . corporibus non tactis:** Cf. *Ars Am.* 2.633, *corpora si nequeunt, quae possunt nomina tangunt.* This emphasis on the despicable nature of false claims to love conquest is reflected in Andreas, whose fifth precept of love (1.6E.268) is *mendacia omnino vitare memento*; see also no. 37 below.

eheu, etc.: Cf. Ovid *Ars Am.* 2.625, *at nos nocturnis titulos imponimus actis.* In Andreas 2.7.43–44, in the eighteenth love judgment, the knight who publicized his conquest was condemned to be denied all hope of love thereafter.

11. **prostat in prostibulo, redigitur in pactum:** The poet condemns equally the roles of the courtesan and the married lady.

1a. Vacillantis trutine
     libramine
mens suspensa fluctuat
     et estuat
in tumultus anxios,
     dum se vertit
     et bipertit
motus in contrarios.

Refl. O, o, o, o, langueo!
     causam languoris video,
          nec caveo,
     videns et prudens pereo.

1b. Me vacare studio
     vult ratio.
sed dum amor alteram
     vult operam
in diversa rapior;
     ratione
     cum Dione
dimicante crucior.

Refl.

2a. Sicut in arbore
     frons tremula,
     navicula
levis in aequore,
dum caret ancore
     subsidio,
     contrario
flatu concussa fluitat;
     sic agitat,
sic turbine sollicitat
     me dubio
hinc amor, inde ratio.

Refl.

2b. Sub libra pondero
     quid melius,
     et dubius
mecum delibero.
nunc menti refero
     delicias
     venerias,
que mea michi Florula
     det oscula,
qui risus, que labellula,
     que facies,
frons, naris aut cesaries.

Refl.

3a.   His invitat
          et irritat
Amor me blanditiis.
     sed aliis
ratio sollicitat
     et excitat
     me studiis.

Refl.

3b.   Nam solari
          me scolari
cogitat exilio.
     sed, ratio,
procul abi! vinceris
     sub Veneris
     imperio.

Refl.

1a. My purpose hangs in the balance of the wavering scales; it is wave-tossed and boils over in troubled confusion as it twists and splits into opposing emotions.

Refrain. How listless I am! I see the cause of my listlessness but do not guard against it. With eyes open and of sound mind I seek destruction.

1b. Reason desires me to devote myself to study. But since love desires the other activity, I am dragged in opposing directions. I am tortured as reason grapples with Venus.

Refrain.

2a. As a trembling leaf on a tree, or as a ship without ballast on the sea, lacking the help of an anchor, is battered by conflicting squalls and tosses about; in the same way, Love on the one side, and Reason on the other, assail and afflict me with a whirlwind of doubt.

Refrain.

2b. Before the scales I weigh which is the better, and in doubt I ponder within me. Now I set before my mind the delights of love, the kisses which my dear Flora offers me; her smile, dear lips, face, forehead, nose, or hair.

Refrain.

3a. Love entices me and makes me itch with these allurements, but Reason nags and fires me with researches of another kind.

Refrain.

3b. For she thinks to console me with the scholar's exile. But away, far away with you, Reason! You are defeated and lie beneath Venus' dominion.

Refrain.

THE POEM IS incomplete in B, which has only 1a.1–4, 1b.5–8, 2b, and 2a, in that order. The complete text is in London Arundel 384 (A); there is another (defective) version in Cambridge Ff.1.17 (Ca).

This is the most celebrated and the most accomplished of the poems composed by Peter of Blois. Dronke suggests in his excellent critique ("Peter of Blois," 200ff.) that it is "Peter's recreation of the ancient motif of Hercules at the crossroads, being tempted by Virtus and Voluptas," a theme which he suggests was known to Peter through Cicero's *De Officiis* (1.118). It is perhaps worth qualifying this judgment by observing that virtue nowhere raises its head here, nor does Peter in his other lyrics show much preoccupation with it. The tension is between *amor* and *ratio*, between the beckoning attractions of the fair Flora and the pull of the spokesman's studies, to which reason draws him because they will advance him on a career in the Church for which celibacy was the prudent norm. The dilemma is precisely that examined in no. 1: the attachment to Pallas Athene versus the attachment to Venus.

As Dronke well puts it, "The quivering of the balance, the tossing and turning of the mind, the shivering branch and the anchorless skiff . . . all these are mirrored in the texture of the language, its rhythms and rhymes. . . . Yet the inner conflict here is only a pretence, the result a foregone conclusion."

1a. Cf. Virgil *Aen.* 12.486, *vario nequiquam fluctuat aestu.*

Ref. **videns et prudens pereo**: (A and Ca have *videns*, B *vivens*). Cf. Terence *Eun.* 72, *prudens sciens vivos vidensque pereo*. Peter expects his readers to visualize the spokesman as a second Phaedria, who likewise in that play ponders the alternatives of love and reason.

1b. **alteram . . . operam**: I.e., the pursuit of love.

2a. **sicut in arbore, etc.**: These parallels of the leaf in the wind and the anchorless ship on the sea go back to Scripture (cf. Job 13:25, *folium, quod vento rapitur*) and to Ovid (*Am.* 2.4.8, *auferor ut rapida concita puppis aqua*; cf. *Met.* 8.470–71, *utque carina / quam ventus ventoque rapit contrarius aestus*). The Archpoet likewise assembles these images in his *Confession* (*CB* 191 = *Thirty Poems*, no. 2).

2b. **labellula**: The ML diminutive of the CL diminutive ("those dear little lips") accentuates the tenderness of the description.
naris aut: So A and Ca; *naris quae* Ehrenthal; *narisque* B, Schmeller, and Dronke.

3a. **aliis . . . studiis**: The alternative of a life of study in another region (see stanza 3b) has its attractions.

3b. **cogitat**: The subject is *ratio*.

34 (111)

1. O comes amoris, dolor,
   cuius mala male solor,
      an habes remedium?
   dolor urget me, nec mirum,
   quem a predilecta dirum,
      en, vocat exsilium.
   cuius laus est singularis,
   pro qua non curasset Paris
      Helene consortium.

2. Sed quid queror me remotum
   illi fore, que devotum
      me fastidit hominem,
   cuius nomen tam verendum
   quod nec michi presumendum
      est, ut eam nominem?
   ob quam causam, mei mali,
   me frequenter vultu tali
      respicit, quo neminem?

3. Ergo solus solam amo,
   cuius captus sum ab hamo
      nec vices reciprocat.
   quam enutrit vallis quedam
   quam ut paradisum credam
      in qua pius collocat
   hanc creator creaturam
   vultu claram, mente puram,
      quam cor meum invocat.

4. Gaude, vallis insignita,
   vallis rosis redimita,
      vallis, flos convallium;
   inter valles vallis una
   quam collaudat sol et luna,
      dulcis cantus avium!
   te collaudat philomena,
   vallis dulcis et amena,
      mestis dans solacium!

1. Sorrow, love's companion, for whose ills I find poor consolation, is there any remedy for you? Sorrow oppresses me, and not surprisingly, for grim exile, as you see, summons me away from my beloved. Her fame is unique; Paris would not have preferred Helen's company to hers.

2. But why do I lament that I shall be far from her, when she holds this devoted suitor in contempt? Her name is so venerable that I must not even presume to name her. Why to my despite does she often eye me with a look which she directs at no other?

3. I alone, then, love her alone. I am caught on her hook, but she does not reciprocate my feelings. She is nurtured by a certain vale which I am to consider a paradise, in which the devoted Creator sets this creature, bright of countenance and pure of heart, on whom my own heart calls.

4. Rejoice, egregious valley, valley wreathed in roses, valley, flower of valleys; among valleys the one valley praised by sun and moon and the sweet song of birds. The nightingale praises you, sweet and pleasant valley, offering consolation to those sad at heart.

THE POEM APPEARS in fuller form in the *Fragmenta Burana*, no. 8* (*CB*, vol. 1.3).

The theme of the sorrows of love is a frequent feature in these lyrics (see Dronke, *Medieval Latin and the Rise of European Love-Lyric*, index s.v. "sorrows"). In this poem it inspires a reversal of the conventional presentation. In place of the initial description of the transformation in nature followed by the quickening of human love, the spokesman begins with emotional lament and follows with a description of the earthly paradise in which his unattainable maiden dwells. In this sense the glories of nature offer a consolation for unrequited love. This lack of fulfillment is a common thread in the courtly love experience; the lady shows haughty disdain to the lowborn suitor (see comments below on stanza 2).

1. **dirum . . . vocat exsilium**: The implication of the exile is that he must distance himself from the hazards of courting this highborn lady, whose rank is specified in stanza 2.
   Paris Helene: For Paris as a sobriquet of the courtly lover, and Helen as the epitome of feminine beauty, cf. 17.8, 17.14, 29.12, etc. The love liaison between them is the theme of *CB* 101–3.

2. **cuius nomen . . . ut eam nominem**: A leading motif in courtly wooing is the discretion by which the suitor refrains from identifying the object of his affections (cf. 17.2, *nomen tamen domine serva palliatum*); the injunction is intensified here by the high status of the lady. The analogue of the troubadour comes readily to mind, and there are obvious parallels in other lyrics in this collection, as at no. 55: *me sciat ipsa magnanimum, / maiorem meo corpore, / qui ramum scandens altissimum / fructum queram in arbore*. See further Dronke, *Medieval Latin and the Rise of European Love Lyric*, 305.
   quod . . . est: Frequently used for the consecutive construction in ML (= CL *ut . . . sit*).
   mei mali: The genitive of exclamation is familiar to writers in ML through their knowledge of Roman comedy (cf. Plautus *Most.* 912, *Truc.* 409, etc.).
   neminem?: I add the note of interrogation.

3. **amo . . . hamo**: The fanciful etymology of *amo/amor* is found in Isidore *Etym.* 10.1.5. Cf. Andreas Capellanus 1.3, *dicitur autem amor ab amo verbo, quod significat capere vel capi. nam qui amat . . . alium desiderat suo capere hamo.*

paradisum: The Greek sense of "park" is compounded for the medieval reader by the notion of Eden, in which this second Eve (hence evoking the Virgin Mary) is set.

4. **mestis dans solacium:** See the introductory comments above.

35 (113)

1. Transit nix et glacies
   spirante Favonio;
   terre nitet facies
   ortu florum vario;
   et michi materies
   amor est, quem sentio.

   > *Refl.*   ad gaudia
   >   temporis nos ammonet
   >   lascivia.

2. Agnosco vestigia
   rursus flamme veteris;
   planctus et suspiria
   nove signa Veneris.
   a, que manent tristia
   amantes pre ceteris!

   > *Refl.*

3. Illa, pro qua gravior
   mens amorem patitur,
   iusto plus asperior,
   nec michi compatitur.
   amans, et non mentior,
   nec vivit nec moritur.

   > *Refl.*

4. Hic amor, hic odium;
   quid eligam nescio.
   sic feror in dubium,
   sed cum hanc respicio,
   me furatur inscium
   et prorsus deficio.

   > *Refl.*

5. Non est finis precibus,
   quamvis cantu finiam;
   superis faventibus
   adhuc illi serviam,
   unde letis plausibus
   optata percipiam!

   > *Refl.*

1. Snow and ice are passing away under the breath of the south wind. The face of the earth gleams with sprouting flowers of many hues, and what is growing in me is the love which I feel.

   Refrain. The playful sport of the season turns our thoughts to joy.

2. I recognize the traces of the old fire once again. Grief and sighs are the marks of a new love. What sadness awaits lovers above all others!

Refrain.

3. The lady for whom my heart, now more oppressed, suffers love, is harsher than is right and does not share my pain. A lover—I do not lie—neither lives nor is dead.

Refrain.

4. On one side is love, on the other hatred; I know not which to choose, so that I am cast into doubt. But when I look upon this lady, she steals my heart without my knowing, and I am wholly without resource.

Refrain.

5. There is no end to my prayers, though I end my song. With the support of the gods above I shall continue to serve her, so that from that source with joyful approbation I may attain my longing.

As in the previous lyric, the central theme is the sorrows of love. The motif of quickening nature offers the barest of introductions, for the spokesman begins to detail his personal love experience in the very first stanza. Though his present plight is grievous (stanzas 2–4), he nurtures obstinate hope that all may eventually turn out well. The literary patterning of the poem, with its successive evocations of Horace, Virgil, and Ovid, warns us against regarding it as an expression of spontaneous emotion.

1. **Transit nix . . . spirante Favonio, etc.**: A Horatian exordium: cf. *Carm.* 1.4.1, *solvitur acris hiems grata vice veris et Favoni*; 4.7.1–2, *diffugere nives, redeunt iam gramina campis, / arboribusque comae.*
   et michi materies: The scholastic term reflects the poet's clerical ambience; the "matter" of the poet is the quickening love which is the counterpart of the "matter" of the earth, the sprouting flowers.

2. **agnosco vestigia . . . flamme veteris**: The love-weary spokesman adopts the persona of Dido. Cf. Virgil *Aen.* 4.23, *agnosco veteris vestigia flammae.* Like Dido he experiences the "signs of a new love."
   a, que manent: My emendation of the corrupt *a quo monet* of the manuscript.

3. **nec vivit nec moritur**: This depiction of the limbo between life and death is a cliché of the courtly love experience.

4. **hic amor, hic odium:** Ovid *Am.* 3.11.33–34, *pectusque leve in contraria tendunt, / hac amor, hac odium,* is a more likely influence than Catullus 85, *odi et amo,* as the latter was virtually unknown at this period.

me furatur inscium: Cf. Horace *Carm.* 4.13.20, *quae me surpuerat mihi.*

5. **superis faventibus:** The phrase reinforces the Classical ethos achieved by the evocations from Horace, Virgil, and Ovid.

36 (114)

> 1. Tempus accedit floridum,
>   hiems discedit temere;
>   omne quod fuit aridum
>   germen suum vult gignere.
>   quamdiu modo vixeris
> semper letare, iuvenis, quia nescis cum deperis!
>
> 2. Prata iam rident omnia,
>   est dulce flores carpere;
>   sed nox donat his somnia
>   qui semper vellent ludere.
>   ve, ve, miser, quid faciam?
> Venus, michi subvenias! tuam iam colo gratiam.
>
> 3. Plangit cor meum misere,
>   quia caret solacio;
>   si velles, hoc cognoscere
>   bene posses, ut sentio.
>   o tu virgo pulcherrima,
> si non audis me miserum, michi mors est asperrima!
>
> 4. Dulcis appares omnibus,
>   sed es michi dulcissima;
>   tu pre cunctis virginibus
>   incedis ut castissima.
>   o tu mitis considera,
> nam pro te gemitus ⟨edens⟩ passus sum et suspiria.

1. The season of blossoms draws near; winter readily departs. All that has withered seeks to bring forth its buds. For the full course of your life here and now, young sir, you must be happy, for you know not when you die!

2. All the meadows now smile; it is sweet to pluck the blossoms. But night bestows dreams on those whose desire would be always for innocent sport. Alas, alas, what in my wretchedness must I do? Venus, come to my aid! It is your favor which I now cultivate.

3. My heart feels wretched sorrow because it lacks consolation. If you were willing you could, I feel, graciously acknowledge this. Maiden most fair, if you do not hearken to my unhappy plea a most harsh death awaits me.

4. You are sweet in the eyes of all, but most sweet in mine. In your progress you outshine all maidens in perfect purity. Be gentle and give thought to me, for I utter groans and have borne sighs on your behalf.

As in the previous two poems, the "sorrows of love" motif again dominates in this conventional presentation of the natural world's burgeoning juxtaposed with the spokesman's fervid love feelings, so that as suitor he proclaims himself at odds with the regeneration in nature. This emotional discord is subtly introduced in the second stanza; *est dulce flores carpere* hints at the second level of meaning, the pleasures of love so far denied him. The lines that follow develop his disquiet in an original direction, hinting at the sexual pressures experienced by the clerical suitor who wishes to go no further than innocent flirtation (*ludere*).

1. **temere:** For the sense of "readily" already in CL, but usually in negative contexts, see *OLD* s.v. temere 4.

2. **ludere:** See the introductory comments above.

4. Schumann obelized the last two lines as metrically defective. The two-syllable rhyme evident in the earlier stanzas is not achieved by *considera / suspiria*; more important, *nam pro te gemitus* requires a supplement of two syllables. Other possibilities besides my offering, *edens,* which appears with *gemitus* at Lucretius 4.1015, are *ciens* and *trahens.* But it is quite possible that the original version of these final two lines was lost and that the stanza has been completed by a later contributor whose technical skill does not match his nice sense of an appropriate ending.

37 (117)

1. Lingua mendax et dolosa,
   lingua procax, venenosa,
   lingua digna detruncari
   et in igne concremari,

2. Que me dicit deceptorem
   et non fidum amatorem,
   quam amabam, dimisisse
   et ad alteram transisse!

3. Sciat deus, sciant dei:
   non sum reus huius rei!
   sciant dei, sciat deus:
   huius rei non sum reus!

4. Vnde iuro Musas novem,
   quod et maius est, per Iovem
   qui pro Dane sumpsit auri,
   in Europa formam tauri;

5. Iuro Phebum, iuro Martem
   qui amoris sciant artem;
   iuro quoque te, Cupido,
   arcum cuius reformido;

6. Arcum iuro cum sagittis
   quas frequenter in me mittis;
   sine fraude, sine dolo
   fedus hoc servare volo!

7. Volo fedus observare,
   et ad hec dicemus quare:
   inter choros puellarum
   nichil vidi tam preclarum.

8. Inter quas appares ita
   ut in auro margarita.
   humeri, pectus et venter
   sunt formata tam decenter.

9. Frons et gula, labra, mentum
   dant amoris alimentum;
   crines eius adamavi
   quoniam fuere flavi.

10. Ergo dum nox erit dies,
    et dum labor erit quies.
    et dum aqua erit ignis,
    et dum silva sine lignis,

11. Et dum mare sine velis,
    et dum Parthus sine telis,
    cara michi semper eris;
    nisi fallar, non falleris!

---

1. What a lying, crafty tongue, a wanton, poisonous tongue, a tongue deserving to be cut out and consumed by fire!

2. For it says that I am a deceiver and not a faithful lover, that I have abandoned the girl I loved and have passed on to another.

3. I call God, I call the gods to witness: I am not guilty on this charge! I call the gods, I call God to witness: on this charge I am not guilty!

4. So I swear by the nine Muses, and more important by Jupiter, who took the shape of gold for Danaë's sake, and that of a bull for Europa.

5. I swear by Apollo, I swear by Mars, for they know the art of love; I swear by you too, Cupid, of whose bow I stand in fear.

6. I swear by your bow and arrows which you keep discharging against me; I wish to preserve this compact without deceit and guile.

7. I wish to maintain this compact. Moreover, I shall tell you why: among all the bands of maidens I have seen none so outstanding.

8. Among them you appear like a pearl set in gold. Your shoulders, breast, and belly are so beautifully shaped!

9. Forehead, throat, lips, and chin add fuel to my passion. Her hair, too, I have come to love because of its blonde color.

10. So until night becomes day, till toil becomes rest, till water becomes fire, till the forest becomes woodless,

11. Till the sea has no sails, till the Parthian has no missiles, you will always be dear to me. If I'm not deceived, you will not be deceived either!

No. 32 (*Dum curata vegetarem*) was interpreted as a playful treatment in the Ovidian manner of the solemn injunctions of courtly love theory. This marvelously witty poem is likewise a sardonic mockery of one of the central preoccupations of that theory, condemnation of malevolent gossip. The spokesman's protestations of fidelity to his lady, and his rejection of allegations about his promiscuous behavior, are anything but persuasive. The oaths which he swears inclusively by the Christian god and the pagan gods (stanza 3) have a comic ring, and they are followed by citation of a string of heavenly witnesses all notorious for their roving eye (stanza 4–6; on this see Elliott, "The Art of the Inept Exemplum"). The two ensuing stanzas which detail the lady's physical attractions (8–9) sound suspiciously like parody of such conventional descriptions. The poem ends on a suitably ambivalent note, for the spokesman expresses his conviction that the lady will not be deceived—by his assurances rather than by his behavior!

1. **lingua . . . lingua**: The exordium inevitably calls to mind Hilarius *Carm*. 6 (text conveniently in *OBMLV*, no. 168), *Lingua servi, lingua perfidie*; see Lipphardt, "Unbekannte Weisen zu den *Carmina Burana*," who suggests that this is one of a block of poems (*CB* 116–22) reflecting connections with Hilarius. On Hilarius' career see Luscombe, *The School of Peter Abelard*, 52ff.

3–4. In the manuscript these stanzas are reversed, but this would disturb the sequence of adjurations in stanzas 4–6.

3. **reus . . . rei**: Because the words are etymologically connected, they are often juxtaposed in CL (cf. Plautus *Trinummus* 234; Cicero *Verr*. 2.2.94).

4. **Dane:** = CL *Danaë*. The story of Jupiter's seduction of Danaë by entering her guarded tower as a golden shower is a favorite of Ovid's (*Met.* 4.697ff., *Am.*, 2.19.27ff., *Ars Am.* 3.631ff.) and appears also in Horace (*Carm.* 3.16.1ff.) and other authors.
   Europa: This second notable instance of Jupiter's amatory exploits (cf. Ovid *Met.* 2.836ff.; Horace *Carm.* 3.27.25ff.) makes the oath risibly dubious.

5. **Phebum:** Apollo was an even more promiscuous lover; Ovid in the *Metamorphoses* details among his quarries Daphne, Coronis, Leucothoë (1.453ff., 2.542ff., 4.196ff.).
   Martem: The famous account of his amour with Venus is at Ovid *Met.* 4.171ff.; he also fathered Romulus (and Remus) by Ilia (*Met.* 15.863).
   Cupido: The inflammatory love god, traditionally characterized as *qui malis suis moribus, contempta disciplina publica, flammis et sagittis armatus, per alienas domos nocte discurrens et omnium matrimonia corrumpens* (Apuleius *Met.* 4.30.4), is an equally disreputable witness to fidelity.

6. **quas frequenter in me mittis:** The allegedly faithful suitor pleads guilty to his wayward disposition.

8. **humeri . . . tam decenter:** The catalogue of physical attributes has a parodic ring, and the rhyme *venter / decenter* becomes a cliché in these lyrics. Vollmann well cites the St. Martial poem *fronsque labra pectus venter / sunt formata tam decenter,* and the Ripoll Collection (on which see Raby, *SLP,* 2:236ff.), *nasus dentes labra venter / sunt formata tam decenter* (12.33–34). Cf. Spanke, "Zum Thema 'Mittelalterliche Tanzlieder,'" 12.

9. **quoniam fuere flavi:** The perfect tense should perhaps be regarded as jocose; dramatic transformations in hair color are one of the female enticements addressed in *De Vita Monachorum* (ed. Wright in *Anglo-Latin Satirical Poets*): *arte quidem videas nigros flavescere crines.*

10. The catalogue of *adynata* is a technique adopted from antiquity (e.g., Virgil *Ecl.* 1.59ff., 8.52ff.) which became popular in ML from the Carolingian age onward; see Curtius, 95ff.

11. **Parthus sine telis:** Cf. Ovid *Ars Am.* 1.210, *telaque ab adverso quae iacit Parthus equo.*
    non falleris: See the introductory comments above.

38 (119)

1. Dulce solum   natalis patrie,
   domus ioci,   thalamus gratie,
   vos relinquam   aut cras aut hodie,
   periturus   amoris rabie.

2. Vale tellus,   valete socii,
   quos benigno   favore colui,
   et me dulcis   consortem studii
   deplangite,   qui vobis perii!

3. Igne novo   Veneris saucia
   mens, que prius   non novit talia,
   nunc fatetur   vera proverbia:
   "ubi amor,   ibi miseria."

4. Quot sunt apes   in Hyble vallibus,
   quot vestitur   Dodona frondibus,
   et quot natant   pisces equoribus,
   tot abundat   amor doloribus.

1. Sweet soil of my native land, house of sportive wit, chamber so pleasing, this day or tomorrow I shall abandon you, for I am doomed to die through the madness of love.

2. Farewell, my land; farewell, my comrades, whom I have cultivated with gracious goodwill. Grieve for me, your companion in pleasurable study, for I am dead so far as you are concerned.

3. My mind, wounded by a new flame of love and inexperienced in such things before, now confesses the truth of the proverb: "Where there is love, there is wretchedness."

4. As many as are the bees in the vale of Hybla, as many as are the leaves in which Dodona is clad, as many as are the fish that swim in the seas, so many are the sorrows in which love abounds.

THIS POEM is found in five other manuscripts besides B. In B and L (Linz Studienbibl. Cc III 9) stanza 4 appears before stanza 3, but the order here is preferable. B and C (Chartres Bibl. Munic. 223) have an extra word appended to each of the first three stanzas (1 *exul,* 2 *igne,* 3 *gravis*), and B alone has *usque* appended to stanza 4. B is also unique in having a further stanza (4a), clearly spurious.

The creators of these lyrics constantly seek techniques of variation in presenting their stylized messages; as in nos. 34–36, the central theme is the sorrows of love, but the poet has enclosed the motif in the form of a *syntaktikon,* or speech of reluctant departure, in which the spokesman lauds the country left behind. The love affair is the cause of the departure; we are left to infer that the suitor is in physical danger, just as in no. 41 the pregnant girl's lover has been forced to exile himself. A further refinement in presentation is observable in the fact that here there is not a choice between love and study, as often elsewhere; the spokesman must abandon both.

1. **dulce solum:** The poet evokes Ovid in exile: *Pont.* 1.35–36, *nescio qua natale solum dulcedine cunctos / ducit.*
   domus . . . thalamus: The choice of *thalamus* (strictly a bridal chamber) suggests that this has been the scene of the love encounter.

3. **igne novo Veneris saucia:** The combination of flame and wound evokes the image of Dido at Virgil *Aen.* 4.1–2: *iamdudum saucia cura / vulnus alit venis, et caeco carpitur igni.*
   ubi amor, ibi miseria: Cf. Plautus *Persa* 179, *miser est qui amat.*

4. **quot sunt apes, etc.:** The stanza is a pastiche of Ovid: cf. *Ars Am.* 2.517ff., *quot apes pascuntur in Hybla, / caerula quot bacas Palladis arbor habet, / . . . tot sunt in amore dolores*; and *Pont.* 2.7.28, *quot natant pisces in aequore.* The poet has replaced the olive tree in Ovid with the oak grove of Zeus at Dodona, which makes a frequent appearance in other Ovidian contexts (*Met.* 7.623, 13.716, etc.).

39 (120)

1. Rumor letalis	tibi novercatur;
me crebro vulnerat,	cautius ama
meisque malis	ne comperiatur!
dolores aggerat.	quod agis, age tenebris,
me male multat	procul a Fame palpebris!
vox tui criminis,	letatur amor latebris
que iam resultat	cum dulcibus illecebris
in mundi terminis.	et murmure iocoso.
invida Fama	

2.   Nulla notavit
   te turpis fabula,
     dum nos ligavit
   amoris copula.
     sed frigescente
   nostro cupidine,
     sordes repente
   funebri crimine.
     Fama letata
   novis hymeneis
     irrevocata
   ruit in plateis.
   patet lupanar omnium
   pudoris, en, palatium,
   nam virginale lilium
   marcet a tactu vilium
     commercio probroso.

3.   Nunc plango florem
   etatis tenere,
     nitidiorem
   Veneris sidere,
     tunc columbinam
   mentis dulcedinem,
     nunc serpentinam
   amaritudinem.
     verbo rogantes
   removes hostili,
     munera dantes
   foves in cubili.
   illos abire precipis
   a quibus nichil accipis;
   cecos claudosque recipis,
   viros illustres decipis
     cum melle venenoso.

1. Death-bearing gossip repeatedly wounds me, heaping sorrows on my evil plight. Word of your sinning, now resounding throughout the boundaries of the world, punishes me sorely. Jealous Rumor deals with you harshly. Love more circumspectly, that discovery may not overtake you! Do what you do in the dark, far from the eyes of Gossip! Love with its sweet allurements and sportive whispers rejoices in hiding places.

2. No foul gossip besmirched you as long as we two were fastened in the bonds of love. But now that our desire grows cold, you are suddenly blackened by the indictment that spells death. Rumor, which takes joy in a new marriage union, rushes irrevocably through the streets. See how your palace of chastity is exposed as a brothel for all, for the virginal lily withers in shameful transactions from the touch of tawdry men.

3. Now I mourn for the bloom of your innocent youth, which shone more brightly than Venus' star, that erstwhile dovelike sweetness of heart which is now the bitterness of the snake. You repel with aggressive words those who entreat you, but you caress in bed those who bring you gifts. Those from whom you get nothing you bid depart, but the blind and lame you take in, and you beguile men of fame with your poisonous honey.

THE POEM APPEARS in one other manuscript, Stuttgart Landesbibl. H.B. 1.95 (S).

This is a notably original composition, wholly different in theme and structure from the common run of these lyrics. On the one hand, as Dronke observes (*Medieval Latin and the Rise of European Love-Lyric,* 302), there is a Catullan flavor about it; the spokesman bitterly contemplates the indiscriminate award of the lady's favors to all who arrive with gifts, just as Catullus 11 (*Furi et Aureli*) bids Lesbia *cum suis vivat vale- atque moechis, / quos simul complexa tenet trecentos, / nullum amans vere, sed identidem omnium / ilia rumpens.* On the other hand, the spokesman is concerned with the pernicious effects of common gossip (a frequent motif in courtly love theory: Andreas Capellanus repeatedly condemns such scandal-mongering, and no. 37 is a humorous disquisition on such malicious gossip), to some extent upon himself but more markedly on the lady, whose reputation in his keeping had earlier been unspotted. It is the combination of these two themes, the pain of contemplating the girl's promiscuity and the distress at the common talk which it provokes, which lends the poem its distinctive originality.

1. **Rumor**: This reading of B is clearly to be preferred to *humor* in S, since a leading theme of the poem is the increasing notoriety attached to the lady; note especially the references to Fama in stanzas 1–2 and the mention of *turpis fabula* in stanza 2.
meisque malis . . . aggerat: "Heaps pains on my ills"; notoriety is superimposed on the spokesman's sense of desertion and desolation. In CL the ablative with this verb normally expresses means, as at Virgil *Aen.* 4.197, which has perhaps inspired this passage: [*Fama Iarbae*] *incenditque animum dictis atque aggerat iras.*
vox tui criminis: *Crimen* is occasionally found even in CL in the sense of fornication; cf. Ovid *Met.* 9.24, *Iuppiter aut falsus pater est, aut crimine verus; / matris adulterio patrem petis.* In ML, under the influence of Christian Latin, this sense becomes more frequent; cf. no. 26, refrain: *aro non in semine, / pecco sine crimine.*
invida Fama: Here, as in stanza 2, the poet evokes Virgil's description of the *dea foeda* at *Aen.* 4.173ff.
novercatur: This deponent verb first appears in Late Latin (cf. Sidonius Apollinaris *Ep.* 7.14), the meaning of "treat harshly" being a natural development from the secondary sense of *novercalis* in CL.
palpebris: This word for the eyelids in CL (cf. Cicero *Nat. D.* 2.143) is commonly used for the eyes themselves in Late and Christian Latin; cf. the Vulgate of Ps. 10:5, *palpebrae eius interrogant filios hominum.*
letatur . . . murmure iocoso: The poet may have had Horace *Carm.* 1.9.18ff. in mind: *lenesque sub nocte susurri / composita repetantur hora, / nunc et latentis proditor intimo / gratus puellae risus ab angulo.*

2. **frigescente nostro cupidine:** According to the grammarian Nonius Marcellus, *cupido* when feminine = *cupiditas*, and when masculine indicates the god Cupid himself. But the masculine often appears in Horace, Ovid, and Seneca without such personification. *Frigescere* is often applied to *libidines* and to emotions generally, especially in Christian Latin.

irrevocata: In the sense of *irrevocabilis*, found in Statius *Achil.* 1.791, *Theb.* 7.773.

Fama . . . ruit in plateis: Virgil *Aen.* 4.184ff. is doubtless in the poet's mind.

patet . . . pudoris palatium: *Pudor* is one of the words whose meaning is transformed in Christian Latin to denote virginity. In Ambrose's celebrated hymn *Intende, qui regis Israel* the Virgin's womb is called *pudoris aula regia* (Walpole, *Early Latin Hymns*, no. 6, line 18). At 12.4b above *regia Diones* is a grandiloquent phrase for the female pudenda, and the same sense is evident here, as is clear from the next line.

virginale lilium: The lily as a symbol of virginity goes back to early commentaries on the Song of Solomon (2:2, *sicut lilium inter spinas, sic amica mea inter filias*); it was early applied to the Virgin Mary. Ambrose, perhaps influenced by Origen's *Commentary* (in Migne, *PG*, 13:149–50), extends the symbolism to sacred virginity generally: *lilia sunt; specialiter sacrae virgines* (*Inst. Virg.* 93).

marcet . . . probroso: For *commercium* in this sense of venal sex see stanza 3 below, *munera dantes foves in cubili*, and 60.1, *hac in parte fortior quam Iupiter / nescio procari / commercio vulgari*.

3. **columbinam . . . serpentinam:** The inspiration for the dove-serpent contrast is clearly Matt. 10:16, *estote ergo prudentes sicut serpentes, et simplices sicut columbae*; but here it is used to denote that the lady's kiss is transformed from the dove's innocent affection to the snake's lethal bite.

rogantes: "Mere requests" (without an accompanying gift).

cecos claudosque: Cf. Matt. 11:5, *caeci vident, claudi ambulant*. The implication is that the lady indiscriminately entertains all who are willing to be paying guests; "the blind and lame" symbolize men of defective vision who cannot see through her, and those who cannot escape her.

cum melle venenoso: Perhaps the poet has an eye on Ovid *Am.* 1.8.104, *impia sub dulci melle venena latent*.

1. "Tange, sodes, citharam   manu letiore,
   et cantemus pariter   voce clariore!
   factus ab amasia   viduus priore
   caleo nunc alia   multo meliore.

      clavus clavo retunditur,
      amor amore pellitur.
      iam nunc prior contemnitur,
      quia nova diligitur.
            igitur
        leto iure psallitur.

2. Prior trux et arrogans,   humilis secunda;
   prior effrons, impudens,   nova verecunda.
   prior patet omnibus   meretrix immunda,
   hec me solum diligit   mente pudibunda.

      prior pecuniosior,
      rapacior, versutior;
      hec nova curialior,
      formosior, nobilior,
            letior
      ⟨omni modo⟩ potior.

3. Hec quam modo diligo,   cunctis est amanda,
   nulla de nostratibus   ei comparanda.
   communiter omnibus   esset collaudanda,
   sed tractari refugit;   in hoc est damnanda.

      mittam eam in ambulis
      et castigabo virgulis,
      et tangam eam stimulis
      ut facio iuvenculis;
           vinculis
      vinciam, si consulis."

4. "Non erit, ut arbitror,   opus hic tanta vi;
   nam, cum secum luderem   nuper in conclavi,
   dixit: 'tractas teneram   tactu nimis gravi!
   tolle, vel suavius   utere suavi!'

exierat de balneo;
nunc operit quo gaudeo.
non ferreo, sed carneo
calcanda est calcaneo.
                    ideo
         valeas, quam valeo!"

1. "Strum your guitar, I beg you, with a more joyous touch, and let us sing
   together with voices less restrained. Deprived of an earlier mistress I am
   now flushed with passion for another and much better. One nail is blunted
   by another; one love is expelled by another. Now that earlier girl is
   spurned, for a new lady has my love. So our hymn is one of justified joy.

2. That first girl was sultry and proud; this second is unassuming. The first
   was barefaced and shameless; my new love is shy. The first is exposed as a
   filthy harlot before all; my present girl with modesty of heart loves me and
   no other. The earlier one was more mercenary, greedy, crafty; this new girl
   is more courtly, beautiful, noble, joyful—preferable in every way.

3. The girl whom I love now is deserving of all men's affections—none of our
   local girls can be compared with her. She would be worthy of the general
   praise of all except that she shrinks from being handled, and for this merits
   condemnation. I shall set her with the ponies, discipline her with the rod
   and flick her with the whip, as I do with bullocks. If you advise it, I will
   put straps on her."

4. "My view is that in this case there will be no need for such great force, for
   when I sported with her in her chamber the other day, she said: 'Your han-
   dling of a young girl is far too rough! Take your hands off, or apply their
   pleasurable touch more pleasurably!' She had just emerged from the bath
   and was now concealing the focus of my joy. You must goad her not with
   the iron spur but with the prick of the flesh. So may your success match
   mine!"

SEVERAL OF THESE love lyrics (e.g., nos. 32, 37, 60) have a comic or
ironical thrust; as was observed in nos. 16 and 17, the "goliardic" meter is
a favored medium for such treatment, and it is notable that the first four
lines of each stanza in this poem are in this measure. The spokesman gush-
ingly contrasts the infidelity and venality of his earlier girl with his idealized
new partner; but the bubble is abruptly burst in the final stanza, when the
friend, who is being consulted on how to make the girl more responsive,
casually offers advice based on his own love experience with her.

Within this comic frame the poet introduces a theme which undercuts yet again the idealized version of courtly love: how to bring a love-shy girl to heel. The explicit comparison made between the girl and a farm animal evokes the cruder courtship of antiquity as described in Horace *Carm.* 3.11. That ode, addressed to Mercury and the lyre, solicits guidance on how to break the innocent resistance of Lyde, *quae velut latis equa trima campis / ludit exultim metuitque tangi / nuptiarum expers et adhuc protervo / cruda marito.* In this poem the introduction of *cithara* in the first line, and the request for guidance of a similar sort, encourages such speculation about Horatian influence.

1. **tange, sodes, citharam:** Cf. Ovid *Rem.* 336, *non didicit chordas tangere, posce lyram.* Fischer and Vollmann interpret *sodes* dubiously as = *sodalis*; the sense of "I beg you" was familiar to twelfth-century literati from both Terence and the satirists.
   amasia: See comments at 12.5a.
   caleo nunc alia: Cf. Horace *Carm.* 4.11.33–34, *non enim posthac alia calebo / femina.* Also Ovid *Am.* 3.6.83.
   clavus clavo retunditur: For this medieval proverb see Singer, *Sprichwörter des Mittelalters,* 3:88.

2. Such catalogues of female frailties at greater length are found in John of Salisbury *Policraticus* 8.1; Walter Map *De Nugis Curialium* 4.30; and Andreas Capellanus 3.65ff.
   pecuniosior: The word does not have this derogatory sense in CL.
   curialior: In CL the word means "belonging to the same parish" and in LL "belonging to the imperial court," but in ML under the influence of courtly love theory it contains overtones of piety, generosity, prudence, and honesty.
   ⟨**omni modo**⟩: Schumann's suggestion for filling out the lacuna in the manuscript.

3. **tractari:** The word is often used in CL for putting an animal through its paces; the image of the recalcitrant filly is sustained throughout the stanza.
   in ambulis: *Ambulus* is a rare colloquialism in ML for *mannus,* or pony; *ambulum* is occasionally found for *ambitus,* or walkway. The phrase therefore means "among the ponies" or possibly "on the walkways." In either case the implication is that he will train the girl as he would an undisciplined farm animal.
   tangam eam stimulis: Cf. Horace *Carm.* 3.26.11–12, *flagello / tange Chloen.*

ut facio iuvenculis: In the Latin Vulgate, Jeremiah addresses the Lord: *castigasti me, et eruditus sum quasi iuvenculus indomitus* (31:18).

4. With Schumann I allot the entire stanza to the friend's response. Bischoff suggests that his words end at line 4; Spanke at line 5, with the remaining lines uttered by the spokesman; but this undercuts the poem's irony.
in conclavi: Cf. 60.5, *penitentem corripe, si placet, in conclavi.*
non ferreo . . . calcaneo: The friend humorously alludes to the suitor's complacent suggestion for bringing the girl to heel in stanza 3.
valeas quam valeo: This is Lundius' emendation of *valeat quam valeo*; by this change the line is attributed to the friend and not the suitor. Bischoff, who regards the line as having been spoken by the suitor, proposes *valeat quam video*, but that would be a prosaic close to a witty poem.

41 (126)

1. Huc usque, me miseram,
   rem bene celaveram,
   et amavi callide.

2. Res mea tandem patuit;
   nam venter intumuit,
   partus instat gravide.

3. Hinc mater me verberat,
   hinc pater improperat;
   ambo tractant aspere.

4. Sola domi sedeo;
   egredi non audeo
   nec inpalam ludere.

5. Cum foris egredior,
   a cunctis inspicior,
   quasi monstrum fuerim.

6. Cum vident hunc uterum,
   alter pulsat alterum;
   silent dum transierim.

7. Semper pulsant cubito,
   me designant digito
   ac si mirum fecerim.

8. Nutibus me indicant;
   dignam rogo iudicant
   quod semel peccaverim.

9. Quid percurram singula?
   ego sum in fabula
   et in ore omnium.

10. Ex eo vim patior;
    iam dolore morior.
    semper sum in lacrimis.

11. Hoc dolorem cumulat,
    quod amicus exsulat
    propter illud paululum.

12. Ob patris sevitiam
    recessit in Franciam
    a finibus ultimis.

13. ⟨Iam⟩ sum in tristitia
    de eius absentia,
    in doloris cumulum.

1. Poor wretch that I am, until this time I had successfully hidden this affair, and my love was craftily concealed.

2. But my condition at last became clear with my swollen belly and my imminent childbirth pressing sorely.

3. On the one side my mother beats me; on the other my father reproaches me. Both treat me harshly.

4. I sit alone at home, not venturing to go out or to have fun openly.

5. When I do go out, I am the object of all eyes, as though I were a monster.

6. When they notice my belly, one nudges another, and they fall silent till I pass by.

7. They keep elbowing each other and point a finger at me, as though my feat were extraordinary.

8. They point me out with their nods and judge me worthy of death on the pyre, because I have sinned just once.

9. Why should I recount each detail? I figure in the gossip on the lips of all.

10. The result is that I suffer violence. My sorrow brings me death; I am ever shedding tears.

11. What compounds my grief is that my boyfriend is in exile, just because of this peccadillo.

12. He has retired to the furthest borders of France because my father dealt with him harshly.

13. His absence is the cause of my melancholy and increases my pain.

THE POEM APPEARS only in B, which has a wholly inapt additional stanza at the beginning and a refrain (*Eya / qualia / sunt amoris gaudia*) which one can charitably regard as ironical.

The theme of pregnancy and the choice of the girl as spokeswoman offers welcome variation. The poignancy of the situation and the beguiling simplicity of the presentation should not lead us to underestimate the art of the poet, reflected in both subtlety of rhyme and clarity of structure. The causes of the girl's misery extend in an outward pattern. She begins with her own discomfort (stanza 2), passes to ill treatment by her parents (stanza 3), then retails the reactions of the neighbors (stanzas 4–9), and finally journeys abroad with her lover's exile (stanzas 10–13).

1. **rem**: Ambivalently indicating the love affair and the disastrous outcome.

3. **improperat**: Primarily biblical (Matt. 27:44, etc.) and liturgical.

4. **inpalam**: *Palam* is found in the Vulgate as an indeclinable noun: Luke 8:17, *quod non cognoscatur et in palam veniat*. *Inpalam* is subsequently found as an adverb.

6. **dum transierim**: The perfect subjunctive is required by the rhyme scheme.

9. **quid percurram singula?**: Raby (*SLP*, 2:275) remarks on the Ovidian flavor of this *interrogatio*; it reinforces the impression of the poet as a man of detached learning.

12. **a finibus ultimis**: In *CL* such expressions as *a cornu dextro* express place where; so, here, "on the furthest borders."

13. **iam**: Some such supplement as this of Peiper's is required before or after *sum* for the demands of the rhythm.

42 (135)

1. Cedit, hiems, tua durities;
   frigor abit, rigor et glacies,
   brumalis et feritas, rabies,
   torpor et improba segnities,
   pallor et ira, dolor, macies.

2. Veris adest elegans acies,
   clara nitet sine nube dies,
   nocte micant Pliadum facies;
   grata datur modo temperies,
   temporis optima mollities.

3. Soluta mundi superficies,
   gramine redolent planities,
   induitur foliis abies;
   picta canit volucrum series.
   prata virent, iuvenum requies.

4. Nunc, Amor aureus, advenies,
   indomitos tibi subicies.
   tendo manus; michi quid facies?
   quam dederas, rogo, concilies,
   et dabitur saliens aries!

1. Winter, your severity now gives place. The cold, the stiffness, the ice are departing, as are the wintry wildness and the rage, the numbness and unremitting sluggishness, the wanness and anger, the grief and barrenness.

2. Spring's tasteful array is at hand. The bright, unclouded daylight gleams forth, and at night the Pleiades make their shining appearance. Now welcome warmth is accorded us, the unsurpassed balminess of the season.

3. The world's surface is loosened. The plains diffuse the scent of plants; the fir clothes itself in leaves. A succession of colorful birds sings its songs. The meadows where the young recline are green.

4. Now, golden Cupid, you will come and subject to you those who have not yielded. I stretch out my hands; what will you do for me? Win over for me, I beg you, the girl you had bestowed on me, and your offering will be a mounting ram!

AT FIRST SIGHT the originality in what seems scarcely more than an amusing piece of doggerel appears to reside solely in the poet's virtuosity in assembling twenty rhyming words. The poem follows the conventional order of the love lyric, with greater emphasis on the transformation in nature, and the spokesman's appeal to Cupid in the final stanza is hardly anguished. There is, however, a greater subtlety than at first appears; the imagery of winter and spring has an implicit application to love relationships; this is especially true of the nouns descriptive of winter in stanza 1.

Stanza 3 appears after stanza 4 in the manuscript, but the latter provides a more apt close. The manuscript has suffered damage at each side of the third stanza, so that reconstruction is speculative. The surviving fragment, written as continuous prose, is as follows:

> ura mundi superfi
> s gramine redo
> t. induitur foliis abi
> picta canit volu
> i series. prata vi
> it juvenum requies

1. **improba**: For the sense of "unremitting" cf. Virgil G. 1.146–47, *labor omnia vincit / improbus*.

2. **Pliadum**: The rising of the Pleiades (the native Latin term is *Vergiliae*) in mid-May marked the beginning of safe seafaring and intensive cultivation; hence its aptness as a learned formulation of the arrival of the new season.

3. For the problems of text see the introductory comments above; *soluta* is my tentative suggestion. Bischoff's *est pura* is closer to the text; Schumann prints Meyer's *libera*. Meyer also proposed *planities*; Schumann prints *graminee redolent species*.

4. For *aureus* as an epithet of Cupid cf. Ovid *Am.* 2.18.36.

indomitos . . . subicies: For the sentiment cf. 26.2, lines 3–4, *rigidos et asperos / duro frangit flexu.*

saliens aries: An apt sacrificial victim for Cupid, as *salire* is often found in the agricultural writers to describe the copulation of animals.

43 (136)

1. Omnia sol temperat
   purus et subtilis,
   novo mundo reserat
   faciem Aprilis;
   ad amorem properat
   animus herilis,
   et iocundis imperat
   deus puerilis.

2. Rerum tanta novitas
   in sollemni vere,
   et veris auctoritas
   iubet nos gaudere,
   vices prebet solitas;
   et in tuo vere,
   fides est et probitas
   tuum retinere.

3. Ama me fideliter!
   fidem meam nota!
   de corde totaliter
   et ex mente tota,
   sum presentialiter
   absens in remota.
   quisquis amat aliter
   volvitur in rota.

1. The sun, so clear and fine, lends warmth to all things and unbars the face of April to a transformed world. Our mistress's spirit propels us toward love, and the boy-god bestows his commands on the glad at heart.

2. Such great renewal in the world at the annual springtime, and the authority of the spring, bid us rejoice. Spring demonstrates its customary changes; and in the spring that is yours there is the good faith and the decency to hold fast to your lover.

3. Love me faithfully, and mark my own good faith! Though I am absent far away, in my heart I am wholly with you, in my whole mind present with you. The one who loves in any other way is whirled round upon the wheel.

THIS IS THE example par excellence of the conventional love lyric, in which the two balancing elements of renewal in nature and the love relationship are accorded one and one-half stanzas each; the theme of nature's spring and the girl's spring effects a skillful joining of the two in the second stanza. Unlike several of our earlier lyrics, the spokesman dilates not on the sorrows of love but on a love secure; his confidence in the *fides* of his lady is matched by the protestation of his own.

1. **purus et subtilis**: The first adjective suggests the absence of cloud, the second the absence of the oppressive heat of the dog days; together they depict the ideal weather of spring.
   herilis: = "belonging to the mistress." It is clear from the next lines that the mistress is Venus and that just as Cupid commands his subjects to love, so Venus hastens them on likewise.

2. **in tuo vere**: For the metaphorical sense of *ver* cf. Ovid *Met.* 10.85, *aetatis breve ver*; Catullus 68.16, *iucundum cum aetas florida ver ageret*.
   tuo: Emphatic, relating the girl's burgeoning to that in nature.
   probitas: The honesty of manners which makes a partner dependable is one of the salient features of courtly love.

3. **sum presentialiter absens in remota**: That is, *in remota parte*. This is the authentic *amor de lonh* of the troubadours, a concept closely comparable with the *caritas Christiana* of a Paulinus of Nola (cf. comments at 56.1), who repeatedly stresses that his affection transcends all space and time.
   volvitur in rota: The image is that of Ixion's wheel, the infernal punishment (he was strapped to it, revolving eternally, for having assaulted Hera) described in Ovid *Met.* 4.461. The image was familiar from Roman comedy; cf. Plautus *Cist.* 206ff.: *iactor, agitor, stimulor, versor / in amoris rota. . . .*

44 (138)

1. Veris leta facies
     mundo propinatur;
   hiemalis acies
     victa iam fugatur.
   in vestitu vario
     Flora principatur,
   nemorum dulcisono
     que cantu celebratur.

2. Flore fusus gremio
     Phebus novo more
   risum dat, hoc vario
     iam stipate flore.
   Zephyrus nectareo
     spirans it odore.
   certatim pro bravio
     curramus dulciore!

3. Litteratos convocat
      decus virginale;
   laicorum exsecrat
      pecus bestiale.
   cunctos Amor incitat
      per iubar estivale;
   Venus se communicat,
      ut numen generale.

4. Citharizat cantico
      dulcis philomena;
   flore rident vario
      prata iam serena.
   ⟨turba⟩ psallit avium
      silve per amena;
   chorus promit virginum
      iam gaudia millena.

1. The glad face of spring attends upon the world. The sharp edge of winter is now overcome and put to flight. Flora plays the queen in her dappled garments, and she is hymned by sweet-sounding song from the woodland glades.

2. Phoebus, extended in Flora's lap, bestows an unaccustomed smile on her, engulfed as she is now with this varied array of flowers. The West Wind approaches, his breath endowed with the fragrance of nectar. So let us vie in our haste to win a sweeter prize!

3. The beauteous band of maidens summons the men of letters, and curses the uncivilized herd of laymen. Cupid by means of the summer's radiance rouses us all, and Venus, the divine power throughout the world, imparts herself to all.

4. The sweet nightingale strums an accompaniment to the song. The meadows, now sunny, smile with assorted blossoms. The crowd of birds hymns in harmony throughout the charming woodland, and the band of maidens now recounts its thousandfold joys.

IN THIS SIMPLE composition the love theme is subordinated to the description of the renewal in nature. The spokesman expresses no personal longing but instead prefers to stress the superior learning of the cleric and his preferred status as suitor in the eyes of the maidens.

1. **propinatur:** Though emendations have been proposed (*propitiatur* Schumann; *propinquatur* Schreiber), the reading of B can stand; medieval composers are not averse to forming deponents out of active verbs.
   acies: Here the "sharp edge," in contrast to *veris acies* in 42.2.
   Flora: So Schumann, rightly, for *Phebus* in B, retained by Vollmann.
   principatur: The deponent verb is frequent in Ecclesiastical Latin.

2. **Flore fusus gremio:** The image of the sun stretched out in Flora's lap is a bold and happy one.

novo more: The smile has not been habitual during the winter months.

bravio: For the Graecism, familiar from Paul's letters, cf. comments at 15.31.

dulciore: B has *in odore* repeated from two lines earlier; *dulciore* is one of several remedies suggested by Schumann; Schmeller prints *in amore*.

3. **litteratos:** The lettered men are the clerics, contrasted as elsewhere with the brute laity; see especially 52.5.

pecus: Schumann retains *pectus* from B, but *pecus* is to be preferred not only because of the rhyme with *decus* but also as enhancing the withering tone of contempt; see Spanke, 44.

Amor: Surely a personification (*pace* Schumann), in view of *Venus* following.

ut numen: Schumann's emendation of *per nomen,* retained by Vollmann.

4. **citharizat:** The image of the nightingale strumming the lyre is bold. The verb was familiar to ML readers through Rev. 14:2–3.

turba: Meyer's suggested supplement; Schmeller has *salit ⟨cetus⟩ avium.*

psallit: My suggested reading for *salit* is appropriate after *citharizat* above, for it means "to sing to the *cithara*"; cf. Ps. 32:2, *confitemini Domino in cithara, in psalterio decem chordarum psallite illi.* The error could easily arise if the scribe took down the poem by dictation.

45 (139)

1. Tempus transit horridum,
    frigus hiemale;
   redit, quod est placidum,
    tempus estivale.
   quod cum Amor exigit
    sibi principale,
   qui Amorem diligit,
    dicat ei vale!

2. Mutatis temporibus
    tellus parit flores;
   pro diversis floribus
    variat colores.
   variis coloribus
    prata dant odores;
   philomena cantibus
    suscitat amores.

3. Quisquis amat, gaudeat
tempus se videre,
in quo sua debeat
gaudia tenere!
et cum amor floreat
qui iubet gaudere,
iam non sit, qui audeat
inter nos lugere!

4. Vnam quidem postulo
tantum michi dari,
cuius quidem osculo
potest mors vitari.
huic amoris vinculo
cupio ligari;
dulce est, hoc iaculo
velle vulnerari!

5. Si post vulnus risero,
dulcis est lesura;
si post risum flevero
talis est natura.
sed cum etas venerit
senectutis dura,
lugeat quod fecero
pro pena futura.

6. Sed quod eam diligo
mira res videtur;
onus est, quo alligor,
et vix sustinetur.
unum de me iudico
quod verum habetur:
morior, quam eligo
nisi michi detur.

1. The grisly time of the winter's cold is passing, and the summer season of balmy weather returns. Now that Cupid is demanding this season as his before all others, any lover of Cupid must hail its coming.

2. With the transformation of the seasons, the earth brings forth its blossoms, diversifying the colors according to the variety of flowers. The meadows with their blossoms of diverse hue bestow fragrant scents. The nightingale rouses love feelings with its songs.

3. Each and every lover must rejoice that he beholds the day on which he is to grasp his joys. And since the love which bids us rejoice is blossoming, there must not now be a single soul who among us dares to lament!

4. My request is that there be granted me that girl, and no other, by whose kiss death can be evaded. To her I long to be united by the bond of love. How sweet is the aspiration to be wounded by this dart!

5. Should the smile of content attend upon the love-wound, that injury is sweet; but should weeping pursue that smile, such is the natural course of things. But once the grim period of old age approaches, my deeds must bring grief in the light of the punishment to come.

6. Yet my love for her seems a wondrous thing, a burden by which I am enchained and which can be barely endured. I make but one judgment in my own case which is accounted true: unless the girl of my choice is granted me, I am doomed to die.

THOUGH AT FIRST SIGHT this lyric seems to lack distinctive originality as it follows the conventional sequence (transformation of the season, consequent dominion of Cupid, confession of the spokesman's personal longing), there is a subtlety in the expression of these ideas. Summer's colors and songs usher in the joys over which Cupid presides. The suitor avows that his wound is sweet, and if pain must follow, that is acceptable as nature's dispensation. Old age will be early enough to feel the remorse which will annul eternal damnation (an uncommon motif). The final stanza, confessing to a burden which the suitor can scarcely endure, yet stressing that a continuation of life is dependent on the realization of his love, is a fine depiction of the psychology of such infatuation. The pleasing technique of repetition of words to establish the continuity of the imagery, and the balance between the two halves of the poem, is notable: *flores . . . floribus* and *colores . . . coloribus* in stanza 2 are set against *gaudeat . . . gaudia . . . gaudia* in stanza 3 and *vulnerari . . . vulnus* in stanzas 4 and 5.

1. **dicat ei vale:** As Schumann notes, there are two possible interpretations here. Either *vale* is taken in the less usual sense of *salve* (as in epistolary greetings: *si vales, bene est,* etc.), in which case *ei = tempori estivali.* Or *vale* retains its more regular sense of "farewell," and *ei = frigori hiemali.* The second interpretation would be attractive if Schumann's suggested *illi* for *ei* were accepted; but *ei* must be correlative with *quod* and refer to *tempus estivale.*

3. The sensation of the joys of love awakened by the sights and sounds of summer underlines the role of Cupid as the harbinger of such happiness. **floreat:** The verb carefully connects the growth in nature and in love feelings.

5. The stanza nicely balances the temptations of youthful ardor against the remorse of old age. The clerical spokesman is willing to anticipate the pain of rejection (*talis est natura*) rather than forgo the love experience.
   lesura: First in Christian Latin; cf. Wisd. of Sol. 11:20.
   lugeat: If the text is sound (Schumann tentatively suggests *lugeam*), the word must be taken as the equivalent of *pigeat/paeniteat.*

6. This is a splendid stanza, distilling the experience of youthful passion. It is a *mira res* that the suitor's aspiration is on the one hand a burden barely endurable but, on the other, the prelude to death through despair if not attained.

46 (143)

1.
Ecce gratum
et optatum
ver reducit gaudia;
purpuratum
floret pratum;
sol serenat omnia.
iam iam cedant tristia!
estas redit,
nunc recedit
hiemis sevitia.

2.
Iam liquescit
et decrescit
grando, nix ex ethera;
bruma fugit,
et iam sugit
veris tellus ubera.
illi mens est misera
qui nec vivit
nec lascivit
sub estatis dextera.

3.
Gloriantur
et letantur
in melle dulcedinis,
qui conantur
ut utantur
premio Cupidinis.
simus iussu Cypridis
gloriantes
et letantes
pares esse Paridis!

1. See how the spring, so welcome and so much desired, restores our joys. The crimson meadow is a feast of flowers; the sun makes all things bright. Sadness at this very moment must give place. The summer returns, and the savagery of winter is now in retreat.

2. The hail and snow now melt and subside from the sky. The winter flees, and now the earth sucks the paps of spring. Wretched is the heart of him who under summer's guiding hand fails to live and frolic!

3. Those who strive to enjoy Cupid's reward exult and rejoice in honeyed sweetness. Let us with exultation and joy at Venus' command show ourselves a match for Paris!

THIS ATTRACTIVE LYRIC, familiar to a wide circle from its association with Orff's infectious melody, reveals the classic pattern of the medieval lyric at its simplest. Note the exact division between the manifestation of spring's joys and their desired effect on the love lives of the youth.

1. **purpuratum**: In CL the word means "clad in purple"; in ML it becomes an alternative form for *purpureus* with its range of meanings (purple, crimson, bright). Perhaps crimson is the likeliest sense, with its image of fields of poppies in the springtime.
serenat omnia: Cf. Virgil *Aen.* 1.255; Walter of Châtillon, St. Omer 24.1.4, *sol serenat aëra.*

2. **ex ethera**: Schumann's hesitant suggestion for *et ethera* in B. It assumes a ML variation of *ex aethere* in CL; but this is surely preferable to Schmeller's *et cetera*, which is intolerably prosaic.
sugit . . . ubera: This striking image is achieved by Schumann's fine emendation of *surgit / ver estatis ubera* in B. He well compares St. Omer 24.1.5–6, *tument veris ubera, / tellus impregnatur.*

3. **in melle dulcedinis**: Cf. Ps. 118:103, Rev. 10:9–10.
Cypridis: Cypris, the Cyprian goddess, is found as a title for Venus first in LL (cf. Ausonius *Epigr.* 55.1, etc.), and it appears frequently in ML.
pares esse Paridis: Paris is repeatedly cited in these lyrics (e.g., 16.10, 29.12, 34.1; *CB* 142.3, 147.2) as the model for the courtly lover. The jocular pun on the name forms a splendid final flourish.

47 (145)

1. Musa venit carmine;
dulci modulamine
pariter cantemus!
ecce, virent omnia   prata, rus et nemus.

2. Mane garrit laudula,
lupilulat acredula;
iubente natura
philomena queritur   antiqua de iactura.

3. Hirundo iam finsat,
cygnus dulce trinxat
memorando fata,
cuculat et cuculus   per nemora vernata.

4. Pulchre cantant volucres;
terre ⟨nitet⟩ facies
vario colore,
et in partum solvitur   redolens odore.

5. Late pandit tilia
    frondes, ramos, folia;
        thymus est sub ea
viridi cum gramine,   in quo fit chorea.

6. Patet et in gramine
    iocundo rivus murmure;
        locus est festivus.
ventus cum temperie   susurrat tempestivus.

1. The Muse attends by way of song. Let us sing together in sweet harmony. Look how all things sprout green—meadows, countryside, and glade!

2. In the early morning the dear lark chatters, and the goldfinch cries *lupiloo.* At nature's command the nightingale laments her ancient loss.

3. Now the swallow *finces,* the swan sweetly *trinxes,* telling of her imminent death, and the cuckoo cries *cuckoo* through the verdant glades.

4. The birds sing sweetly. The earth's surface gleams with diverse colors, and parts to give birth, diffusing its fragrance.

5. The lime tree spreads wide its foliage, branches, leaves; below it is thyme and the green turf on which the dance takes place.

6. Over this turf too extends a stream with its pleasing murmur. This is a cheerful spot; the seasonal breeze whispers with its warm breath.

IN HER ATTRACTIVE collection of texts and translations of Medieval Latin lyrics entitled *The Virgin and the Nightingale*, Fleur Adcock presents a short anthology of bird poems dating from the seventh century (Eugenius of Toledo) to the twelfth. In the conventional pattern of the twelfth-century lyric the motif of the birdcall in the rejuvenation of nature is an integral strand and appears in many of the poems in the *Carmina Burana*. On occasion scholarly lore gets the upper hand over romanticism and a poem becomes little more than an ornithological catalogue; witness 3.4, *Mergus aquaticus, / aquila munificus, / bubo noctivagus, / cygnus flumineus*, and so on, a collection of fifteen birds each with its appropriate epithet. A similarly amusing treatment appears in *CB* 132, where every bird (and animal) is apportioned an appropriately onomatopoeic verb: *Merulus cincitat, / acredula rupillulat, / turdus truculat / et sturnus pusitat*, two stanzas of birdcalls being followed by two of animal sounds in this compilation of fun-learning. That composition is followed by *Hic volucres caeli* (CB 133), with a list of birds nicely assembled in hexameter verses.

The present poem seeks its originality in isolating, so to say, the songs and sounds which herald the spring. Human participation is fleetingly mentioned in stanza 1 and recalled with mention of the dance in stanza 5, but the birdcalls in stanzas 2 and 3, onomatopoeically described, and the murmur of the stream and whisper of the breeze, as climax in stanza 6, are the poet's central concern.

1. **Musa venit carmine:** Meyer's *veni* is attractive, but "The Muse comes by way of song" (*venit*) can be taken as a programmatic prelude to the sounds which follow.

2. The sounds allotted to the birds (cf. Wackernagel, *Voces Variae Animantium*) are mostly untranslatable in ML formulations.
   laudula: ML, a diminutive form of *alauda*.
   lupilulat acredula: The distinctive call of the goldfinch is expressed as *rupillulat* at CB 132.2a; it is impossible to pronounce on whether a single form of the verb should be read in both contexts.
   philomena queritur: See comments at 3.1.

3. **Hirundo . . . finsat:** Cf. CB 132.2a, *hirundo et trisphat*. As with the goldfinch's sound in stanza 2, it is justifiable to leave the two forms unchanged.
   cygnus . . . trinxat: At CB 132.2a *cygnus drensat* is the reading; see comments just above.
   memorando fata: The tradition that swans sing before their death is prominent in Greek literature; cf. Plato *Phaedo* 85B, "foreseeing the blessings in Hades."
   cuculat: This verb is found as early as Suetonius; see *TLL*.
   vernata: The verb is frequent from Ovid (*Met.* 7.284) onward, but it is always intransitive in CL.

4. **in partum solvitur:** The image of the earth softening and opening to give birth to its blossoms is a frequent one in these lyrics.

5. **in quo fit chorea:** One can regard the structure as a ring composition: the human participation urged in stanza 1 is reintroduced here with mention of the dance.

6. As a pleasing variation on the order of topics, the *locus amoenus* is set at the end of the poem in these final two stanzas. The "joyful murmur" of the stream and the "whisper of the seasonal breeze with its seasonal warmth" complete the catalogue of captivating sounds of spring.

48 (148)

1a. Floret tellus floribus,
    variis coloribus,
    floret et cum gramine.
1b. Faveant amoribus
    iuvenes cum moribus
    vario solamine!

2a. Venus assit omnibus
    ad eam clamantibus,
    assit cum Cupidine!
2b. Assit iam iuvenibus
    iuvamen poscentibus,
    ut prosint his domine!

3a. Venus, que est et erat,
    tela sua proferat
    in amantes puellas!
3b. Que amantes munerat,
    iuvenes non conterat,
    nec pulchras domicellas!

1a. The earth blooms with blossoms of diverse hues; it blooms also with grass.
1b. Young men of good manners must promote love affairs with their varied consolations.

2a. May Venus attend on all who cry to her; may she attend with Cupid!
2b. May she now attend on youths who beg her aid, that their ladies may bring them help!

3a. May Venus, who is and always was, brandish her darts against maidens to make them love!
3b. May she who rewards lovers not bruise the young or their beautiful damsels!

RABY (*SLP*, 2:267) exploits this poem to illustrate "the nature-introduction, the conjunction of spring and love, . . . which must have come direct from the vernacular. . . . It had acquired an almost ritual significance from its relation to the immemorial *fêtes de mai*. . . . This is a humble piece mixed with others of the same kind, simple and pleasing, having nothing more to say than the plain facts of spring and love." The poem is set in a self-contained group within the whole collection (*CB* 135–55), all of them evincing a similar simplicity, and all of them (as is the case with several others later) followed by a stanza in German. This suggests that they are (in Dronke's phrase) "a local repertoire" and that the German stanzas were added to allow participation in the songs by singers ignorant of Latin. While the basic conceptions propounded by Raby of vernacular origin and simple formulation are acceptable, there are elements of sophistication introduced when these themes are handled in Latin by scholarly craftsmen; see below at stanza 1a.

1a. **floret . . . floret**: The repetition moved Spanke to propose *viret* in line 3, but the repetition is deliberate; cf. *assit . . . assit* in stanza 2a. A further example of such balanced repetition can be seen in 2a.3–2b.1, *assit . . . Assit*, and 3a.3–3b.1, *amantes . . . amantes*.

1b. **faveant**: The manuscript has *caveant*, but Peiper's emendation is certain. **cum moribus**: A strange phrase, doubtless promoted by the trisyllabic rhyme scheme. The sense must be "Young men of good manners," and the poet may have intended a connection with *vario solamine* which follows; this hints at the two forms of love, *amor purus* and *amor mixtus* (on which see introductory comments to no. 4). As in no. 26, the moral men go for *amor purus*.

2b. **iuvamen**: The word appears first in LL and is especially frequent in Christian writers; the poet deploys it here to achieve the *iuvenibus/iuvamen* jingle.

3a. **est et erat**: The phrase has rightly troubled commentators, but the emendations suggested—*recesserat* (Schumann), *se reserat* (Spanke), *absconderat* (Bischoff)—are none of them persuasive. Perhaps *quieverat*? **tela sua proferat**: Cupid usually fires the darts; but cf. 16.6, *asto vulneratus / a sagitta Veneris*. **in amantes puellas**: *Amantes* is proleptic.

3b. The spokesman shows the customary ambivalence toward Venus, hoping that she will be benign but apprehensive of her hostility. **domicellas**: = ML "damsels"; initially as *dominicella,* diminutive of *domina.*

49 (151)

1. Virent prata, hiemata
        tersa rabie,
   florum data mundo grata
        rident facie.
        solis radio
   nitent albent rubent candent;
   veris ritus iura pandent
        ortu vario.

2. Aves dulci melodia
        sonant garrule,
   omni via voce pia
        volant sedule.
        et in nemore
   frondes, flores et odores
   sunt; ardescunt iuniores
        hoc in tempore.

3. Congregatur, augmentatur
　　　　cetus iuvenum,
adunatur, colletatur
　　　chorus virginum;
　　　et sub tilia
ad choreas Venereas
salit mater, inter eas
　　　sua filia.

4. Prestat una, quam Fortuna
　　　　dante veneror,
clarens luna, oportuna,
　　　ob quam vulneror,
　　　dans suspiria.
preelecta, simplex, recta
cordi meo est invecta
　　　mutans tristia.

5. Quam dum cerno, de superno
　　　　puto vergere.
cunctas sperno, donec sterno
　　　solam Venere.
　　　hanc desidero
ulnis plecti et subnecti,
loco leto in secreto
　　　si contigero.

1. Now that the madness of winter is erased, the meadows are green, and they smile with the welcome bloom of flowers bestowed upon the world. Beneath the sun's rays they gleam, shining white, glowing red, all aglitter. The rites of spring will reveal their rights of tenure with their diverse growth.

2. The loquacious birds resound with sweet melody; they diligently fly in all directions with devoted cries. In the glade are leaves and blossoms, and the scents which they diffuse. At this time those of younger years burn with passion.

3. The crowd of young men gathers and swells; the band of maidens is united with them, sharing their joy. Beneath the lime tree a matron prances amongst Venus' bands, and amongst them too her daughter.

4. There is one surpassing maiden whom I revere as Fortune's gift, my shining moon appearing seasonably. She is the cause of my wound and of the sighs which I utter. She is my chosen one, ingenuous, upright; she has invaded my heart and transformed my sadness.

5. When I behold her, I believe that she has swooped down from heaven. All maidens do I scorn until I bed her alone in an act of love. I long to have her in my arms, enfolded and entwined beneath me, if I chance upon her in isolation in some delightful spot.

THOUGH THIS LYRIC is conventional in structure (two stanzas devoted to the transformation in nature, the third to the general elation among the youth, the final two to the personal feelings of the spokesman; the final couplet of the second stanza linking the theme of renewal in nature with that of human emotions), there is a pleasing originality in the diction and in the rhyme scheme which reveals the superior craftsman. This prompted Schumann to air the possibility that the composer is identical with the author of *Hebet sidus* (no. 57), which some critics speculatively ascribe to Abelard; see the introductory comments there. Schumann further claims affinities with *CB* 165 and 168.

1. **hiemata:** The participle of *hiemare* is pressed into service as substitute for *hiemali* to accommodate the rhyme.
pandent: The future tense, which Schumann regards as strange, is necessary to achieve the rhyme.

2. **garrule . . . sedule:** Best taken as feminine plurals.
voce pia: Their devotion is perhaps to Mother Nature generally rather than specifically to the demands of their young.

3. **mater . . . filia:** In these dance lyrics old and young together are depicted in the celebrations; see 21.4.

4. **prestat:** Vollmann's fine emendation of *restat* in B.
clarens luna: The image is of the chosen lady surrounded by lesser stars. Just as in the *Aeneid* Dido is depicted as Diana (the moon) to Aeneas' Apollo (the sun), so in the Fathers the Virgin is accorded the same image with relation to Christ the *sol verus*. This evocation of the Virgin here is reinforced by the word *preelecta* at the beginning of the next stanza.

5. **vergere:** Schumann's preferred reading for *vigere* in B (*vivere* Martin).
cunctas: Schumann's emendation is preferable to *cuncta* in B.
donec sterno solam Venere: The sentiment seems crude after the propriety of what goes before; but it is difficult to improve on *sterno* (so Patzig; *cerno* in B is already used in line 1 of the stanza), and on Schumann's *Venere* for *tenere* in B.

50 (157)

1. Lucis orto sidere,
   exit virgo propere
      facie vernali,
   oves iussa regere
      baculo pastorali.

2. Sol effundens radium
   dat calorem nimium.
      virgo speciosa
   solem vitat noxium
      sub arbore frondosa.

3. Dum procedo paululum,
   lingue solvo vinculum:
       "salve, rege digna!
   audi, queso, servulum,
       esto michi benigna!"

4. "Cur salutas virginem
   que non novit hominem
       ex quo fuit nata?
   sciat Deus: neminem
       inveni per haec prata."

5. Forte lupus aderat,
   quem fames expulerat
       gutturis avari.
   ove rapta properat
       cupiens saturari.

6. Dum puella cerneret
   quod sic ovem perderet,
       pleno clamat ore:
   "si quis ovem redderet
       me gaudeat uxore!"

7. Mox ut vocem audio,
   denudato gladio
       lupus immolatur;
   ovis ab exitio
       redempta reportatur.

1. When the star of morning had risen, a maiden with the bloom of spring emerged in haste; she had been bidden to govern the sheep with shepherding crook.

2. The sun poured out its rays and caused excessive heat. The beautiful maiden avoided the harmful sun by sitting beneath a shady tree.

3. As I advanced a step or two, I loosed the restraints of my tongue: "Greetings, lady worthy of a king! I beg you, hearken to your poor servant, and be kind to me!"

4. "Why do you greet a maiden who has known no man since the day she was born? God must know that I have found no man in these meadows."

5. It chanced that a wolf lurked near, driven out by the hunger of its greedy maw. Grabbing a sheep it hastened off, wishing to fill its belly.

6. When the girl realized that she was losing a sheep in this way, she cried at the top of her voice: "The man who gets back my sheep can have the joy of me as his wife!"

7. As soon as I heard this, I unsheathed my sword. The wolf was sacrificed. The sheep was restored, redeemed from death.

THIS ATTRACTIVE POEM belongs to the genre of the pastourelle, on which see the Introduction, section 6. As is suggested there, the genre be-

gan as a vernacular form; when it emerges in Latin dress, authors seem
mostly content to retain the purely secular flavor of lighthearted entertain-
ment in the pastoral mode. Of the four examples in the *Carmina Burana,*
the other three are clearly of that type, and Dronke argues (in "Poetic
Meaning") that the fourth is essentially no different. I have argued, to the
contrary (Walsh, "Pastor and Pastoral"), that the poet is here Christianiz-
ing the genre, just as Endelechius in the fourth century, and Alcuin and the
author of *Ecloga Theoduli* (Gottschalk?) in the Carolingian age, Christianized Virgilian pastoral. Though at one level the poem can be interpreted as
a secular lyric exploiting the wolf motif popular in vernacular versions, it is
striking how the shepherdess appears through biblical and liturgical evocations as a Virgin Mary who is frequently represented as a type of the
Church. When the girl begs that the sheep be rescued from the ravages of
the wolf and promises herself as bride to the savior, it is difficult not to interpret this as the Church's plea to Christ her Bridegroom to redeem the
human soul from the devil's power, or at the lower level a plea to the priest,
who is an *alter Christus,* to undertake his pastoral duty of saving the human soul.

1. **Lucis orto sidere:** The initial words seem to signal religious intent, for there
are several hymns with this exordium, notably the traditional hymn for
Prime (Walpole, *Early Latin Hymns,* no. 81), *Iam lucis orto sidere / Deum
precemur supplices. . . .*
oves iussa regere baculo pastorali: The "pastoral" role of the Church
seems to be clearly alluded to here.

2. **virgo speciosa:** The twelfth-century reader would surely connect this with
Song of Sol. 2:13, *surge amica mea, speciosa mea,* and the Beloved of the
that book is regularly identified with the combined persona of Mary and
the Church.

3. **lingue solvo vinculum:** The expression is biblical. Cf. Mark 7:35, *et solu-
tum est vinculum linguae eius.*
salve, rege digna: The words surely evoke *Salve regina,* one of the oldest
Marian antiphons, which is ascribed to Herman the Cripple and was popular in twelfth-century devotion.

4. **virginem que non novit hominem:** So Mary replied to Gabriel when told
that she was with child: *Quomodo fiet istud, quoniam virum non cog-
nosco?* (Luke 1:34).

5. *lupus . . . ove rapta*: The equation of the *lupus* with the devil, and of the sheep with Christ's faithful, became a commonplace in scriptural exegesis of Luke 2 and John 10. These images were carried over into Christian poetry and hymnology: e.g., Prudentius' *Cathemerinon* 8.37ff. and, especially, Venantius Fortunatus' *Crux benedicta nitet* (*crux benedicta . . . / traxit ab ore lupi qua sacer agnus oves*).

6. **me gaudeat uxore**: The promise of marriage suggests the mystical wedlock of Christ with his Church (Eph. 5:25ff.).

7. **lupus immolatur . . . ovis . . . redempta**: The allegory of the wolf does not of course extend to the extinction of Satan, but the use of the theological word *redempta* for the rescue of the sheep is suggestive.

51 (158)

1. Vere dulci mediante,
   non in Maio, paulo ante,
   luce solis radiante,
   virgo vultu elegante
   fronde stabat sub vernante
         canens cum cicuta.

2. Illuc veni fato dante.
   nympha non est forme tante,
   equipollens eius plante;
   que me viso festinante
   grege fugit cum balante,
         metu dissoluta.

3. Clamans tendit ad ovile,
   hanc sequendo precor: "sile!
   nichil timeas hostile!"
   preces spernit, et monile
   quod ostendi tenet vile
         virgo, sic locuta:

4. "Munus vestrum" inquit "nolo,
   quia pleni estis dolo!"
   et se sic defendit colo.
   comprehensam ieci solo;
   clarior non est sub polo
         vilibus induta!

5. Satis illi fuit grave,
   michi gratum et suave.
   "quid fecisti" inquit "prave?
   ve ve ⟨tibi⟩! tamen ave!
   ne reveles ulli cave,
         ut sim domi tuta.

6. Si senserit meus pater
   vel Martinus, maior frater,
   erit michi dies ater!
   vel si sciret mea mater,
   cum sit angue peior quater,
         virgis sum tributa!"

1. In the middle of the pleasant spring (not in May, but a little earlier), under the sun's beaming light a maiden of refined countenance stood under the green foliage, making music with her pipe.

2. Fortune guided me to that spot. No nymph has such beauty as hers, or is comparable to the sole of her foot. When she saw me hastening up, she took to her heels with her bleating flock, unhinged by fear.

3. Crying out, she made for the sheepfold. I followed her and pleaded: "Hush, now; don't be afraid of any violence!" The maiden scorned my plea, and held cheap the necklace that I proffered. These were her words:

4. "I don't want this gift of yours," she said, "for I know that you are full of guile." Saying this, she used her staff to defend herself. I grabbed her and threw her to the ground. No more radiant creature exists under heaven, though she was clad in tawdry garments.

5. For her it was quite oppressive, but for me satisfying and sweet. "What is this dirty trick you have played?" she asked. "Shame on you. Still, God be with you. Be sure not to disclose this to anyone, so that I may not suffer at home.

6. If my father or elder brother Martin gets wind of this, it will be a black day for me. Or if my mother should get to know, I am in for a beating, for she is four times worse than a raging snake."

THIS IS A FURTHER example of the genre of the pastourelle (see the Introduction, section 6), here in its purely secular garb. As Dronke ("Poetic Meaning") well observes, there is an exact metrical correspondence between this and no. 19. The similarities between the two go beyond the meter. They are of exactly the same length, and of similar structure: in both, after the initial description of the *locus amoenus,* the gallant seeks to persuade the shepherdess to dally with him. In no. 19 she rejects him, pleading the anger of her parents, and there the poem abruptly ends. Here the gallant applies force, and her subsequent rebuke similarly emphasizes the wrath of her family should they discover her downfall. The identically abrupt close to both poems militates against Schumann's suggestion that further stanzas have been lost. In the treatise of Andreas Capellanus it is suggested that country girls are fair game for the predatory male (see my introductory comments to no. 12); one suspects that this is a further facet of the literary fantasy which is courtly love theory.

1. **Vere dulci mediante:** Biblical Latin inspires this use of *mediare*; cf. John 7:14, *iam autem die festo mediante.*

cicuta: The secondary sense of "pipe" (originally made from the hemlock stem) is already common in pastoral poetry in CL (Virgil *Ecl.* 2.36, 5.85, etc.).

2. **equipollens eius plante:** *Equipollens* in this sense is found first in Apuleius (*De Dogmate Platonis* 3). Doubtless John the Baptist's demeaning self-comparison with Christ (*cuius ego non sum dignus ut solvam eius corrigiam calceamenti,* John 1:27) is in the poet's mind.

3. **sequendo:** The ablative of the gerund in a purely participial sense is common from the Silver Age onward.
nichil timeas hostile: Cf. 19.5, *non sum predo, / nichil tollo, nichil ledo.*
monile: Fate may have guided him (stanza 2), but he has come well-equipped!

4. **pleni estis:** By this date the plural is often used in address to one of higher social status. It is amusing to note that after the confrontation the girl no longer addresses the gallant in the obsequious plural; see stanza 5, line 3.
et se sic defendit: Pillet's emendation, *etsi sic defendit,* is hardly necessary.

5. **prave:** Possibly vocative, but *prave facere* is common in both comedy and satire (both genres much read at this time) in CL.
tibi: Preferable to Manitius' *mihi* because of the following *tamen* (so Schumann).
ave: An expression of goodwill in Ecclesiastical Latin; cf. 2 John 10:11, *nec ave ei dixeritis.*

6. **angue:** The symbol of fury in Ovid *Met.* 3.52ff., 4.483.

52 (162)

1.   O consocii,
     quid vobis videtur?
     quid negotii
     nobis adoptetur?
   leta Venus ad nos iam ingredietur;
   illam chorus Dryadum sequetur.

2.   O vos socii,
     tempus est iocundum;
     dies otii
     redeunt in mundum.
   ergo congaudete, cetum letabundum
   tempus salutantes ⟨ob⟩ iocundum.

3.   Venus abdicans
     cognatum Neptunum,
     venit applicans
     Bacchum oportunum,
   quem dea pre cunctis amplexatur unum,
   quia tristem spernit et ieiunum.

4.   His numinibus
     volo famulari,
     (ius est omnibus
     qui volunt beari)
   que dant excellenti populo scolari
   ut amet et faciat amari.

5.   Ergo litteris
      cetus hic imbutus,
      signa Veneris
      militet secutus!
estimetur autem laicus ut brutus;
nam ad artem surdus est et mutus.

1. Fellow scholars, what have you in mind? What business shall we put in hand? Venus will come into us at any moment, and the chorus of wood nymphs will follow behind her.

2. Comrades, this is a pleasant season; the days of leisure are returning to the world. So as you greet the happy band, join in the rejoicing because of the pleasant season.

3. Venus, disowning her relative Neptune, comes bringing Bacchus aptly in tow. The goddess embraces him alone before all others, because he scorns the gloomy teetotaler.

4. I wish to enter service to these deities, as is right for all who wish to attain blessedness, for they grant the faculty of loving and being loved to the outstanding nation of scholars.

5. So this band of ours, steeped as we are in polite letters, must campaign following the standards of Venus. As for the laity, they must be accounted oafish, for they are deaf and dumb so far as the art of love is concerned.

As in the better-known *Omittamus studia* (no. 15), the theme of this poem is the pursuit of relaxation by scholars after study. Inevitably their thoughts turn to the pursuit of love; they transfer their allegiance from Pallas to Venus. The theme of spring's renewal is ritually introduced in stanza 2 but has a subsidiary role; the poet's leading preoccupation (and the element of originality in this composition) is the alliance of love and wine. The closed circle of clerics here as elsewhere flaunts its superior knowledge in love lore over the hapless laity; the jocular metonymy in stanza 3 underlines this learning.

1. **nobis**: Schumann's emendation of *vobis* in B.
Venus . . . chorus Dryadum: While it is possible to interpret this as an imaginary vision of Venus with the wood nymphs, it is more natural to assume that they represent a band of maidens, as in *CB* 110.2: *Ad Dryades veni, / iamque visu leni / cepi speculari / quasque decoris ameni; / sed unam inveni / pulchram absque pari.*

2. **ob iucundum**: The addition of *ob*, necessary for sense and meter, was Spanke's; Meyer and Patzig earlier suggested *et*.

3. **abdicans cognatum Neptunum**: Neptune is Venus' uncle as the brother of her father Jupiter; the purposely pompous metonymy renounces water for wine. The theme of wine versus water is popular in the humorous poetry of the age; most celebrated is the *Dialogus inter Aquam et Vinum* (ed. Wright, *Poems of Walter Mapes*, 87ff.), and another is one by Hugh Primas at *CB* 194.
   applicans Bacchum: The combination of Venus and Bacchus, already a commonplace in Classical poetry, is equally popular in medieval lyric; e.g., *CB* 200.3: *Bacchus sepe visitans mulierum genus / facit eas subditas tibi, o tu Venus.*
   spernit: The subject could be equally Venus. For the sentiment cf. Horace *Carm.* 3.21.29, *te, Liber, et si laeta aderit Venus.* . . .

4–5. The stanzas, in reverse order in B, were rightly adjusted by Herkenrath.

5. **estimetur**: Meyer's *exturbatur* sharpens the sense but is hardly justified.
   ad artem: That is, *artem amatoriam*. It is the boast of the cleric here as elsewhere (e.g., 29.41) that his knowledge of love lore raises him above the ignorant layman.

53 (163)

1.   Longa spes et dubia
       permixta timore
      solvit in suspiria
       mentem cum dolore,
     que iam dudum anxia
       mansit in amore.
   nec tamen mestum   pello dolorem.

2.   Heu, cure prolixitas
       procurata parum
     et loci diversitas
       duxerunt in rarum
   quod pre cunctis caritas
       cordis habet carum!
   omne ⟨cor⟩ largum   odit avarum

3.   In hoc loro stringitur
       nodus absque modo,
     nec ullus recipitur
       modus in hoc nodo;
   sed qui nunquam solvitur
       plus constringit modo.
   lodircundeia!   lodircundeia!

4.   Hanc amo pre ceteris,
       quam non vincit rosa;
     nec proferre poteris
       cantibus nec prosa,
   nec voce nec litteris,
       quam sit speciosa.
   flos in amore   spirat odore.

5. Inopino saucius
        hesito stupore,
    stulto carpor anxius
        animi furore,
    amens amans amplius
        obligor amore.
    nec tamen mestum   pello dolorem.

1. The long period of doubtful hope, mingled with fear, causes my mind, which has for long remained exercised with love, to dissolve into sighs with their accompanying distress. Yet I cannot dispel my sad sorrow.

2. Sadly, the redoubling of my cares, too little remedied, and the physical distance between us have put in short supply what the heart's affection above all holds dear. Every generous heart loathes the miser.

3. The knot in this thong is mercilessly tightened, and this knot grips ever tighter. Since it is never loosened, it now bites more than ever. Indeed it does, indeed it does!

4. This girl I love before all others; the rose does not excel her. You will not be able to describe her peerless beauty in lyrics or in prose, in utterance or with the pen. She is a blossom who in love exhales her fragrance.

5. I am at a loss, wounded by a numbness unforeseen, troubled and enfeebled by this doltish passion of the heart. In my crazy loving my hands are tied still further by this love, yet I cannot dispel my sad sorrow.

THIS AND THE following poem in the collection explore the psychological strains endured by the suitor who has embarked upon the complex rigmarole of courtship. This is detailed in the treatise of Andreas Capellanus: when the lady is solicited, she may reject the suitor *tout court*, or alternatively offer him hope (*spem largiri*). If she offers him hope, he must prove his worthiness by undertaking appropriate action in her name. She may pronounce a moratorium on the relationship, or even test him by deceit (*fallacia*). Thus the conferment of hope signals an indefinite period of probation without possibility of intimacy or guarantee of ultimate acceptance. Several poems in the collection emphasize the frustration or exultation experienced on the conferment of hope (see 54.2, *spes dari*; 59.1, *animata/ spei merito*), but this poem is the most explicit expression of the sorrows of love induced by the agony of uncertainty.

Spring and its renewal have no part in this composition. The spokesman finds no uplifting of the spirit in nature; the sustained lament is relieved only by the description of the lady's idyllic beauty. Before we signal the poem as emotional release from personal frustration, we should note the art of the craftsman conspicuous in the alliterative balance, the dexterity of verbal interchange worthy of a Walter of Châtillon, and the literary reminiscence; the composition is a memorable achievement on a less usual theme.

1. Every line in this programmatic stanza builds up the sense of anxiety and pain; mingled hope and fear create the angst clouding the suitor's existence.

2. **cure:** So Schumann for *cui est* in B.
The elaborately patterned alliterative effects (*prolixitas procurata parum*; *diversitas duxerunt*; *pre cunctis caritas cordis habet carum*) achieve the result of concentrating the reader's attention on the three factors contributing to the spokesman's depression: the waiting, the separation, the absence of physical affection.
omne ⟨cor⟩ largum odit avarum: This is my hesitant suggestion to remedy the syllabic balance and the internal rhyme. B has *omnis largus odit avarum*.

3. **loro:** (So Schumann; *loco* B.) The image is of the lover as beast of burden constrained by the knotted thong of the reins.
absque modo . . . in hoc nodo: (B has *absque nodo . . . in hoc modo*; Schumann suggested the necessary change without incorporating it into his text.) The leather thong is knotted mercilessly (*absque modo* = "without limit"), and the repetitive interchange of words intensifies the sense of the tightening of the knot. The image of the reins was perhaps suggested by Ovid's depiction of the opposite situation at *Ars Am.* 1.41: *dum licet, et loris passim potes ire solutis. . . .*
plus constringit modo: The never-loosened knot now (*modo*) bites more than ever.
lodircundeia: = Provençal "lo dir cuideie" (Bernt), "I should say so." Several of the later love lyrics in the collection have such ejaculations in the vernacular.

5. **saucius . . . carpor . . . animi furore:** The exemplar of Dido as unfulfilled lover once again emerges in the "sorrows of love" motif. Cf. the parallel vocabulary at Virgil *Aen.* 4.1–2, *at regina gravi iamdudum saucia cura / . . . caeco carpitur igni*, and 4.298ff., *furenti . . . inops animi.*
amens amans: Following Plautus *Merc.* 82, *amens amansque*, this verbal play is repeatedly found in CL and then in ML.

54 (164)

1. Ob amoris pressuram
    medentis quero curam
    amanti valituram.
    cor estuat interius,
    languet mens quondam pura,
    affligor et exterius
    propter nature iura.

2. Si cupio sanari
    aut vitam prolongari,
    festinem gressu pari
    ad Corinne presentiam,
    de qua potest spes dari,
    eius querendo gratiam.
    sic quero reformari.

3. Hec dulcis in amore
    est et plena decore,
    rosa rubet rubore,
    et lilium convallium
    tota vincit odore;
    favum mellis eximium
    dulci propinat ore.

4. Non in visu defectus,
    auditus nec deiectus;
    eius ridet aspectus.
    sed et istis iocundius:
    locus sub veste tectus.
    in hoc declinat melius,
    non obliquus, sed rectus.

5. Vbi si recubarem,
    per partes declinarem,
    casum pro casu darem,
    nec presens nec preteritum
    tempus considerarem,
    sed ad laboris meritum
    magis accelerarem.

1. Through the exigencies of love, I seek a healer's remedy which will avail a lover. My heart seethes within; my mind once unsullied is enervated; and in my outer appearance I am haggard through nature's dominion.

2. If I seek to be healed or to extend my life, I must hasten with fitting step to the presence of Corinna. Hope can be gained from her by my seeking her favor; this is how I seek renewal.

3. She is sweet in love, and beautiful; with her ruddy complexion she is a blushing rose, and with her fragrance she wholly excels the lily of the valleys. From her sweet lips she proffers a peerless honeycomb.

4. There is no stigma in her gaze, nor disappointment to our ears; her appearance beams on us. But there is also something more delightful than these, the region concealed beneath her garments. In this respect her declension is better, is straight and not oblique.

5. If I reclined there, I would go over the parts, cite case for case, and take no thought for present or past tense, but make more haste to gain the reward of my toil.

THOUGH THE EXORDIUM proclaims the spokesman's distress in the toils of love, a reading of the whole poem soon convinces us that this is not a cry from the heart but a humorous and risqué composition which assembles conventional motifs after the manner of Peter of Blois, who could well be the author. The first hint of academic playfulness comes with the identification of the girl with Ovid's Corinna (see below at stanza 2). The two stanzas which describe the spokesman's pains are followed by two more which dwell upon the lady's attractions; the catalogue of her external beauty is followed by contemplation of her hidden charms, in which the crudity of the boy's aspirations is palliated by a description of them in grammatical terms. Such deployment of "erotic grammar" is a commonplace in the lyrics of this era; we may compare feebler modern ditties such as "*Amo, amas,* I love a lass / As a cedar tall and slender; / Sweet cowslip's grace is her nominative case, / And she's of the feminine gender."

1. **quero:** Herkenrath's emendation of *gero* in B. The tenor of the exordium suggests that the spokesman needs to seek the succor of one who can heal his lovesickness. The theme of *querere* is prominent in stanza 2, lines 6–7; *curam gero* (= "I take thought for"; cf. *CB* 191.5) is possible but less apposite.
   mens quondam pura: Unsullied, that is, with preoccupations of sex.
   et exterius: This suggests the pallor of the haggard lover but also the physical responses (caused by the "dominion of nature") activated by his love obsession.

2–5. Hilka and Schumann's edition encloses stanzas 2–5 within quotation marks, presumably regarding these as a soliloquy; but the whole poem is a self-address in this sense, so that this separation of stanzas 2–5 seems to have little point.

2. **festinem gressu pari:** The urgency of his journey is to match the urgency of his situation.
   Corinne: Corinna is the ubiquitous lady who appears in twelve of Ovid's *Amores*; whether she really existed is a matter of dispute (see Wilkinson, *Ovid Recalled,* chap. 4). She also appears in *CB* 103; the citation of her name, like that of Coronis (also Ovidian) in nos. 7 and 12, where the author is probably Peter of Blois, is the scholar's flourish, her flesh-and-blood existence equally in doubt.

spes dari: For the importance of *spes* in courtly love theory see introductory comments to no. 53.

querendo . . . quero. See comments above at stanza 1.

3. **rosa . . . lilium:** (Meyer's *rose*—genitive—has much to recommend it.) For the rose-lily combination in conventional descriptions of beauty see comments at 3.2, 7.5a, etc. Here there is variation with emphasis on fragrance.
favum mellis: See comments at 9.3.
propinat: The image is of the serving maid proffering sweet honey, but from her lips.

4. **declinat, etc.:** The grammatical punning begins at this point. The girl's hidden figure is amusingly described in terms of the declension of a noun; the *casus rectus* is the nominative case (cf. Quintilian 1.5.61), and the other cases are "oblique" (Quintilian 1.6.22; *obliquus* is used also of tenses of verbs other than the present indicative, Quintilian 1.6.10). But of course the words *non obliquus sed rectus* literally imply that her figure is straight and slim rather than twisted and bulging.

5. **per partes declinarem:** Again the double entendre. The spokesman would stray downward *per partes corporis*; in grammar he would conjugate a verb by citing its parts, or decline a noun by citing its cases.
casum pro casu darem: At one level, "I would cite case for case" (i.e., in declining a noun at the behest of a teacher); at another, "I would offer one outcome in response to another."
nec presens nec preteritum tempus: For the three tenses of past, present, and future see, e.g., Varro *De Lingua Latina* 8.20; cf. Quintilian 9.3.11.

55 (166)

1.   Iam dudum Amoris militem
        devotum me exhibui,
    cuius nutu me precipitem
        stulto commisi ausui,
          amans in periculo
unam que nunquam   me pio respexit oculo.

2. Si adhuc cessarem penitus
        michi forte consulerem,
    sed non fugat belli strepitus
        nisi virum degenerem.
          fiat quod desidero!
vitam fortune   casibus securus offero.

3.   Me sciat ipsa magnanimum
          maiorem meo corpore,
    qui ramum scandens altissimum
          fructum queram in arbore,
          allegans: ingenio
nunc esse locum   in amante metus nescio.

1. For long now I have shown myself Cupid's devoted knight. At his bidding I have embarked headlong on a crazy act of daring, loving at great hazard a woman who never looks on me with kindly eye.

2. I should doubtless consult my own welfare if I now desisted entirely. But only the coward is put to flight by the din of war. Oh, may my longing reach fulfillment! Untroubled, I offer my life to the hazards of fortune.

3. She must know of my greatness of soul, greater than my frame, for I climb the highest branch in searching for fruit on the tree, claiming that in a lover who knows no fear there is now a role for native talent.

SEVERAL OF THE POEMS in the collection expatiate on the classic themes of courtly love, in which "the lady stood in a position of superiority to her lover as uncontested as the position of inferiority in which a wife stood towards a husband" (Power, *Medieval Women*, 24). But beyond the higher eminence accorded to ladies in general, a popular theme both in these poems and in the vernacular poetry of the troubadours, was the aspiration of the lowborn suitor toward a lady of higher social standing in castle or court. So in *O comes amoris, dolor* (no. 34) the suitor laments the disdain of a lady beyond his social standing; in the dialogues of Andreas Capellanus suitors and ladies of different social stations converse. It is clear that this poem belongs to a familiar genre and need not represent an actual experience.

There is a further stanza in the manuscript between stanzas 2 and 3, but its content breaks the flow of courtly argument, and defective rhyme further indicates that it is spurious.

1. **Amoris militem**: The phrase sounds the keynote of the poem; this is to be the proclamation of the courtly lover. His textbook is Ovid's *Ars Amatoria*, the guide for one *qui nova nunc primum miles in arma venis* (*Ars Am.* 1.35), a description echoed by Andreas in his preface: *Asseris te namque novum amoris militem*. . . . But the spokesman here has already embarked on his campaign.

in periculo: It is often suggested (e.g., Lazar, *Amour courtois et fin'amors*, 60; Power, *Medieval Women*, 23ff.) that courtly love is of its nature adulterous. But in the poetry of the troubadours, though some lyrics are addressed specifically to married ladies, the great majority are not (Press, "The Adulterous Nature of Fin'Amors," 327ff.). So the danger here may be visualized as from a husband poised for punitive action, but alternatively from the indignant lady.

2. **non fugat . . . nisi virum degenerem**: Cf. Andreas Capellanus 2.1.8, *set et si talis sit amator cui congruat bellatorem exsistere, studere debet ut eius cunctis appareat animositas manifesta, quia plurimum cuiusque probitati detrahitur, si timidus proeliator exsistat.*

3. **maiorem meo corpore**: This could be interpreted metaphorically with reference to his social status, but *magnanimum* earlier suggests a diminutive suitor.
   ramum . . . in arbore: The motif of gathering fruit from high branches is echoed in Provençal lyric; cf. Peire Vidal 6.9–10.
   ingenio . . . locum: There is an allusion here to the ancient dispute on the true nature of nobility, the classic statements of which come in Marius' speech in Sallust's *Jugurthine War* 85.15ff. (known to some twelfth-century readers) and in Juvenal's eighth satire, *Stemmata quid faciunt?* (esp. 20, *nobilitas sola est atque unica virtus*). Marius' claim that nobility took its origin from *virtus* and does not depend on superior social status became the keynote. It is taken up by Andreas Capellanus 1.6.13–14: *morum atque probitas sola est quae vera facit hominem nobilitate beare.* He continues: "Since all of us are descended initially from the same stock, it was only honesty of character which originally brought distinction of nobility, and introduced difference of class." The argument is extended here from *virtus* ("excellence") in general to *ingenium* ("native talent") in particular.
   nunc: With some hesitation I print *nunc* for *non* in the manuscript (so Spanke). Schumann suggests that *non* can stand if *ingenium* bears the sense of rank or social status, but this is impossible. Elsewhere, however (see Walsh, *Courtly Love*, 8), I suggest a possible defense of *non*, interpreting *ingenium* as craftiness: "I am boldly making for the highest branch; in a lover who knows no fear, there is no place for the crafty approach."

56 (167a)

1. Laboris remedium,
   exsulantis gaudium,
   mitigat exsilium
   virginis memoria;
   unicum solacium
   eius michi gratia.

2. In absentem ardeo;
   Venus enim aureo
   nectit corda laqueo.
   corporis distantia
   merens, tamen gaudeo
   absentis presentia.

(167b)

1. Nil proponens temere,
   diligebam tenere
   quam sciebam degere
   sub etate tenera,
   nil audens exigere
   preter mentis federa.

2. Iam etas invaluit,
   iam amor incaluit;
   iam virgo maturuit,
   iam tumescunt ubera;
   iam frustra complacuit
   nisi fiant cetera.

3. Ergo iunctis mentibus
   iungamur operibus!
   mellitis amplexibus
   fruamur cum gaudio!
   flos pre cunctis floribus,
   colluctemur serio!

4. Vvam dulcem premere,
   mel de favo sugere,
   quid hoc sit, exponere
   tibi, virgo, cupio;
   non verbo, sed opere
   fiat expositio!

56 (167a)

1. The cure for my toil, the joy experienced in my exile, is the recollection of the maiden which assuages that exile. The one consolation is the favor which she shows to me.

2. My heart burns for this absent girl, for Venus binds our hearts with her noose of gold. Though I grieve at her separation from me in body, I nonetheless rejoice at her absent presence.

(167b)

1. No rash proposal did I make, but I loved innocently the girl who I knew was still close to the years of innocence. I dared demand nothing but a compact of the heart.

2. But now her years have matured, and love's flame has intensified. The maiden now has ripened, and her breasts are now swelling. The pleasure she afforded me is now vain unless the remaining course ensues.

3. So since our hearts are one, let us make ourselves one in the flesh! Let us take joy and pleasure in honeyed embraces! Blossom superior to all blossoms, let us wrestle together in earnest!

4. To squeeze the sweet grape, to suck the honey from the comb—the meaning of these things, dear girl, I wish to explain to you. But I pray that my explanation may be by deed and not word!

THESE CLEARLY SEPARATE compositions appear as one poem in the manuscript, with the first comprising stanzas 1 and 3, the second stanzas 2 and 4–6. The meter and the rhyme scheme are identical; both may stem from the same pen. But the cause of the intermingling of the stanzas remains a puzzle.

56 (167a) *Laboris remedium*

The theme of *Laboris remedium* is that *amor de lonh* which is a feature of contemporary troubadour poetry, and in a sense the counterpart of the *amicitia Christiana* which claims to transcend boundaries of space and time. The concept is encapsulated in the moving poem of Paulinus of Nola addressed to Ausonius, *Ego per te omne quod datum mortalibus* (*Carm.* 11.49–68). So in this poem (which some suspect to be a fragment, but which still stands as a full treatment of the theme) the recollection of the girl's favor sustains the spokesman.

1. **laboris remedium, etc.:** This stanza strikes the ear as a courtly litany, evoking such prayerful address to the Virgin as the eleventh-century *Salve regina* (*Ad te clamamus, exsules . . .*), the *Ave Maria* (*gratia plena*), and the Litany of Loreto (*consolatrix afflictorum*).

2. By contrast, the second stanza is uncompromisingly secular.
aureo . . . laqueo: Like Aphrodite in Homer (*Il.* 3.64, *Od.* 8.337), Venus in Virgil is *aurea* (*Aen.* 10.16), and her weapons, like her son Cupid, are correspondingly golden; see, e.g., 18.3 above.
absentis presentia: A favorite oxymoron; cf. 43.3 above.

167b. *Nil proponens temere*

Though in several of these poems the clerical spokesmen advocate *amor purus* against *amor mixtus* (see introductory comments at no. 26), others countenance *amor purus* for the present but hold out the prospect of *amor mixtus*. So in *Amor habet superos* (no. 26) the spokesman proclaims that his present liaison is innocent but envisages future development. The present poem (strikingly similar in imagery, thereby suggesting identical authorship or the tribute of imitation) declares that the moratorium should now be ended.

1. **temere:** Hinting at the rashness of *amor mixtus.*
   tenere: Cf. 26.9, *ambo sumus teneri; tenere ludamus.*

2. **incaluit:** The verb is found in Ovid (*Met.* 3.371) describing the nymph Echo's passion for Narcissus; here it is the spokesman's love that is inflamed.
   maturuit: *Maturesco* is likewise Ovidian (*Met.* 14.335); note the further connection with 26.3, *donec sit matura.*

3. **operibus:** Schumann emends to *corporibus,* but unnecessarily, as *opus* is frequently found in both CL and ML for sexual intercourse; see Adams, *The Latin Sexual Vocabulary,* 157.
   flos: The word symbolizes virginity, as at Catullus 62.46. Note the further correspondence with 26.7, *flos est; florem tangere / non est res secura.*
   colluctemur: For this verb used of the love encounter see Adams, *The Latin Sexual Vocabulary,* 157–58. The wrestling image is notable at *CB* 147.2a (rightly excluded from the text by Schumann): *in palestra, Clytemestra, / lude fortius.*
   serio: Implicitly in contrast to innocent flirtation (*ludere*).

4. **uvam dulcem premere:** The imagery of the ripe grape, pervasive in CL (e.g., Catullus 17.16; Ovid *Met.* 13.795) and in the Bible (Song of Sol. 7:8), is another feature shared with no. 26 (stanza 7, *uvam sino crescere*).
   mel de favo: See comments at 9.3.
   opere: See comments at stanza 3 above.

1. Hebet sidus leti visus
      cordis nubilo,
   tepet oris mei risus
      carens iubilo;
      iure mereo,
   occultatur nam propinqua,
   cordis vigor floret in qua;
      totus hereo.

2. In Amoris hec chorea
      cunctis prenitet,
   cuius nomen a Phebea
      luce renitet
      et pro speculo
   servit solo; illam colo,
   eam volo nutu solo
      in hoc seculo.

3. Tempus queror tam diurne
      solitudinis.
   quot furabar vi nocturne
      aptitudinis
      oris basia!
   a quo stillat cinnamomum,
   et rimatur cordis domum
      dulcis cassia.

4. Tabet illa tamen, caret
      spe solacii;
   iuvenilis flos exaret.
      tanti spatii
      intercisio
   annulletur, ut secura
   adiunctivis prestet iura
      hec divisio!

1. The bright star of my joyful countenance is dulled by my heart's cloud. The smile on my lips loses its warmth, for it forgoes its joy. I rightly grieve, for my nearest and dearest lies hidden. In her my heart's strength blossoms; I am fixed fast to her entirely.

2. In Cupid's dance she excels all others. Her name brightly reflects the light of Phoebus, and she serves the earth as mirror. I worship her, long for her, acknowledging her alone in this world.

3. I lament the period of solitude so long extending. How many kisses from her lips did I steal through the impulse of opportunity by night! From her lips drips cinnamon, and sweet cassia insinuates itself into my heart's home.

4. But she wastes away, lacking the hope of consolation. Her youthful bloom is withering. Would that our separation at this great distance could be expunged, so that the sundering we endure may bestow unchallenged rights on us when we are united!

THIS IS ONE of the most original and arresting of the love lyrics in the collection. Many scholars (Ehrenthal, Meyer, and Allen among them) have suggested that the author is Abelard, who was celebrated for his poems to

Heloïse (see the Introduction, section 2 and note 10). The ascription to Abelard is based on a possible pun on the name Heloïse in stanza 2, just as in a letter to her he plays on her name in a different way (*PL* 178:207D). In a notable critique (*Medieval Latin and the Rise of European Love-Lyric*, 313ff.), Dronke revives the speculation by emphasizing the aptness of the poem to the situation of the lovers; Abelard had removed Heloïse to a convent at Argenteuil pending arrangements for their future life (*Historia Calamitatum* 7–8). As Dronke well observes, the final stanza is especially apt to their situation, in that the spokesman's description of the lady's wasting beauty might otherwise seem unflattering and inappropriate. Spanke's rebuttal, on the grounds that the stanza pattern is too complex for such an early date, is inconclusive given the complex texture of Abelard's hymns, but the ascription can remain only at the level of attractive speculation, for the liaison attracted such attention as a cause célèbre that a later composer of comparable talent could have been inspired by it.

1. **cordis vigor:** "*My* heart's strength"; the whole stanza is directed to the spokesman's own feelings.

2. **In chorea:** The description of the girl outshining all companions in the dance contrasts effectively with the dark, oppressed appearance of her lover in stanza 1. *Chorea* is often used of the movement of the stars (see *TLL*), so that *prenitet* is appropriate, and there may be deliberate contrast with *hebet sidus* in stanza 1.
   nomen: This is the manuscript reading, and the possibility of a play on the name of Heloïse (*a Phebea luce* as translation of Greek *hēlios*) encourages its retention. But Heinrich's *lumen* is attractive in view of Ovid *Met.* 4.347ff., *flagrant lumina nymphae, / non aliter quam cum . . . / opposita speculi referitur imagine Phoebus*. The Ovidian context (the Salmacis myth) would make the reminiscence apt.
   servit solo: The temptation to emend to *soli* (suggesting that she serves the sun by reflecting his light) should be resisted. Her role as mirror of the sun is to brighten the earth. For the image of girl as mirror see comments at 17.12.

3. **quot:** Herkenrath's happy emendation of *quo* (*qui* Manitius).
   cinnamomum . . . cassia: Song of Sol. 4:11ff., *favus distillans labia tua . . . emissiones tuae . . . cinnamomum*, and Ps. 44:4, 9, *diffusa est gratia in labiis tuis . . . casia a vestimentis tuis*, both eulogies of women, are the more likely inspiration than Plautus *Curc.* 100–101, *tu cinnamum, tu rosa, / tu crocinum et casia es.*

rimatur cordis domum: Such images as this distinguish the poet from the honest craftsman.

4. **spe**: Sedgwick's improvement on *spes* in B.
   adiunctivis: The word is normally used for "conjunction" by the grammarians but is here pressed into service *metri gratia* for *adiunctis*.

58 (170)

1. Quelibet succenditur   vivens creatura
   ad amoris gaudia;   meque traxit cura
   insignite virginis,   in cuius figura
   laboravit deitas   et mater natura.

2. Facies est nivea   miranda decore;
   os eius suffunditur   roseo rubore.
   consurgenti cernitur   similis aurore,
   irriganti climata   matutino rore.

3. Tota caret carie;   lampas oculorum
   concertat carbunculo;   sicut flos est florum
   rosa, supereminet   virginalem chorum.
   ⟨silici⟩ scintillulas   excitat amorum.

1. Each and every living creature is inflamed to gain the joys of love, and I have been attracted by my regard for an outstanding maiden, who was lent her shape by the toils of the Godhead and of Mother Nature.

2. Her snowy complexion is wondrous in its beauty. Her face is tinged with the crimson of the rose. She appears before our eyes like the rising dawn, as it waters the earth's regions with the morning dew.

3. She is untainted with any stain. The luster of her eyes vies with the ruby. She stands out above the band of maidens as the rose is the flower of all flowers. She awakes the sparks of love feelings even from a rock.

IN THIS SEEMINGLY artless but elegant poem the composer has dispensed with the conventional salutation of the spring to focus the reader's attention upon the peerless beauty of the lady. A single line suffices to proclaim love's dominion over all living creatures, and thereafter the spokesman devotes himself to the object of his own amorous feeling. The description of her incorporates clear echoes of the Song of Solomon (see below, on stanzas 2 and 3), which implicitly link her person with that of the Virgin Mary. The image of love's flame with which the poem begins (*succenditur*) is neatly reawakened at the close in *scintillulas*.

1. **insignite**: The adjective is used more commonly of objects in CL, in which *insignis* is regular in this sense of "striking" personal beauty.
    deitas et . . . natura: As was noted in the introduction to no. 7, in several twelfth-century philosophical poems Nature is visualized as God's agent in the creation of beauty in the world.

2. **facies, etc.**: For the frequent motif of the lineaments of the lady in these love lyrics see comments at 4.3–5.
    facies nivea . . . roseo rubore: So in 7.3a, *frons nivea*, and 7.5a, *rosam maritans lilio*; the combination of red and white is a cliché in these poems (4.2, 7.5a, 54.3; *CB* 156.4, *nivei candoris / rosei ruboris / sunt maxille*).
    miranda decore: So also at *CB* 65.4a.
    consurgenti . . . similis aurore: The inspiration is clearly Song of Sol. 6:9, *quae est ista quae progreditur quasi aurora consurgens?*
    climata: The Greek word *clima* is frequently used in LL for the regions of the heavens, and similarly for the regions of the earth (see *TLL*).

3. **tota caret carie**: *Caries* ("dry rot," and subsequently the shriveling of old age, in CL) is here virtually identical with *macula*. Cf. *CB* 155.2, *hec est, que caret macula*, evoking Song of Sol. 4:7, *tota pulchra es, amica mea, et macula non est in te*.
    concertat carbunculo: The *carbunculus* or ruby, which owes its name to its likeness to a burning coal (*carbo*), was regarded by the ancients as the most outstanding of precious stones (Pliny *HN* 37.92ff.).
    flos . . . florum rosa: See also 17.6.
    ⟨silici⟩ scintillulas: This is my speculative supplement; cf. Virgil *Aen.* 1.174, *silici scintillam excudit Achates*. The beauty of the maiden is such that she can rouse sparks of love even from a rock. The comparison of the cold lover to flint is a commonplace in Classical poetry (see *Aen.* 6.471, etc.). Other suggested supplements—*undique* (Schmeller), *sedulas* (Schumann), *varias* (Bischoff), *spectanti* (Vollmann)—are harder to account for paleographically. For *scintillulas* cf. *CB* 165.5, *ardoris scintilla . . . cor meum ignivit*.

59 (171)

1. De pollicito
   mea mens elata,
   in proposito
   vivit, animata
   spei merito;
   tamen dubito
   ne spes alterata
   cedat subito.

2. Vni faveo,
   uni, dico, stelle,
   cuius roseo
   basia cum melle
   stillant oleo.
   in hac rideo;
   in ipsius velle
   totus ardeo.

3. Amor nimius
   incutit timorem;
   timor anxius
   suscitat ardorem
   vehementius.
   ita dubius
   sentio dolorem
   certo certius.

4. Totus Veneris
   uror in camino.
   donis Cereris
   satiatus, vino
   parco; ceteris
   et cum superis
   nectare divino
   fruor; frueris!

1. My mind is overjoyed with the promise given. It lives in the prospect of what is to come, enlivened by the hope it has won. But I am apprehensive that this hope may suffer change, and suddenly give place.

2. One single maiden is my delight, one star, I say, and no other. Her kisses with their rosy honey ooze with the oil that charms. She elicits my smile; I am all aflame to perform her will.

3. My exceeding love induces fear, and that troubled fear rouses more insistently the heat of passion. So it is that in my uncertainty I feel the pain—nothing could be surer than that!

4. I am wholly aflame in Venus' furnace. I have had my fill of the gifts of Ceres, and I am sparing with wine; in company with the other deities above, I enjoy the nectar divine. You too must enjoy it!

As was explained in the introduction to no. 53, one of the central motifs in twelfth-century discussions of courtly love is the conferment of hope (*spei largitio*) by the lady on the suitor (see, e.g., Andreas Capellanus *De Amore* 1.6C.127, 130). Even after the lady has conferred hope, the suitor must still prove himself, and the tension felt, between elation and the possibility of acceptance on the one hand and, on the other, the fear endemic in the uncertainty during probation, is a fruitful theme in many of these lyrics. The tension is well described by Andreas at the outset of his treatise: "It is easy to see that love is a suffering, for until it is equally balanced on both sides there is no greater discomfort. The lover is in perpetual fear that his love may not be able to attain its desired end" (1.1.2). This suffering (cf. stanza 3, *sentio dolorem*) is the theme of this poem.

1. **alterata**: This verb first appears in LL.

2. **uni, dico, stelle**: I follow Schumann's punctuation; others take *dico* as "I address myself to."
   roseo basia cum melle: The conjunction of the adjective and noun is bold; *roseus* is descriptive of the lady's lips (rather than of the honey) as in Catullus 63.74, *roseis labellis*, and Virgil *Aen.* 9.5, *roseo ore*.
   stillant oleo: For *stillare* cf. 37.3. The imagery of oil, so pervasive in the Old Testament (*oleum laetitiae*, etc.), is developed further in the Fathers from Origen onward; for example, both Augustine and Cassiodorus in their glosses on Ps. 108:18 suggest that *oleum* denotes spiritual grace. From this it is an easy step to grace in the more general sense.
   in ipsius velle: The substantival use of the infinitive (= *voluntas*) had become regular in ML prose and verse by this date.

3. **amor . . . timor**: (*timor* is Patzig's certain emendation of *amor* in B.) For the juxtaposition of the two in courtly love theory see the citation from Andreas in the introductory remarks above.
   certo certius: The phrase was a feature of colloquial language from the Classical period onward (cf. Apuleius *Met.* 9.41.4, etc.).

4. **Veneris . . . in camino**: The image of Venus' furnace does not appear elsewhere in this collection, but it develops from *ignis Veneris*, which is a commonplace in both CL and ML (cf. *CB* 119.4).
   donis . . . parco: This is a difficult passage, which has given rise to considerable emendation. The manuscript has *donis ceteris / sauciatus vino / parco ceteris*. Peiper's *Cereris* for the first *ceteris* is certain; *satiatus* (Schmeller) for *sauciatus* is also convincing. Schumann proposed *satiatis vino / presto ceteris* = "I am superior to all others who are satisfied with (gifts of bread and with) wine; I enjoy divine nectar with the gods above." There is no doubt that Terence *Eun.* 732, *sine Cerere et Libero friget Venus*, lies behind the stanza (so Bernt). But it is possible to read *satiatus* and to retain *parco* by punctuating with a stop after *parco*: "I have had my fill of the gifts of Ceres, and I am sparing with wine; in the company of the other deities (i.e., other than Venus) I enjoy the divine nectar."

fruor; frueris: There is a hint of "erotic grammar" here (cf. introductory comments to no. 54). As the spokesman here speaks of the lady in the third person, rather than addresses her directly (stanza 2), he presumably exhorts the reader in *frueris,* which is best taken as a future denoting a polite imperative: "And you too must enjoy it!"

60 (178)

1. Volo virum vivere   viriliter;
   diligam, si diligar   equaliter.
   sic amandum censeo,   non aliter.
   hac in parte fortior   quam Iupiter,
       nescio procari
       commercio vulgari;
   amaturus forsitan,   volo prius amari.

2. Muliebris animi   superbiam
   gravi supercilio   despiciam,
   nec maiorem terminum   subiciam
   neque bubus aratrum   preficiam.
       displicet hic usus
       in miseros diffusus;
   malo plaudens ludere   quam plangere delusus.

3. Que cupit ut placeat,   huic placeam;
   ipsa prior faveat,   ut faveam.
   non ludemus aliter   hanc aleam,
   ne se granum reputet,   me paleam.
       pari lege fori
       deserviam amori,
   ne prosternar impudens   femineo pudori.

4. Liber ego liberum   me iactito,
   casto pene similis   Hippolyto,
   nec me vincit mulier   tam subito
   que seducat oculis   ac digito.
       dicat me placere
       et diligat sincere;
   hec michi protervitas   placet in muliere.

5. Ecce, michi displicet   quod cecini,
    et meo contrarius   sum carmini,
    tue reus, domina,   dulcedini,
    cuius elegantie   non memini.
       quia sic erravi
       sum dignus pena gravi;
    penitentem corripe,   si placet, in conclavi.

1. I want to live a man's life, as a man should.
I'll plight my love if I'm loved on equal terms.
This is my idea of right loving, no other way.
To this extent I'm a better person than Jupiter—
I can't woo a woman by a common transaction.
Perhaps I'll give my love, but I want to be loved first.

2. I shall despise the hauteur of the female mind with stern brow;
I'll not put a distant limit on my love, nor put the plow before the oxen.
This practice extended to wretched men annoys me;
I prefer happy flirtation to the grief of being mocked.

3. I want to please the lady who wants to please me;
let her first show affection so that I may do so.
We won't play this game of chance any other way—
then she won't count herself as grain, but me as chaff.
I'll submit myself to love on the equal terms of the courts,
so that I may not have to prostrate myself without shame before female modesty.

4. I'm a free man, and I boast of my freedom;
I'm almost as chaste as the chaste Hippolytus.
No woman can win me over so fast as to lead me astray with beckoning eye and finger.
She must say I pass muster, and love me honestly;
that's the wantonness I like in a woman.

5. But look, I don't like the song I've sung; I now oppose my own words.
I'm a prisoner to your charms, my lady. I was forgetting how exquisite you are.
For this sin of mine I deserve heavy chastisement.
I'm sorry. Rebuke me, if you will, in your chamber.

THE POEM IS found in one other manuscript besides B: Basel Univ.-Bild VI 4, of the fourteenth century.

As is explained in the Introduction (sections 2, esp. 5), several of the poems in the collection are witty and ironical commentary on courtly love theory, which is literary fantasy rather than a mirror to actual life; see especially nos. 32 and 37. This poem initially purports to be a declaration of revolt against the conventions of courtly wooing, but the *recusatio* in the final stanza overturns the passionate plea for equality so loudly voiced earlier. The sequence of humiliating dependence on the lady is outlined by Andreas Capellanus in his treatise: when the suitor requests his lady's ear, she may reject him or offer him hope (*spem largiri*). If she offers him hope, he must prove his worth (*probitas*) by unceasing labor in her name. She may test him by declaring a moratorium on their relationship, or even by employing deceit (for example, by pretending that he has rivals for her affection). Against this vision of courtship is implicitly set the doctrine of Ovid in his *Ars Amatoria*. True, *vir prior accedat, vir verba precantia dicat* (*Ars Am.* 1.709), but the lady's response should be gracious (*excipiat blandas comiter illa preces*), for *tantum cupit illa rogari* (1.710–11). In antiquity the man firmly has the upper hand, but there should be "due respect to the decencies on both sides" (Hollis, in his commentary ad loc.)

The structure of the poem is clear. After recounting the conduct which he wishes to impose on himself, and rejecting the haughty conduct of ladies (stanzas 1–2), the spokesman belabors their exalted status and demands the equality appropriate to his own *probitas* (stanzas 3–4). But the final stanza renounces this claim, and the palinode has more in it than abject surrender, for if the lady accedes to the suitor's plea to "rebuke him in her chamber," she will be tacitly accepting him as her *amator*, as Andreas Capellanus makes clear (1.6H.531).

1. **virum vivere viriliter:** The alliteration and repetition conspire to present an inflatedly manly figure, later to be punctured in stanza 5.
procari commercio vulgari: The connection of this phrase with Jupiter is established at Ovid *Met.* 4.697ff., in which that god seduced Danaë by appearing to her as a golden shower (cf. *Am.* 2.19.27ff., *Ars Am.* 3.631ff.; Horace *Carm.* 3.16.1). The story became a parable for money prevailing over virtue; hence "sordid transaction" here.

2. **maiorem terminum:** The moratorium mentioned in the introductory remarks above.
plaudens ludere quam plangere delusus: The elegance of the chiasmic antithesis is accentuated by the fact that *plaudere* and *plangere* both have the primary sense of "to beat."

3. **granum . . . paleam:** For the wheat-chaff contrast cf. Matt. 3:12, *congregabit triticum suum in horreum, paleas autem comburet igni inextinguabili.*

4. **casto pene**: There may be a double entendre in *pene* here.

   Hippolyto: For Hippolytus, son of Theseus, as a symbol of chastity in his devotion to the virgin goddess Diana and his rejection of the advances of his stepmother Phaedra cf. Ovid *Met.* 15.497ff., etc.

   digito: The gesture with the middle finger (the *impudicus*) was well known in antiquity: cf. Juv. 10.53, *medium ostendere unguem*; Martial 6.70.5–6, *impudicum ostendis digitum mihi*; and the Archpoet's *Confession* (*CB* 191.8), *ubi Venus digito iuvenes venatur*.

5. **corripe**: The full sense is "rebuke and correct"; see the introductory comments just above for the artful invitation.

Bibliography

Manuscripts Cited

Sigla are as in *CB* vol. 1.2, where the same letter occasionally denotes different manuscripts, but never with reference to the same poem.

A   London Arundel 384
B   Munich, Codex Buranus, Clm. 4660
B¹   B, corrected by the same hands
C   Chartres Bibl. Munic. 223
Ca   Cambridge Ff.1.17
E   Erfurt Amplon. Oct. 32
E   Escorial Z II 2
G   St. Gall Stiftsbibl. 383
F   Florence Laur. PL 29.1 (contains six of the lyrics in *CB*)
F   Florence Laur. Edili 197 (contains one of the lyrics in *CB*)
L   Linz Studienbibl. Cc III 9
M   Diessen, Clm. 5539
P   Paris B.N. lat. 1139
P   Paris B.N. lat. 3719
S   Stuttgart Landesbibl. H.B. 1.95
V   Vat. Reg. Christ. 344

Basel Univ.-Bild VI 4
Heidelberg 357

Ancient and Modern Works Cited

Adams, J. N. *The Latin Sexual Vocabulary.* London, 1982.
Adcock, Fleur. *The Virgin and the Nightingale.* Newcastle, 1983.
Alan of Lille. *Anticlaudianus.* Edited by R. Bossuat. Paris, 1955. Translated by J. Sheridan. Toronto, 1973.
———. *De Planctu Naturae.* Edited by N. Häring. *Studi Medievali* 19, no. 2 (1978): 797–879. Translated by J. Sheridan. Toronto, 1980.
———. *Liber Poenitentialis.* Edited by J. Longère. Louvain, 1965.
Allen, P. S. *Medieval Latin Lyrics.* Chicago, 1931.
Andreas Capellanus. *Andreas Capellanus on Love.* Edited by P. G. Walsh. London, 1982.
Apuleius. *Apuleius of Madauros: The Isis-Book (Metamorphoses Book XI).* Edited by J. Gwyn Griffiths. Leiden, 1975.
Arundel. *See* McDonough.

Ashcroft, J. "'Venus' Clerk': Reinmar in the *Carmina Burana*." *Modern Language Review* 77 (1982): 618–28.

Avicenna. *The Treatise on Love. See* Fackenheim.

Bate, Keith. "La littérature latine d'imagination à la cour d'Henri d'Angleterre." *Cahiers de civilisation médiévale* 34 (1991): 3-21.

———. "Ovid, Medieval Latin and the Pastourelle." *Reading Medieval Studies* 9 (1983): 16–33.

———. *Three Latin Comedies.* Toronto, 1976.

Bäuml, Franz H. *Medieval Civilisation in Germany.* London, 1969.

Beare, W. *Latin Verse and European Song.* London, 1957.

Benton, J. F. "Clio and Venus: An Historical View of Medieval Love." In *The Meaning of Courtly Love,* edited by F. X. Newman. Albany, 1968.

Bernard Silvestris. *Cosmographia.* Edited by P. Dronke. Leiden, 1978. English translation by W. Wetherbee. New York, 1973.

Bernt, G. *Carmina Burana: Die Gedichte des Codex Buranus lateinisch und deutsch.* Übertragen von C. Fischer, Übersetzung der mittelhochdeutschen Texte von H. Kuhn, Anmerkungen und Nachwort von G. Bernt. Zurich, 1974.

Bezzola, R. R. *Les origines de la formation de la littérature courtoise en occident.* Paris, 1963.

Bischoff, B. *Carmina Burana: Einführung zur Faksimile-Ausgabe der Benedikt-beurer Liederhandschrift.* New York, 1967.

Blaise, A. *Manuel du latin chrétien.* Turnhout, 1955.

Boase, Roger. *The Origin and Meaning of Courtly Love.* Manchester, 1977.

Boncompagno da Signa. *Rota Veneris.* Edited and translated by J. Purkart. New York, 1975.

Brewer, D. S. "The Ideal of Feminine Beauty in Medieval Literature." *Modern Language Review* 50 (1955): 257–69.

Brost, E. *Carmina Burana: Lieder der Vaganten.* 4th ed. Heidelberg, 1961.

Cairns, F. "The Archpoet's Confession: Sources, Interpretation and Historical Context." *Mittellateinisches Jahrbuch* 15 (1980): 87–103.

Carmina Burana. Edited by A. Hilka, O. Schumann, and B. Bischoff. Heidelberg, 1933–70.

Chenu, M. D. *La théologie au douzième siècle.* Paris, 1957.

Clemencie, R. *Carmina Burana: Gesamtausgabe der mittelalterlichen Melodien mit den dazuhehörigen Texten.* Munich, 1979.

Cremaschi, G. *Guido allo studio del latino medievale.* Padua, 1959.

Curtius, E. R. *European Literature and the Latin Middle Ages.* Translated by Willard R. Trask. London, 1953.

De Ghellinck, J. *L'essor de la littérature latine au douzième siècle.* Brussels, 1954.

Dronke, P. "The Archpoet and the Classics." In *Latin Poetry and the Classical Tradition,* edited by P. Godman and O. Murray, chap. 4. Oxford, 1990.

———. *Medieval Latin and the Rise of European Love-Lyric.* Oxford, 1965. 2d ed. 1968.

———. *The Medieval Lyric.* 2d ed. Cambridge, 1977.

———. "Peter of Blois and Poetry at the Court of Henry II." *Medieval Studies* 38 (1976): 185–235.

———. "Poetic Meaning in the Carmina Burana." *Mittellateinisches Jahrbuch* 10 (1974–75): 116–37.

Duby, G. *The Knight, the Lady and the Priest.* London, 1984.

Elliott, A. G. "The Art of the Inept *Exemplum*: Ovidian Deception in *CB* 117 and 178." *Sandalion* 5 (1982): 353–68.

———. "The Bedraggled Cupid: Ovidian Satire in *CB* 105." *Traditio* 42 (1981): 426–37.

Fackenheim, E. "A Treatise of Love by Ibn Sina." *Medieval Studies* 7 (1945): 208–28.

Fechter, W. "Galle und Honig." *Beiträge zur Geschichte des deutschen Sprache und Literatur* 80 (1958): 107–42.

Fischer, C. *See* Bernt.

Geoffrey of Vinsauf. *Poetria Nova.* Edited by E. Faral in *Les arts poétiques.* Paris, 1924. Translated by M. F. Nims. Toronto, 1967.

Gerald of Wales. *De Mundi Creatione.* In *Opera,* edited by J. S. Brewer, vol. 1. Rolls Series, 21. London, 1861–91.

Godman, P., and O. Murray, eds. *Latin Poetry and the Classical Tradition.* Oxford, 1990.

Haller, R. S. "The *Altercatio Phyllidis et Florae* as an Ovidian Satire." *Medieval Studies* 30 (1968): 119–33.

Häring, N. M. "The Creation and Creator of the World according to Thierry of Chartres and Clarenbaldus of Arras." *Archives d'histoire doctrinale et littéraire du moyen âge* 22 (1955): 137–216.

———. "Die Gedichte und Mysterienspiele des Hilarius von Orléans." *Studi Medievali* 17 (1976): 915–68.

Haskins, C. H. *Studies in Medieval Culture.* Oxford, 1929.

Heer, F. *The Medieval World.* London, 1963.

Helm, K. "Quinque lineae amoris." *Germanisch-Romanisch Monatsschrift* 29 (1941): 236–47.

Hilarius of Orléans. *Hilarii Versus et Ludi.* Edited by J. B. Fuller. New York, 1929.

Hilka, Schumann, and Bischoff. *See Carmina Burana.*

Hugh Primas. *See* McDonough.

Jackson, W. T. H. "The Medieval Pastourelle as a Satirical Genre." *Philological Quarterly* 31, no. 2 (1952): 156–70.

Jones, W. P. *The Pastourelle.* 2d ed. New York, 1973.

Laistner, L., E. Brost, and W. Bulst. *Carmina Burana: Lieder der Vaganten.* 5th ed. Heidelberg, 1974.

Langlois, E. *Les origines et les sources de la Roman de la Rose.* Paris, 1891.

Langosch, K. *Hymnen und Vagantenlieder.* Basel, 1954.

Lazar, M. *Amour courtois et fin'amors.* Paris, 1964.

Lehmann, P. *Die Parodie im Mittelalter.* 2d ed. Stuttgart, 1963.

Lewis, C. S. *The Allegory of Love.* Oxford, 1936.

Lindsay, J. *Medieval Latin Poets.* London, 1934.

Lipphardt, W. "Unbekannte Weisen zu den *Carmina Burana.*" *Archiv für Musikwissenschaft* 12 (1955): 122–42.

Löfstedt, E. *Late Latin.* Oslo, 1959.

Luscombe, D. *The School of Peter Abelard.* Cambridge, 1970.

McDonough, C. J., ed. *The Oxford Poems of Hugh Primas and the Arundel Lyrics.* Toronto, 1984.

Manitius, M. *Geschichte der lateinischen Literatur des Mittelalters.* 3 vols. Munich, 1911–31. Reprinted 1964.

Map, Walter. *Poems of Walter Mapes.* Edited by T. Wright. London, 1841.

Massa, E. *Carmina Burana e altri canti della goliardia medioevale.* Rome, 1979.

Matthew of Vendôme. *Ars Versificatoria.* Edited by F. Munari. Rome, 1988. Translated by A. E. Galyon. Ames, Iowa, 1980.

Meyer, W. *Gesammelte Abhandlungen zur mittellateinischen Rythmik.* 3 vols. Berlin, 1905–36.

Munari, F. "Mediaevalia I–II." *Philologus* 104 (1960): 279–92.

Newman, F. X., ed. *The Meaning of Courtly Love.* Albany, 1968.

Norberg, D. *Manuel pratique de latin médiéval.* Paris, 1968.

Ovid. *Ars Amatoria, Book I.* Edited by A. S. Hollis. Oxford 1977.

The Oxford Book of Medieval Latin Verse. Edited by F. J. E. Raby. Oxford, 1959.

Pamphilus. See Bate, *Three Latin Comedies.*

Parlett, D. *Selections from the Carmina Burana.* Harmondsworth: Penguin, 1986.

Patch, H. R. *The Goddess Fortuna in Medieval Literature.* Cambridge, Mass., 1927.

Patzig, H. "Zu Guiraut de Cabreira." *Romanische Forschungen* 4 (1891): 549–50.

Peter of Blois. *Opera.* Edited by J. A. Giles. 4 vols. Oxford, 1846.

Piguet, E. *L'évolution de la pastourelle du XIIe siècle à nos jours.* Basel, 1927.

Pirot, F. *Recherches sur les connaissances littéraires des troubadours occitans et catalans des XIIe et XIIIe siècles.* Barcelona, 1972.

Power, Eileen. *Medieval Women.* Edited by M. Postan. Cambridge, 1975.

Press, A. R. "The Adulterous Nature of Fin Amors: A Re-examination of the Theory." *Forum for Modern Language Studies* 6 (1970): 327–41.

Raby, F. J. E. *Christian Latin Poetry.* 2d ed. Oxford, 1953.

———. *Secular Latin Poetry.* 2 vols. Oxford, 1934.

Rahner, H. *Greek Myths and Christian Mystery.* London, 1962.

Reynolds, L. D., ed. *Texts and Transmission.* Oxford, 1983.

Rigg, A. G. "Golias and other Pseudonyms." *Studi Medievali* 18 (1977): 65–69.

Riquer, M. de. *Les chansons de geste françaises.* 2d ed. Paris, 1957.

Robertson, D. W. "Two Poems from the *Carmina Burana.*" In *Essays in Medieval Culture,* 131–50. Princeton, 1980.

Rossi, P., ed. *Carmina Burana.* Milan, 1989.

Salzer, A. *Die Sinnbilder und Beiworte Mariens in der deutschen Literatur und lateinischen Hymnenpoesie des Mittelalters.* Darmstadt, 1967.

Sayce, O. *The Mediaeval German Lyric.* Oxford, 1982.

Schaller, D. "Bauformeln für akzentrhythmische Verse und Strophen." *Mittellateinisches Jahrbuch* 14 (1979): 9–21.

Schmeller, J. A., ed. *Carmina Burana.* Stuttgart, 1847. Reprinted 1904.

Schütt, M. "The Literary Form of Malmesbury's *Gesta Regum.*" *English Historical Review* 46 (1931): 255–60.

Singer, S. *Sprichwörter des Mittelalters.* Bern, 1947.

Southern, R. W. *Medieval Humanism and Other Studies.* Oxford, 1970.

Spanke, H. "Die älteste lateinische Pastorelle." *Romanische Forschungen* 56 (1942): 257–65.

———. "Der Codex Buranus als Liederbuch." *Zeitschrift für Musikwissenschaft* 13 (1931): 241–51.

————. Review of *CB* 1.2. *Literaturblatt für germanische und romanische Philologie* (1943): 35–46.

————. "Zum Thema 'Mittelalterliche Tanzlieder.'" *Neuphilologische Mitteilungen* 33 (1932): 1–22.

Stock, Brian. *Myth and Science in the Twelfth Century.* Princeton, 1972.

Strecker, K. *Introduction to Medieval Latin.* Translated by R. B. Palmer. Berlin, 1957.

————. "Walter von Châtillon und seine Schule." *Zeitschrift für deutsches Altertum und deutsche Literatur* 64 (1927): 97–125, 161–89.

Symonds, J. A. *Wine, Women and Songs.* 2d ed. London, 1925.

Szövérffy, J. *Peter Abelard's Hymnarius Paraclitensis.* 2 vols. Albany, N.Y., and Brookline, Mass., 1975.

Tarrant, R. J. "Ovid." In *Texts and Transmission,* edited by L. D. Reynolds, 257–84. Oxford, 1983.

Theobald. *Physiologus.* Edited by P. T. Eden. Leiden, 1972.

Thirty Poems from the Carmina Burana. Edited by P. G. Walsh. Reading, 1976; now Bristol Classical Press.

Vigneron, P. *Le cheval dans l'antiquité.* Nancy, 1968.

Vita Gosvini. Edited by M. Bouquet in *Recueil des historiens des Gaules et de la France.* Paris, 1869.

Vollman, B. K., ed. *Carmina Burana.* Frankfurt, 1987.

Wackernagel, W. *Voces Variae Animantium.* Basel, 1869.

Waddell, Helen. *Medieval Latin Lyrics.* 4th ed. London, 1947. Often reprinted.

————. *The Wandering Scholars.* 6th ed. London, 1932.

Walpole, A. S. *Early Latin Hymns.* Cambridge, 1922.

Walsh, P. G. "Amor Clericalis." In *Author and Audience in Latin Literature,* edited by Tony Woodman and Jonathan Powell, 189–203. Cambridge, 1992.

————. *Courtly Love in the Carmina Burana.* Inaugural Lecture, University of Edinburgh. Edinburgh, 1971.

———— (with James Walsh). *Divine Providence and Human Suffering.* Wilmington, 1985.

————. "Golias and Goliardic Poetry." *Medium Aevum* 52, no. 1 (1983): 1–9.

————. "Pastor and Pastoral in Medieval Latin Poetry." In *Papers of the Liverpool Latin Seminar 1976,* 157–69. ARCA Monograph, 2. Liverpool, 1977.

Walter of Châtillon. *Alexandreis.* Edited by M. L. Colker as *Galteri de Castellione, Alexandreis.* Padua, 1978. Translated as *Walter of Châtillon, The Alexandreis* by R. T. Pritchard. Toronto, 1986.

————. *Carmina.* Edited by K. Strecker as *Moralisch-satirische Gedichte Walters von Châtillon aus deutschen, englischen, französischen und italienischen Handschriften.* Heidelberg, 1929.

————. *Die Lieder Walters von Châtillon in der Handschrift 351 von St Omer.* Edited by K. Strecker. Berlin, 1925.

Walther, H. *Lateinische Sprichwörter und Sentenzen des Mittelalters.* Göttingen, 1963.

————. *Das Streitgedicht in der lateinischen Literatur des Mittelalters.* Munich, 1920.

Watenphul, H., and H. Krefeld. *Die Gedichte des Archipoeta.* Heidelberg, 1958.

Wetherbee, Winthrop. *Platonism and Poetry in the Twelfth Century*. Princeton, 1972.

Whicher, G. F. *The Goliard Poets: Medieval Latin Songs and Satires with Verse Translations*. Cambridge, Mass., 1949.

White, T. H. *The Book of Beasts*. London, 1954.

Wilkinson, L. P. *Ovid Recalled*. Cambridge, 1955.

Wright, T. *Anglo-Latin Satirical Poets of the Twelfth Century*. 2 vols. London, 1872.

Zeydel, Edwin H. *Vagabond Verse: Secular Latin Poems of the Middle Ages*. Detroit, 1966.

Index of First Lines

A globo veteri, 24
Amor habet superos, 94
Anni novi redit novitas, 73
Anni parte florida, 101
Axe Phebus aureo, 39
Bruma, veris emula, 4
Cedit, hiems, tua durities, 159
Clauso Cronos et serato, 46
Cum Fortuna voluit, 126
Cur suspectum me tenet domina?, 129
De pollicito, 196
Dulce solum natalis patrie, 149
Dum caupona verterem, 55
Dum curata vegetarem, 132
Dum Diane vitrea, 15
Dum prius inculta, 89
Ecce, chorus virginum, 11
Ecce gratum, 167
Estas in exsilium, 31
Estatis florigero tempore, 34
Estivali gaudio, 77
Estivali sub fervore, 75
Exiit diluculo, 99
Floret tellus floribus, 171
Frigus hinc est horridum, 81
Grates ago Veneri, 42
Hebet sidus, 192
Hortum habet insula, 125
Huc usque, me miseram, 157
Iam dudum Amoris militem, 186
Iam ver oritur, 8

Ianus annum circinat, 1
Iove cum Mercurio, 98
Laboris remedium, 189
Letabundus rediit, 50
Lingua mendax et dolosa, 146
Longa spes et dubia, 181
Lucis orto sidere, 174
Musa venit carmine, 168
Nil proponens temere, 189
Ob amoris pressuram, 184
O comes amoris, dolor, 140
O consocii, 179
Olim sudor Herculis, 19
Omittamus studia, 52
Omnia sol temperat, 161
Quelibet succenditur, 194
Rumor letalis, 150
Saturni sidus lividum, 28
Sevit aure spiritus, 85
Si linguis angelicis, 62
Solis iubar nituit, 79
Tange, sodes, citharam, 154
Tempus accedit floridum, 144
Tempus transit horridum, 164
Transit nix et glacies, 142
Vacillantis trutine, 137
Vere dulci mediante, 177
Veris dulcis in tempore, 93
Veris leta facies, 162
Virent prata, hiemata, 172
Volo virum vivere viriliter, 198

Index of Authors and Passages

Abelard, xv–xvii, xxvi, xxxiif., 128, 131, 174, 192ff.
Hist. Calam. 7f., 193
Adam of St. Victor, xxix
Aeschylus, 117
Alan of Lille, xvi, xxiv, 26, 77, 120
Anticlaudianus 1.281f., 123; 2.486ff., 122; 3.436f., 124; 4.465ff., 30
De Planctu Naturae, prosa 1, 10; Meter 1, 130; 8.208ff., 6
Albertus Magnus, 69
Alcuin, 117, 176
Altercatio Ganymedis et Helenae, 117, 120, 130
Ambrose, xxviii, 153
Comm. Ps. 118.37, 72
Inst. Virg. 93, 153
Andreas Capellanus, xvi, xix, xxiff., 37, 79, 96, 152, 178, 187, 200
De Amore
  1.1.1, 125; 1.1.2, 197; 1.1.8, 91; 1.2.1, 131; 1.3, 141; 1.6.1, 120; 1.6.13f., 120, 188; 1.6.20, 121; 1.6.39, 3; 1.6.40, 71; 1.6.50, 120; 1.6.77, 3; 1.6.115, 71; 1.6.127, 196; 1.6.130, 196; 1.6.229ff., 123; 1.6.242, 135; 1.6.260, 123; 1.6.268f., 134, 136; 1.6.429f., 119; 1.6.470ff., 13, 18; 1.6.487, 118; 1.6.490, 119, 120; 1.6.493, 121; 1.6.531, 200; 1.6.533, 121; 1.7.1, 121; 1.7.4, 119; 1.8, 48; 1.11, 45
  2.1, 121; 2.1.8, 120, 188; 2.3, 120; 2.6.24f., 13; 2.7.43f., 136; 2.8.3ff., 123; 2.8.44ff., 134
  3.65ff., 156
Appendix Probi, xxix
Apuleius, xxx, 136

De Dogmate Platonis 3, 179
Met. 4.30, 148; 6.15, 11; 9.11, 19; 9.41.4, 197
Archpoet, xv, xvii, xxvii, xxxiii
Confession, 139
Aristophanes, 117
Aristotle, xxxvi
Arundel, xvii, 6, 26, 28, 88
Augustine, xxxv, 42, 197
Civ. Dei 5.1ff., 99; 14.8, 119
Conf. 7.6.8ff., 99; 12.11, 3
Ausonius, 14, 190
Avicenna, 96, 121

Baudri, xxiv, xxxiv
Benedict, 11
Bernard de Ventadour, xvi
Bernard of Chartres, xxvi
Bernard Silvestris, xvi, xxvi, 26
Cosmographia 1.1ff., 26; 2.9f., 6; 3.1, 27; 3.445ff., 10
Boethius, xxx
Anal. Post. 2.17, 69
Cons. Phil. 2, 128; 3.8.6, 119
De mus. 1.8, 124
Boncompagno, 38, 48, 70
Book of Beasts, 9

Cassiodorus, xxx, 49, 128, 197
Catullus, xviii, xxviii; 5.7, 73; 11, 152; 17.16, 191; 62.46, 97, 191; 68.16, 51, 54, 162; 85, 144
Celsus, 97
Chaucer, 10
Chrétien de Troyes, xvi, 135
Cicero, 7
De Or. 1.28, 77
Div. 2.90, 99; 2.91, 30
Fin. 3.62, 125

Cicero (*continued*)
 Leg. 1.21, 51
 Nat. D. 2.119, 31; 2.143, 152; 3.59,
  122
 Off. 1.118, 138
 Rep. 6.17, 31
 Tusc. 2.11, 38; 5.87, 119
Clarembald of Arras, xxv
Columella, 6.29.2, 122

De Vita Monachorum, 148
Dialogus inter aquam et vinum, 181
Dietmar von Aist, xxxii
Donatus, 45

Endelechius, 176
Euclid, 121
Eugenius of Toledo, 169
Euripides, 117

Galen, 121
Gautier of Arras, xvi
Gellius, 124
Geoffrey of Vinsauf, 27, 49
Gerald of Wales, xvi, 26, 27f.
Goliae versus de sacerdotibus, 120
Gottschalk, 176
Guiraut de Cabreira, 5

Heinrich von Morungen, xxxii
Henry of Avranches, xvii
Heraclitus, 49, 83
Herman the Cripple, 176
Hilarius, xvi, xxiv, xxxii, 130f., 147
Hippocrates, 121
Homer
 Il. 3.64, 190; 18.478ff., 122
 Od. 8.337, 190
Horace, xxvii, 153
 Ars. P. 17, 77
 Carm. 1.1.31, 52; 1.2.31, 88; 1.4.1,
  143; 1.5.1, 71; 1.9.18ff., 152;
  2.1.39, 3; 2.17.20, 30; 2.19.4, 52;
  3.1.24, 52; 3.11, 156; 3.15.16, 38;
  3.16.1, 89, 148, 200; 3.19.16f.,
  125; 3.21.22, 125; 3.21.29, 181;
  3.26, 127; 3.26.11f., 156;
  3.27.25ff., 89, 148; 4.4.61, 22;

  4.7.1f., 43; 4.11.3, 118; 4.11.33f.,
   156; 4.12.25ff., 54; 4.13.20, 28,
   54, 144
Hrotsvitha, 4
Hugh of Fouilloy, 9
Hugh Primas, xv, xvii, xxxiii
Hyginus, 23

Isidore, 9
 De eccl. off. 4, 120
 Etym. 10.1.5, 141; 12.1.45, 122;
  12.2.13, 97; 12.7.22, 11

Jerome, xxix
John of Salisbury, xv, xvii, xxviii, 130,
 156

Litany of Loreto, 70
Livy 1.7.4, 22; 5.47.4, 11
Longus 2.3ff., 125
Love Council of Remiremont, 117f.
Lucan, xxvii, 122
Lucretius, xxviii, 119; 1.21ff., 127;
 4.1015, 145; 4.1283, 125; 5.96,
 27; 5.610, 18

Macrobius, 124
Map, Walter, 156
Marbod, xxiv
Marner, the, xiii
Martial, xxvii; 6.70.5f., 201; 10.64.1,
 118
Martianus Capella, 6, 48, 123, 124
 Marriage of Philology and Mercury
  1.16f., 49; 1.25, 6; 1.49ff., 7; 1.67,
  7; 1.97ff., 123; 2.181, 6; 9.892ff.,
  123
Matthew of Vendôme, 77
 Ars Versificatoria 1.56ff., 27f., 33, 46,
  72, 87, 88
Maximian
 Elegies 1.9ff., 128; 1.86, 88; 1.93,
  27f.
Mythographus Vaticanus, 49

Neidhart von Reuental, xiv
Nepos, 119
Nigel of Longchamps, xvi

Nonius Marcellus, 153

Origen, 153
Ovid, xvi, xviii, xxvii, 26, 87, 132ff.
 Amores
  1.1.20, 130; 1.4.19, 88; 1.5.17ff.,
   88; 1.5.23f., 73; 1.8.104, 153; 1.9,
   3, 45, 119; 1.14.23, 88; 1.14.33,
   118; 1.15.30, 23
  2.2.43f., 92; 2.4.8, 139; 2.5.1, 135;
   2.18.36, 160; 2.19, xx; 2.19.27ff.,
   148, 200; 2.19.36, 42; 2.29.3, 42
  3.1, 117; 3.2.82, 69; 3.4.17, 42;
   3.6.83, 156; 3.8, 117; 3.11.33f.,
   144; 3.12.33f., 89
 Ars Am.
  1.35, 187; 1.41, 183; 1.45, 54;
   1.210, 148; 1.271, 52; 1.543f.,
   124; 1.669f., 45; 1.675, 92;
   1.709ff., 200
  2.345, 125; 2.493ff., 135; 2.501,
   136; 2.517ff., 150; 2.607ff., 136;
   2.625, 136; 2.633, 136; 2.727f., 45
  3.537, 23; 3.631ff., 148, 200
 Fasti 1.399, 124; 1.405, 124; 1.543f.,
   22; 1.595ff., 118; 2.149, 19; 3.19,
   19; 4.201, 49; 5.183ff., 77;
   5.195ff., 49
 Her. 5.115, 70; 9, 22; 18.177, 97;
   20.45ff., 28
 Met.
  1.452ff., 14, 148; 1.622ff., 10;
   1.624ff., 38; 1.713ff., 38
  2.155, 2, 6; 2.542ff., 28, 148;
   2.769, 61; 2.836ff., 89, 148
  3.52ff., 179; 3.171, 191; 3.272, 97;
   3.310ff., 41; 3.353, 130; 3.402ff.,
   10
  4.30, 124; 4.169, 27; 4.171ff., 148;
   4.173ff., 3; 4.177, 38; 4.196ff.,
   148; 4.347ff., 193; 4.483, 179;
   4.621, 162; 4.697ff., 88, 148, 200;
   4.785f., 122
  5.336ff., 15; 5.341ff., 7; 5.369ff., 96
  6.1ff., 123; 6.97, 11; 6.103ff., 89;
   6.115ff., 122; 6.392, 124; 6.438ff.,
   10
  7.284, 170; 7.623, 150; 7.705, 28

  8.239, 120; 8.256ff., 11; 8.470f.,
   139
  9.1ff., 23; 9.23ff., 23; 9.24, 97, 152;
   9.119f., 23; 9.136ff., 22; 9.183f.,
   23; 9.184f., 23; 9.190, 23; 9.192f.,
   22f.; 9.194ff., 23; 9.197, 23;
   9.198, 22
  10.85, 52, 162; 10.342, 45; 10.525,
   135; 10.529ff., 122
  11.89ff., 24; 11.599, 11
  13.716, 150; 13.795, 191
  14.208, 61; 14.224, 31; 14.335, 191
  15.392, 11; 15.497ff., 201; 15.863,
   148
 Pont. 1.35f., 150; 2.7.28, 150
 Rem. 44, 71; 139, 135; 336, 156;
   749, 120

Pamphilus, 72
Paulinus of Nola, 19, 162, 190
Peire d'Auvergne, xvi
Peire Rogier, xvi
Peire Vidal, 188
Persius, 27
Peter of Blois, xvi, xviiff., xx, xxvi,
   xxxiii, 22, 23, 26, 32, 37, 38, 45,
   87, 91, 138, 185
Peter Riga, 77
Petronius, xxix, 61
Philip the Chancellor, xvii, xxxiii
Physiologus, 9, 97, 128
Plato, xv, xxvi, 75ff., 96, 119
 Phaedo 85b, 170
 Phaedrus 230b, 77
Plautus, xxviii, 23
 Cist. 69, 121; 206ff., 162
 Curc. 100f., 193
 Merc. 82, 183
 Trin. 234, 147
Pliny the Elder, 9, 52
 HN 11.121, 11; 37.92ff., 195
Propertius, xviii, 71; 4.8.88, 92
Prudentius, 42
 Cathem. 8.37ff., 177
 Hamart. 247ff., 27
Ptolemy, 121

Quintilian 1.5.61, 186; 1.6.10, 186; 1.6.22, 186; 9.3.11, 186

Reinmar der Alte, xxxii
Remigius of Auxerre, 48
Ripoll, 148
Robert de Blois, 123
Romance of the Rose, 70

Sallust
  Cat. 20.4, 75; 25.2, 80
  Jug. 85.15ff., 188
Sedulius, xxviii
Seneca, 153
  Ben. 3.13.3, 3
  Oed. 409, 125
Sidonius Apollinaris, 152
Statius, xxvii
  Achill. 1.791, 153
  Theb. 7.793, 153
Stephen of Tournai, 75
Suetonius, 30, 121, 170

Terence, xxiv, xxviii, 156
  Eun. 72, 139; 638, 45; 732, 120, 197
  Phormio 203, 38
Tertullian, 96
Theobald, 9
Theophilus, 123
Thierry of Chartres, xv, xxvi, xxxii
Tibullus, xxviii, 88

Varro, 122, 186
Venantius Fortunatus, xxviii, 69, 177
Virgil
  Aen. 1.4, 88; 1.51ff., 31; 1.174, 195; 1.255, 168; 1.687, 46; 4.1f., 150, 183; 4.2, 50; 4.23, 143; 4.90ff., 15, 118; 4.173, 152; 4.184, 153; 4.197, 152; 4.298ff., 183; 4.695f., 14; 6.467f., 131; 6.471, 195; 8.193ff., 22; 8.626ff., 122; 9.5, 28, 197; 9.619, 124; 10.16, 190; 10.284, 38; 12.486, 139

Ecl. 1.56, 52; 1.59ff., 148; 2.36, 179; 3.78, 118; 3.109f., 42; 5.85, 179; 8.52ff., 148; 10.69, 2
Georg. 1.12ff., 122; 1.146f., 160; 1.473, 26; 2.229, 120; 2.469, 52; 3.72ff., 122; 4.123, 123; 4.535, 50
Vita Gosvini, 128
Vulgate
  Gen. 18:16ff., 131
  Exod. 19:4, 11
  Deut. 32:11, 11
  Judg. 3:36ff., 81
  Job 13:25, 139; 30:31, 135
  Ps. 10:5, 152; 18:11, 33, 73; 19:4, 52; 28:6, 128; 32:2, 164; 44:4, 193; 44:9, 193; 68:26, 81; 118:103, 168; 148:13, 73
  Song of Sol. 1:4, 70; 2:2, 153; 2:13, 176; 3:2, 54; 4:7, 195; 4:11f., 193; 4:12, 127; 6:9, 195; 7:8, 191
  Ecclus. 6:19, 97; 23:6, 3; 24:17, 72
  Wisd. of Sol. 7:26, 71; 11:20, 166
  Jer. 31:18, 157
  Joel 2:23, 37
  Matt. 3:12, 129, 200; 10:16, 153; 11:5, 153; 11:20, 39; 19:24, 121; 27:44, 159
  Mark 7:35, 136; 10:25, 121
  Luke 1:34, 176; 1:39, 71; 1:47, 71; 2:7, 84; 8:17, 159; 15:18, 72
  John 1:27, 179; 7:14, 178
  Rom. 5:11, 72
  1 Cor. 9:24, 52, 73; 13:1, 69
  Eph. 5:1, 54; 5:25ff., 177
  Phil. 2:9, 27
  1 John 2:16, 91
  2 John 10:11, 179
  Rev. 10:9f., 168; 11:10, 77; 14:2f., 164

Walter of Châtillon, xvf., xvii, xxiii, xxiv, xxxiv, 3, 45, 120, 134, 168
Walther von der Vogelweide, xiv, xxxii
William of Malmesbury, 121
William of St. Thierry, 135

Xenophon, 122

General Index

Achelous, 20
Achilles, 107, 123
Adonis, 148
Adynata, 148
Aeneas, 60, 174
Aeolus, 29ff.
Alceus, 21
Alcibiades, 103, 119
Alcmena, 23
Alexander the Great, 120
Amicitia Christiana, 190
Amor (Cupid), 1, 46, 74f., 90, 94, 104ff., 159ff., 163ff., 186f.
Amor de lonh, xxi, 162, 190
Amor purus and *amor mixtus,* xix, xxi, 13f., 96f., 119, 172, 191
Amphitryon, 23
Antaeus, 20, 23
Aphrodite, 190
Apollo, 18, 24, 174. *See also* Cynthian god; Phoebus
Aquilo, 4, 29
Arachne, 89
Argenteuil, 193
Argus, 8, 10, 35ff.
Aries, 1f., 7
Astrology, 98f.
Astronomical motifs, 30, 98
Atlas, 19
"Authoritative" hexameters, 134f.

Bacchus, 41, 109, 125, 179f.
Baldwin of Canterbury, xviii
Bernard of Clairvaux, xv
Birdcalls, 168ff.
Blancheflor, 71
Britannia, 129, 131
Bucephalas, 104, 120

Cacus, 20, 22
Caelus, 7
Calliope, 7, 12, 15
Cecilia, 94ff.
Celibacy, 139
Ceres, 4, 7, 104, 120, 196f.
Champagne, xvi
Charlemagne, xxx
Charles VI, 79
Chronos, 49
Cistercian Order, xv
Cleric and knight, 83, 101ff.
Clerics as suitors, xxii
Copia, 20, 23
Corinna, 184f.
Coronis, xviii, xxvi, 23, 25ff., 43ff.
Courtly love, xxff., 131, 134, 147, 156, 162, 187, 200
Courts of love, xxxiii, 14, 79, 125
Cronos, 46ff.
Cupid, 2f., 8ff., 14, 39ff., 46, 74f., 78f., 84, 103ff., 130, 132ff., 146, 148, 167, 171f. *See also* Amor
Cybele, 7, 39ff.
Cynthian god, 46ff.
Cypris (Venus), 11, 14, 46ff., 167f.
Cythera, 3, 121
Cytherean, the (Venus), 1, 3, 12, 106, 109, 121, 125

Danaë, 86ff., 146, 148
Dance lyrics, xx
Daphne, 1, 4
David, xv
Delos, 49
Diana, 15, 18, 174, 201
Dido, 12, 14, 60, 118, 174, 183
Dione, 1, 3, 4, 7, 39f., 42, 43, 46ff., 89, 102, 106, 121f.

✣ 215

Dis, 7
Dodona, 149f.
Dream framework, 134
Dryads, 46ff., 50ff., 179f.

Echo, 191
Eleanor of Aquitaine, xvi, xviii, xxxii, 75
Epicurus, 103
Ermengarde of Narbonne, xvi, xxxii
Erotic grammar, 185f., 198
Erymanthian boar, 23
Eugenius III, 117
Europa, 86ff., 146, 148
Eurydice, 10
Eurytus, 22
Evander, 22

Fama, 150ff.
Faunus, 8, 10; Fauni, 109, 124
Flora: in CB 83, xviii, 85ff.; and Phyllis, xix, xxii, 12, 14, 84, 101ff.; in CB 108, 137ff.
Flora (goddess), 46ff., 50ff., 76, 77
Fortuna, 126, 128
Frederick I Barbarossa, xvi
Frederick II, xxvii, xxxiii
Frizon, 5

Gabriel, 176
Ganymede, 104, 120
Gemini, 98
German stanzas, xiv
Geryon, 20ff.
Gideon, 81
Glycerium, xxiiif., xxxiv
Goliards, xv; goliardic meter, xxv, 59, 68f., 134, 155
Golias, xv, xxxii
Gossip, xxii, 99, 147, 150ff.
Graces, 25, 109

Hawking, 123
Helen, 3, 63, 71f., 140f.
Heloïse, xvi, xxvi, xxxii, 128, 192f.
Henry II of England, xvi, xviii, 71, 75
Henry the Liberal, xvi
Hercules, xviii, 19ff.

Hesperides, 23
Hesperus, 15
Hippolytus, 198ff.
Homosexuality, xxivf., xxxiv, 130
Hope. See Spes
Hybla, 149f.
Hydra, 19, 22
Hymenaeus, 4ff.

Io, 10, 38
Iole, 19ff.
Isobel of Flanders, xvi, xxxii
Israelites, 81
Itys, 8, 10
Iuliana, 93f.
Ixion, 162

Janus, 1f.
Job, xxvii, 134f.
Juno, 4, 7, 8, 12, 15, 38, 94
Jupiter/Jove, 7, 8, 10, 23, 28f., 46, 49, 50, 57, 85ff., 94, 98f., 148, 198ff.

Knight and cleric, 83, 101ff.

Leda, 86ff.
Leonine hexameter, xxviii
Lesbia, xviii
Lethe, 35ff.
Leto, 18
Libanus, 64, 72
Libra, 98f.
Limoges, 48
Locus amoenus, xxiii, xxiv, 68, 77, 118, 170, 178
Louis VII of France, xvi, 75
Lyaeus, 104, 120
Lycoris, 20, 23

Marie, countess of Champagne, xvi
Marius, 188
Mars, 3, 38, 146, 148
Mars (planet), 98f.
Martial, Saint, 48
Mary, Saint. See Virgin Mary
Matilda, xxxiii
Medusa, 122
Mercury, 28ff., 38, 98f., 107, 156

Metonymy, 49
Midian, 81
Milan, xxxv
Minerva, 23, 107, 123. *See also* Pallas
Morpheus, 16
Morphology, xxx
Mulciber, 107, 123
Music codices, xiv, 48

Naiads, 75
Napeae, 46ff.
Narcissus, 8, 10, 191
Natura, 24ff.
Nemean lion, 23
Neptune, 94, 106, 122, 179ff.
Nereus, 106, 122
Nessus, 20ff.
Neumes, xiii
Noys, 26

Oreads, 50ff.
Orléans, xiv
Orpheus, 8, 10, 19
Orthography, xxx

Pallanteum, 22
Pallas, 1, 12, 15, 139, 180. *See also*
   Minerva
Paris (suitor), 102, 118, 130
Paris (Trojan hero), 3, 56ff., 140f.,
   167f.
Paris, France, xivf.
Parody, 49, 72
Pastourelle, xvii, xxiiif., xxxiiif., 45,
   75ff., 91, 100f., 175ff., 177ff.
Pegasus, 107, 122
Phaedra, 201
Phaedria, 139
Philomela/Philomena, 10, 39ff., 84
Phoebus, 1, 8, 39ff., 50, 146, 148. *See
   also* Apollo
Phrison, 4ff.
Phyllis, xviii, 89ff.; and Flora, xix, xxii,
   12, 14, 61, 101ff.
Pisces, 4, 7
Pleiades, 159f.
Pluto, 62, 70, 94
Poitiers, 69

Poseidon, 122
Procne, 10
Proserpina, 4, 7
Prudentia, 124
Psyche, 11

Quantity and rhythm, xxviii
Quinque lineae amoris, 43ff., 95ff.

Rainald Dassel, xvif., xxxiii
Rhea, 46ff.
Rhinoceros, 94ff., 126, 128
Rhyme, xxviii
Rhythmic verses, xxviii, xxxv
Richard of Canterbury, xviii
Robin (in the pastourelle), xxiii
Rosamund, 71

Salerno, xiv
Salmacis, 193
Satan, 69, 176f.
Saturn, 28ff., 49, 125
Satyrs, 46ff., 50ff., 109, 124
Second Sophistic, xxxv
Semele, 39ff.
Sempronia, 80
Sequence, xxviiif.
Silenus, 109
Sirens, 55ff.
Sodom, 129, 131
Sorrel, xxii, 82ff.
Sorrows of love, xx, 41, 141, 145, 150,
   182
Spes, xxi, 15, 38, 186, 196f.
Stoic physics, 49
Syntaktikon, 150
Syntax, xxx
Syriac hymnology, xxxv

Tantalus, 90ff.
Taurus, 1f., 29ff., 98f.
Tellus, 7
Tempe, 50ff.
Tereus, 8, 10, 39ff.
Terra, 7
Theseus, 201
Thetis, 4, 7
Thisbe, 31, 34ff.

Thracian horses, 20, 23
Thyme, xxii, 82ff.
Troubadours, xvi
Tyndareus, daughter of (Helen), 1,
  130

Vagantes, xiv
Venus, 1ff., 8ff., 12, 15, 16f., 19f.,
  28ff., 34ff., 42ff., 46ff., 50f., 55ff.,
  63ff., 74, 76, 77f., 106, 122, 125,
  139, 149, 162, 163, 171f., 179ff.,

189f., 196f. *See also* Cypris;
  Cytherean, the; Dione
Venus (planet), 98f., 118
Virgin Mary, 70, 72, 142, 153, 174,
  176, 190, 195
Vocabulary, Medieval Latin, xxxi
Vulcan, 3, 35ff., 107, 123

William II of Sicily, xviii

Zephyr, 15, 18, 29ff., 162